The
Musharraf
Factor

The Musharraf Factor

Leading Pakistan to Inevitable Demise

ABID ULLAH JAN

Pragmatic Publishing
Ottawa

National Library of Canada Cataloguing in Publication

Jan, Abid Ullah, 1965-
The Musharraf Factor / Abid Ullah Jan.

Includes bibliographical references and index.
ISBN 0-9733687-1-3

1. Democracy. 2. Democracy—Islamic countries. 3. Islam and state. I. Title.
JC423.A22 2003   321.8'0917'671   C2003-905735-6

All sources have been referenced and acknowledged. The author and publisher
welcome any information enabling them to rectify any error or omission in future
editions.

PRAGMATIC PUBLISHING
Web: http://www.pragmaticpublishings.com/

Musharraf is:

"...a leader with great courage and vision."

— George Bush, February 14, 2003

"[A man] of stature....individual courage, leadership and vision."

— Remarks by Jack Rosen, President Jewish National Congress,
September 17th, 2005

"A man of vision...an indispensable...quintessential Muslim leader of moderation, decency, reason,"

— Out the citation of the US Congress.
September 18, 2005

"[A leader who] showed great courage and foresight."

— Colin Powell, February 05, 2002

"A remarkable figure."

— Condoleezza Rice, September 19, 2005.

"A man of courage, a straight fighter, a responsible and committed leader and an honest man."

When Gen. Musharraf's statement provoked an uproar, he responded with another lie: He claimed that he had never made it. In fact, a recording of him speaking is available on The Post's Web site, washingtonpost.com. His words are quite clear. "These are not my words, and I would go to the extent of saying I am not so silly and stupid to make comments of this sort," the general said. Well, yes, he is.

Editorial, the *Washington Post*,
October 01, 2005.

Contents

"Follow what has been sent down unto you by your Lord-God, and follow no Master other than Him. How seldom do you keep this in mind!"

(Qur'an, 07:03)

The Hard Questions

O N OCTOBER 12, 1999 when the first rumbling of General Parvez Musharraf's thunder disturbed the moldy Islamabad silence, the holy fools in the press and media—the people who always support the person at the top and the sitting regime—predicted that the new dictator would rule for at least seven years. They assured anyone interested in listening that Musharraf was a God-sent figure. He miraculously survived an attempt to crash his plane, he was bold, and he stood up to criticisms at home as well as attacks from the Commonwealth, European Union and America. These were the signs that everyone had searched for in previous leaders, but their approach to governance and obsequiousness to foreign powers was supine. The unusual courage, the ability to speak powerfully, and his radical actions, gave the new General a mystical aura. Writing about General Musharraf—who he was, where he came from, what he was after, where he was heading, and what was his personal stake, became just as intriguing as trying to figure out what Pakistan's future would be.

On October 17, 1999, Musharraf told the nation: "Our aims

and objectives shall be: No. 1- rebuild national confidence and morale; No. 2 - strengthen federation, remove inter-provincial disharmony and restore national cohesion; No. 3 - revive [the] economy and restore investors' confidence; No. 4 - ensure law and order and dispense speedy justice; No. 5 - depoliticize state institutions; No. 6 - devolution of power to the grassroots level; and lastly, No. 7 - ensure swift ... accountability."[1]

More than six years down the road corruption still exists, just as it did under the other governments of the past. Corrupt politicians, whom even Musharraf threw in jail, thrive under his wings. Musharraf's Interior Minister, Aftab Khan Sherpao, is an example, which shows these figures are now more well-off than before. Opportunists from both the Pakistan People's Party and the Muslim League Nawaz group blossomed with new fervor.

Oppressive poverty still exists despite the much-vaunted poverty alleviation initiatives, many funding opportunities and an end to nuclear program related sanctions. If the present trend of inflation and unemployment continue, the situation will soon reach to the level of mass starvation for the poorest. The richest military, on the other hand, has taken land grabs and usurpation of power in civil institutions to a climax.[2] People are more angry and hungry than they were before Musharraf's reign,[3] yet they can hardly raise a voice. Any dissident can now be conveniently labeled as Al-Qaeda sympathizer the moment the regime decides to silence him.

Apparently, Pakistan's problem doesn't seem serious enough to trigger an institutional collapse and the state's breakdown. Nevertheless, there is an indescribable unease among the masses. Some analysts, quoting CIA reports, have expressed concern that Pakistan may not survive past 2015.[4]

Besides the issues raised by the CIA and others, the debate about the causes of Pakistan's predicted failure revolves around two factors in particular: the leadership factor and the collective factor of the nation's attitude. The blame for the failure goes around; some are holding all leaders responsible for their self-centered approach, while others blame the nation for its excessive greed and submissiveness. A parallel debate is underway about Musharraf's transformed role since 9/11. One side argues that he saved Pakistan, whereas the other claims, Musharraf is culminating the more than fifty-eight years' of aimlessness of the nation into total disaster.

Many people are trying to find out if Musharraf is really putting the final nail in the coffin of a nation that has been half dead for a long time. Apparently, Musharraf is no different from Generals Ayub Khan and Yahya Khan before him, who both were "liberal" in their attitude, and thought of the US as a "friend." So what has gone wrong? It is that the US has changed its ways or has the General crossed all limits of surrendering in his compulsive pre-occupation with seeking more legitimacy and continuity? But any dictator would feel such anxiety. Musharraf is not an exception to this rule. Apparently, there seems no reason to believe that his moves would undermine Pakistan.

One may ask, how the nation can be responsible for Pakistan's troubles when the general perception is that the nation hates Musharraf, even calls him a traitor. Moreover, it is nowhere evident that Musharraf is breaking up the state or that there are signs of a situation similar to 1971 under General Yahya Khan, which led to the disintegration of Pakistan. At this point, some analysts argue that unlike his military predecessors, he has become more like Mikhail Gorbachev, who did not want a breakup of the Soviet Union. He only wanted 'glasnost'. Musharraf also didn't want to put Pakistan at stake after 9/11, but probably could not understand that the journey he just embarked upon will, in fact, end up in bringing about unimaginable turmoil in the region.

With strong "constitutional," military and American backing, it makes little sense to predict that Musharraf will soon feel more isolated within Pakistan and will be left to the whims of the Pentagon, the CIA and the intrigues of the US State Department. He will be thrown to the wolves as a liability once he outlives his utility—much like General Zia ul Haq and other American backed dictators in various countries, who were no longer needed by the US.

Many analysts believe that despite the apparent problem with his moves, Musharraf has good intentions for Pakistan. Unfortunately, however, like Gorbachev, he ends up compromising whatever he sets out to defend. He made the US occupation of Afghanistan possible on the plea of national interest: a) security of Pakistan's Northern frontier; b) security of the nuclear deterrent; and c) security of Pakistan's position on Kashmir. The question that begs in-depth response is: why it is so that he continues to try hard but his efforts always end up in failure; such as:

1. There is no security within or outside Pakistan. India is entrenched in Afghanistan and is a friend of Iran, leaving Pakistan surrounded by those who consider it a threat to their security and stability.

2. Most Kashmiris and their sympathizers feel abandoned, thinking that their rights have been bartered for the continuation of Musharraf's presidency.

3. His way of dealing with the nuclear proliferation issue is considered as effectively pleading guilty to criminal proliferation.

4. His actions in the Tribal areas in two provinces are perceived as his declaration of war on his own people.

A study of the politics of leadership and a nation's groping in the dark cannot simultaneously be a study of everything else, although authors criticizing Musharraf's policies and actions tend to be accused (sometimes justly, sometimes not) of ignoring or playing down the importance of available options to him. This work focuses on Musharraf as a factor with distinct contributions to political change in Pakistan and in the world in general.

Musharraf's distinctive contributions to politics lead some

analysts to compare him to General Charles de Gaulle. In fact, in one of his interviews with the *New York Times,* General Musharraf said, "How did General de Gaulle continue in uniform all through his period as president of France, and France is a democratic country?"[5] Earlier, the BBC had compared Musharraf's approach to that of General de Gaulle.[6] In fact, General Musharraf's comparison with General de Gaulle does not fit well.

General de Gaulle did not come to power through a *coup d'etat* by an army chief in a country where coups were a common occurrence. In fact, when he assumed power in 1958, de Gaulle was not a general, commanding French forces at all. He was a national hero in retirement. Many analysts were quick in dismissing Musharraf's comparison with de Gaulle. Unlike Musharraf, as president of France, de Gaulle followed an independent foreign policy, often to the great annoyance of the US. He established relations with Communist China when it was not fashionable amongst the western powers to do so. He opposed the Vietnam War and took France out of NATO's integrated military command. He was very prickly about French honor and dignity.

We will see in the chapters to follow that Musharraf's actions are much more similar to what Gorbachev did in the former Soviet Union. The disintegration of the USSR really started in the Baltic republics. However, what happened there was only a consequence, as a running nose accompanies a cold. The cold should have been treated, but not the nose. The real illness was in Moscow, in the country's leadership, in Gorbachev's surroundings and in the structures of the Russian Soviet Federation Socialist Republic, that started to fight for Russia's sovereignty. What was in the country's outskirts—in the Baltic Republics, in Georgia, in Moldavia, in Ukraine—was serious enough, but would not in itself lead to the dissolution of the giant.

This book examines whether the nation and leaders in Pakistan have abandoned the objective for which the state was established, and what role is Musharraf actually playing as a major factor in the overall equation. What we see in the form of the lack of economic, political and social development are just symptoms of the existing socio-political and economic order. The question is: what is wrong with this order and is there any initiative in order to address the root problem? If not, is the problem severe enough to lead to the demise of Pakistan? Most importantly, what are the factors which lead CIA and others to predict Pakistan's failure and what factors can actually lead to the demise of Pakistan?

Musharraf is the main factor that can break or make Pakistan. We need here to assess whether Musharraf acts like Gorbachev and fundamentally misunderstands the implications of his own actions; if he is acting under pressure, or he acts as he actually believes. Gorbachev did not understand the lessons of Nikita Khrushchev's attempt to de-Stalinize the Soviet Union in the 1953-1964 period. Like Gorbachev, Khrushchev also made efforts to liberalize the Soviet system, but, unlike his later successor, he ultimately backtracked on reform. While Gorbachev believed that an authoritarian power could exist without tight controls, Khrushchev recognized the consequences of his agenda. According to the editor of *Front Page* magazine, Jamie Glazov:

> Gorbachev's moderation inflicted lethal self-destructive blows on the Soviet bloc. Once Moscow ended its total and intrusive control of its satellites, it basically signed its own death warrant. Once the regime allowed free discussion, it committed political suicide. Gorbachev was a tragic figure because his goals and beliefs were incompatible. He hoped to make communism work, but in that effort, it became necessary for him to free himself from Marxist ideology. He sought to de-Stalinize, yet he could not do so without dismantling the regime to which he owed his position.[7]

In the following chapters, we will try to find out if exactly the same is happening in Pakistan under General Musharraf. If it is happening, why is it not generally recognized?

Some analysts argue that once Musharraf ignored the Islamic

identity of Pakistan and allowed the misnomer "enlightened moderation" and the "war on terrorism," the regime literally signed a death warrant for the country. The opposing camp argues that this approach has saved Pakistan from "Talibanization" and Indian and US aggression against it.

Undoubtedly, Musharraf wants to sustain Pakistan. For that he cooperates with the US to save it from direct military attack. However, there is no systematic study available to show that in the process he has actually undermined the very soul of Pakistan. Accusations abound. The self-proclaimed custodians of Islam accuse Musharraf of selling the very identity of his nation for perpetuating himself in power. He wants to secularize the state, yet he cannot do so without dismantling Pakistan's *raison d'être.*

On the other hand, proponents of secularism argue that Islam is considered as *raison d'être* of Pakistan, but that was not the objective of the founding fathers in the first place. In this regard, besides assessing Musharraf's "enlightened moderation," this work attempts to find out if he continues to make some mistakes that can really undermine Pakistan. No doubt, his maneuvering between the Scylla of a totalitarian regime and the Charybdis of democratic ideas is far from irreproachable. No doubt he listens to and trusts the wrong people; no doubt his hearing and sight may be dulled by the enormous pressure, but are his mistakes so crude and irreversible to lead Pakistan towards a demise, or his opponents believe so because in a country not accustomed to the ruler's accountability, not even for surrendering Pakistan's sovereignty and independence, shamanism has always been a trait of the Pakistani national character? They cough and infect everyone around them, but when they all get sick, they throw stones at the shaman because his spells didn't work.

If shaman's intentions are good, then there is only one factor that can surely lead to the demise of Pakistan. That factor is the environment in which any positive development that can put Pakistan on the right track becomes impossible. In this work, we will examine whether certain positive developments are still possible under Musharraf's policies and approach. If not, will it trigger Pakistan's demise?

The first chapter of this book assesses Musharraf's doctrine to see the impact of his words and deeds on state policies and the overall political environment in the country. Particularly, it looks into his "strategy" of "enlightened moderation," its roots, definitions and its different meanings to different people.

The second chapter examines whether achieving the objective behind Pakistan's creation is still possible. Due to political squabbling and the changing strategies of religious political parties, the mass movement towards the objective of Pakistan seems to have completely lost its strength and momentum. Religious parties have exploited mass support in the form of demonstrating street power only to achieve lesser objectives. In the past, the religious parties received substantial support from Pakistan's intelligence agencies, who are now burying the evidence of this cooperation. The US is posing as if it had never pumped millions of dollars into the coffers of religious parties when their services were needed for overthrowing Zulfiqar Ali Bhutto in mid 70s and for the US-sponsored *Jihad* in Afghanistan. The way the present regime manipulated an alliance of the religious parties (MMA) and the way these parties are deluding all those who are struggling for Muslim's self-determination, it seems these parties may never achieve the stated objective. We need to examine whether or not it is possible that the present approach of the religious parties will ever transform Pakistan into the once-desired Islamic State.

Chapter 3 looks at the possibility of full restoration of democratic rule and the efficient rebuilding of the Pakistani State. Although most Pakistanis in the military and civilian establishments are formally committed to the restoration of democracy, many are also uncomfortable with the idea of mass democratic politics. Like anywhere else, in Pakistan, democracy is a vocation of the rich and influential. On the issue of democracy, Pakistan may be somewhat better than many Arab states, but far behind the thoroughly politicized and democratized India or Sri Lanka, and even behind Bangladesh. The question we ask is: Has situation in Pakistan deteriorated to the extent that a truly democratic state is unlikely to emerge? As the US has pinned all its hopes in the military, training it on how to remain loyal and committed to the country's gradual secularization, the hopes of many people are fading away. The United States' lack of trust in politicians and the military's self-interest prevent the army from giving the politicians a free hand. The politicians are so insecure and corrupt that they instinctively turn to the armed forces for political support. In chapter 3 we assess the role of the Musharraf factor on the future of democracy in Pakistan, a state that continues to hover on the edge of a sham democracy.

Chapter 4 assesses the state of collective helplessness and the possibility of any ray of hope in an environment in which many have come to conclude that they are living under a Pak-military led occupation of Pakistan. Various outside actors are challenging the legitimacy of the state. Internally, Pakistan is in the ambivalent position of having an army that can neither govern nor allow civilians to rule. The army itself is established on the foundation of *Iman* (Faith), *Taqwa* (fear of Allah) and *Jihad fee sabeelillah* (*Jihad* in the cause of Allah). It is an inherently Islamic institution. What we need to assess is what has become of this Islamic army in a state, which the commander in chief is not ready to accept as an Islamic State? Is the army still following the motto of *Iman, Taqwa and Jihad fee Sabeelillah* under General Musharraf who profess admiration for Mustafa Ataturk, who was staunchly secular and anti-Islam to the point of fanaticism? Insiders are of the view that only a few of his colleagues share his enthusiasm for militant secularism, which makes radical change inconceivable. This complicates assessing the future. Nevertheless, the potential for polarization is enormous.

Throughout the book, we will try to find out if there is any sign of the emergence of a revolutionary or radical political movement. Pakistan never had a truly leftist political movement; the hostility of the landowners, their alliance with the United States, the dominance of the army, and the *Lassez-faire* attitude of most Pakistanis enfeebled the left. Pakistan came closest to a radical political movement with the socialist government of Zulfiqar Ali Bhutto, who believed that only a populist movement could counter the army's power. There are no signs that such a leftist movement could be repeated in the future. If the present experiment with a mixed military/civilian dictatorship should collapse, an increase in the appetite for pure authoritarianism is more likely. The same is the case with religious organizations. None is in a position of bringing a revolution or capable of undertaking small steps that could lead to a revolution in the future. Small steps by Musharraf's regime, such as changes in the school curriculum, are good enough to close the doors on any possibility of a movement that would challenge the status quo.

One can be Hercules and clean the Augean stable. One can be Atlas and hold up the heavenly vault. But no one has ever succeeded in combining the two roles. Musharraf promised a surgery as he was required. He was expected to clean the Augean stable, not to undermine Pakistan. That's why angry shouts break out whenever he reaches for the scalpel but he ignores them, believing in his approach and thinking his survival lies in the hands of his foreign backers. He is fed with the misconception that he is a Philippine healer who could remove a tumor without blood or incisions. Unfortunately, he is not a Philippine healer. At the same time, what has been identified as a tumor by his foreign advisors could be the only justification for the existence of Pakistan. In the following chapters we will analyze all relevant factors in order to determine if there is still any ray of hope and any possibility that a positive development can take root and save Pakistan from an impending demise.

CHAPTER 1

The Musharraf Doctrine

General Musharraf is the right man in the right place at the right time

Secretary of State Colin Powell[1]

THE MUSHARRAF Doctrine is nothing more than a policy of supporting anything that will prolong his stay in power. The fundamental elements by which his military and civilian associates guide their actions in support of the so-called national objectives are subservience, appeasement and surrender.

In order to place facts in perspective, one needs to have a look at the way Musharraf came to power and how his doctrine evolved during the past six years. Former Pakistani Prime Minister Nawaz Sharif came to power with a massive majority in February 1997. Within months he amended the constitution to prevent the President from sacking an elected government and then in October 1998, possibly emboldened by his successes against the judiciary, Sharif challenged the military establishment.

The army's then chief, General Jehangir Karamat, called for the military to have a greater role in formulating policy through a joint security council with the government. According to reports from the time, Karamat and Sharif held a stormy meeting and, for the first time ever, it was the general who chose to quit.

Sharif moved quickly and appointed General Pervez Musharraf, promoted over the heads of two more senior military figures. Regional analysts say that he chose Musharraf not only to demonstrate his firm grip over the military, but also to put in place a man he believed would be unable to build a powerbase because he did not belong to the dominant Punjabi-officer class in the Pakistani army.

While the military allowed these machinations to take place, the popularity of the Sharif government was plunging amid an economic slump—with foreign debt totaling $32bn, and an ever mounting crisis in law and order. Opposition figures allege that such was the Prime Minister's unpopularity that members of his own parliamentary party now began to conspire with the military, especially as opposition grew in the direction of his peace moves with India, which began in March 1999.

But the turning point was this year's Kashmir crisis, where the Pakistani military believed they could finally score a significant victory over India. Within days of pledging his full support to the Kashmir campaign, viewed by the military as an operation of strategic brilliance, Sharif, under pressure from Washington, made a dramatic U-turn and ordered a full withdrawal.

India's leaders celebrated what they saw as a victory while some of Sharif supporters accused senior Pakistani generals of reckless adventurism. In an interview with the BBC, General Musharraf made clear that all the politicians had been "on board" when the offensive began. He was not going to be blamed.

Shireen Mazari, a Pakistan defense expert, said that the military viewed the pullout as a humiliation. She told BBC that: "A lot of people in the military are unhappy about the fact that after many years, in fact for the first time probably, we had the Indians where we wanted them militarily in Kargil. There is a feeling in the military that had there been proper input into this decision, then maybe the decision (of Sharif) to go to Washington might not have happened."[2]

Sharif was now faced with increasing tension in his own party, the military and among the people. The army takeover began only minutes after General Musharraf was removed from his post on October 12, 1999. Three weeks ago, a senior US State Department official had said that Washington would oppose any attempt by political and military officials to overthrow the Pakistani government through extra-constitutional means.

Musharraf was on a visit to Sri Lanka when he was removed from office. Sharif appointed the head of the country's intelligence service, General Ziauddin, in his place. Sharif was alleged to have ordered the Karachi airport to prevent the landing of the airliner carrying Musharraf from Sri Lanka, which then circled the skies over Karachi. In a coup, the generals ousted Sharif's administration and took over the airport. The plane landed with only a few minutes of fuel to spare, and Musharraf assumed control of the government and promised to bring economic progress and political stability, eradicate poverty, build investor confidence and restore democracy as quickly as possible.

On October 17, 1999, Musharraf addressed the nation and declared he had no intention of remaining in power for longer than it takes to lead the country towards "true democracy." However, he provided no specific date for elections. His spokesman, Brigadier Rashid Qureshi, told the BBC that Musharraf would govern until new elections and the restoration of democracy.[3]

Despite the sheen of democracy, Pakistan remains a military dictatorship in all but name. Musharraf's seizure of power was legitimized by a controversial nationwide referendum in April 2002, but many observers questioned the free and fair nature of this "exercise in democracy."[4]

In the last six years, Musharraf's regime failed to demonstrate that it has a principled position or policy on any issue. His doctrine at best was adumbrated in the issue of *Dawn* (June 2, 2004) in which he authored an article titled "Enlightened Moderation." Obviously written in furtherance of enlightened—read benighted—self-interest, it oozes opportunism in facing up to the harsh realities confronting his illegitimate position in Pakistan today.

To understand Musharraf's doctrine, we will look into the source of his motivation: his attitude as a compulsive gambler. We will then move on to understand his much vaunted "enlightened moderation"; what he implies to offer with it; how is he stabbing the soul of Pakistan and how it can eventually lead to the demise of Pakistan.

1. Attitude of a compulsive gambler

Musharraf's approach is reflective of the attitude of a compulsive gambler, which is the hallmark of the attitude of almost all dictators. Gamblers usually go through the phases of winning, losing, and finally desperation. In the desperation phase, they do not hesitate to put anything at stake for the next bet. Unlike a relapse in alcoholism, where the alcoholic can only see the hangover and devastation of the next drunk, gambling and dictating do, in fact, hold out the elusive hope that "I can win!!" on that next bet.

Scanning the views of some keen observers in the last 6 years reveals that Musharraf has gambled more than steering the country forwards as a principled statesman. Until September 11, 2001, Musharraf had little opportunity to gamble. Despite EU, Commonwealth and Washington's rejection, he was winning at home. The public fully supported his, apparently impersonal, moves. His reason was to win; his attitude was to clean the Augean stables. The driving force was his consuming desire to recreate a model Pakistan. The winning phase, however, ended with the big win: the ensured US backing of his regime.

All along he was making little moves, such as praising Kamal Ataturk's secular model and publicly playing with dogs in order to present himself as a liberal Muslim. He could not, however, sell himself. After September 11, the world witnessed a different Musharraf - a gambler who just entered into his losing phase. This is in total contrast to his apparent success in making himself a darling of Bush and Blair. Far from the edgy, almost apologetic figure that Pakistanis witnessed as he was making the televised announcement of his "full support" for the US, he seemed almost jovial as if the crisis were something he had been waiting for all his life.

In his losing phase of gambling, Musharraf's focus remains getting even with other legitimate leaders and recouping his losses in the first two years of his illegitimate power grab. The driving force in this phase was to recapture the glow of winning - this time abroad - which forced him to bet impulsively and rashly.

The first to identify his gambling attitude was John Zubrzycki of *The Australian* who declared that General Musharraf's "gamble will be welcomed in the US."[5] For winning some concessions, the first rash bet was Musharraf's trashing out his close coup partners, including Lieutenant-General Mahmud Ahmed, chief of Pakistan's Inter-Services Intelligence (ISI), the man who went to Musharraf's aid in the 1999 coup by seizing control of Pakistan's television—and Lieutenant-General Usmani, corps commander of Karachi, who took control of the city's airport when Nawaz Sharif tried to prevent Musharraf's plane from landing just before the coup. This was the period when analysts such as Hannah Bloch, Syed Talat Hussain, Massimo Calabresi, Jeff Chu and Meenakshi Ganguly collectively declared "Western goodwill ... at the core of the Pakistani President's great gamble."[6]

BBC's Stephen Cviic then titled his January 12, 2002 analysis of Musharraf speech as "Musharraf's gamble."[7] This was the moment when Musharraf decided to stake his entire future on a gamble to show that Islam is less important to his fellow countrymen than the convoluted and elusive peace, prosperity and stability. With reference to Palestine he said, "We are not contractors of Islam" to help Muslims all over the world. The same tone continues to this date. His argument is: "Why should Pakistan be more Palestinian than the Palestinians?" Contrast Musharraf's position with Rabbi Yisroel P. Feldman of Neturei Karta International, who protests, "the celebration of the founding of the blasphemous and heretical Zionist state... and the heinous crimes committed in the name of its illegitimate "State of Israel."[8] In fact, many Jewish organizations are documenting and speaking out against daily atrocities and human rights violations against the Palestinian people committed by the Zionist regime.

Mark Baker of the *Age* called the 2002 referendum in Pakistan "Musharraf's boldest gamble" for appointing himself as president in uniform.[9] Baker summed up that the gamble will "be remembered as the moment when another ambitious general began to put personal aggrandizement ahead of a professed commitment to defending democracy." Zaffar Abbas, BBC's Islamabad correspondent, holds the view that "Musharraf's latest gamble [was] anything but a routine flutter."[10]

The elections in Pakistan, and the period since then, mark the desperate phase of General Musharraf's gambling career. In this phase, the gambler simply could not stop. His attitude became unreasonable. His mood swung from blaming to outright lying. Even in his best moments, he was caught in a web of lies. He lied to the *Washington Post* and then condemned the newspaper, not knowing that his comments were on tape with the *Post*.[11] The force that drives him to lying and gambling is his juggling dwindling resources—the limited option for betting. A compulsive gambler will get funds from wherever possible, often through criminal means. Psychologists believe that at this time, a gambler's actions become extremely out of character, unreasonable and desperate.

Jane's Foreign Report titled its March 23, 2003 report as, "Musharraf's High Risk Gamble." The report rightly describes that in utter desperation, Musharraf is pitting himself against Islam. According to the report: "The source of Musharraf's power comes from his control of the army, with the only other source of power coming from religion." The report rightly identifies Musharraf's dwindling resources:

1. By "surreptitiously encouraging mass public demonstrations, [Musharraf] is able to show the international community what he is up against."

2. Musharraf stirred up "mass panic and anti-US feeling by publicly proclaiming that he believes that Pakistan could be the next target of pre-emptive action."

3. Since "US troops were already operating out of Pakistan and Afghanistan," Musharraf had "little extra to offer the Bush administration."

Thus, he "had hoped that a large vote for an extremist religious party would trigger increased US support for his government." That is what he is cashing in on at the moment.

Outsiders picked up Musharraf's signs of desperation well within his losing phase. The *Hindu* called his plans for a praetorian National Security Council and Legal Framework Order (LFO)[12] a reflection of his "sense of political desperation that was totally out of sync with his exudation of confidence as the arbiter of Pakistan's destiny."[13] The whole world watched carefully when Musharraf accentuated his sense of anxiety to safeguard his political flanks for years to come.

The self-deluded potentate is in the final desperate moments of his gamble. He looks around, thinks, and then gambles on almost anything that he considers remotely fit to please his masters. In his promotional, "What I can do for you!" trip to US and UK in 2003, he started talking about diplomatic relations with Israel. He pleaded that he needs "more room to maneuver in Pakistan to develop a national consensus on the [Israel's] recognition question."[14] More room to maneuver means a never-ending dictatorship, like Egypt's Hosni Mubarak, and a continued US sponsorship. He started behind-the-scenes high level meetings with

Israeli counterparts and finally made a "chance meeting" with Ariel Sharon and a presentation of his views at the Jewish National Congress possible in September 2005.

Instead of demanding implementation of the UN resolutions on Kashmir, he proposed an American designed "Road Map." In contrast, *Orient on Line* reports that India has "got recognized Line of Control as a formal dividing line between India and Pakistan." Furthermore, the US "wants Pakistan to seal its border with Iran,"[15] a US dream since the early 1990s. Musharraf has already run out of options. The only card left in his hands is Islam. He declared in 2003: "I am very clear that we cannot allow this thing [the establishment of a vice and virtue department] to happen in our country"[16] and went to the Supreme Court in 2005 to reject a bill passed by an elected provincial assembly. To him, poverty and progress are the issues; not occupations and oppressions.[17] He does not see the root causes of poverty in the exploitative international economic system, but in the "extremist" Islam and lack of will among the poor to get out of the vicious cycle. Therefore, he is ready to assist the US in consolidating its grip on Iraq and he alone considered himself to have the authority to agree in principle for allocating Pakistani troops for America's dirty job in Iraq.

In order to keep gambling, Musharraf has to come up with new services to please his promoters abroad. Having nothing else to offer, he has opted to put Islam on the chopping block. The mantra of "enlightened moderation" is part of the bail-out strategy. When begging, borrowing, and stealing cross the limits, gamblers need a "bailout." When bailouts fail, many desperate gamblers have had to say, "My house is your house." It is difficult for people to understand how a person loses control of his gambling behavior. It just seems like any normal person would know better. After all, no one is making the gambler do it; there is not a chemical addiction; he can see what is happening around him; he must know there is a problem. Like gamblers, Musharraf has lost control in spite of everything he knows or anyone else can tell him. Whatever he does is just not rational.

2. Enlightened moderation or benighted opportunism

Any serious analysis would reveal that Musharraf's "strategy" of "enlightened moderation" is at best, a lamb's logic and, at worst, promotion of the Western warlords' concept of a "war within Islam." The neo-cons of the Western world and the neo-mods of Islam,[18] are promoting "moderate Islam" for justifying perpetual wars, occupations and support of dictatorial regimes.

Since the 2003 OIC Conference, Musharraf has been tirelessly working to get credit for the concept of "enlightened moderation". All he actually achieved was merely adding a word "enlightened" to "moderation"—a term the American warlords have invented to use both as a weapon and a shield for their geopolitical political agenda for a long time. Introducing it is their potent weapon for winning the latest war on Islam. However, it is used as a shield when the crusaders claim to using it not for a war on Islam but only intensifying a "war within Islam,"[19]—a comparatively less offensive phrase for stating the core objective.

Among Muslims, the promoters of "moderate" Islam are considered classic examples of those who do not care about anything other than self-interest. In the following analysis we will see if it is really their benighted opportunism that makes them embrace "moderate" Islam as a tool for self-promotion. Their continually shifting positions, according to the changing priorities of the United States, is an evidence of their self-centered approach in this regard, but an analysis of their approach is necessary.

Before assessing Musharraf's "doctrine" of "enlightened moderation", we need to keep in mind that on the opposite ends of the broad spectrum of anti-Islam views, there are two very general and deep-rooted misconceptions: The first misconception is that the Holy Qur'an preaches intolerance and that Islam is only a religion of peace. Both are misrepresentations of the teachings of Islam.

The basic principle of Islam, a belief in prophethood, including the prophethood of Noah, Abraham, Moses, Jesus, is enough to give the lie to the first misconception. Islam teaches that in times past Allah sent prophets to every nation and their numbers are close to 124,000. Islam also teaches that they essentially taught the same message and, since that is so, to disrespect one of those prophets means to disrespect them all. The Qur'an that preaches not only love and respect for the founders of the great religions of the world, but much more than that—faith in them—could not resort to narrowness of intolerance towards those very religions.

Zero tolerance for *zulm*—injustice and oppression—in Islam negates the second misconception that it is a religion of peace alone. Most importantly, the root word of Islam is *"al-silm"* which means "submission" or "surrender." It is understood to mean "submission to Allah." In spite of whatever noble intention has caused many a Muslim to claim that Islam is derived primarily from peace, this is not true (see Qur'an 2:136).

A secondary root of Islam may be *"Al-Salaam"* (peace); however, the text of the Qur'an (2:136) makes it clear that Allah has clearly intended that the focus of this life should remain submission to Him. This entails submission to Him at all times, in times of peace, war, ease, or difficulty.

To demystify this pair of grand misconceptions, we need to study words and deeds of the present day self-proclaimed "moderates" who are exploiting the second misconception in their favor, which indirectly leads to consolidation of the first.

Musharraf's adding "enlightened" to "moderation" gives the impression that other Muslim opportunists are preaching some kind of inferior moderation. However, his best explanation is hardly different from the confusion spread by several others in the name of moderate Islam.[20]

According to Musharraf, the "suffering" of his "brethren in

faith" at the "hands of militants, extremists, terrorists, have inspired" him to come up with "the strategy of enlightened moderation." Here we must note that Musharraf:

a. tries to kill two birds with one shot, i.e., to please both Muslims and the enemies of Islam;

b. presents "enlightened moderation" as a strategy, not a value, or a form of Islam to avoid annoying Muslims;

c. confirms Islamophobes' perspective that the root of the global turmoil lies with Muslims alone;

d. gives legitimacy to the Islamophobes' classification of Muslims and Islam;

e. attempts to prove Islam and secularism compatible, and

f. hides the source of his inspiration—which is nothing more than his self-interest.

Like other self-proclaimed moderates, Musharraf provides no clarification as to why a true Muslim would not be a moderate without following Musharraf's agenda for the so-called moderation. Instead, Musharraf tries to prove that the world would have been a peaceful place if there were no "plastic explosives, combined with hi-tech, remotely controlled activation means superimposed by a proliferation of suicide bombers." His strategy begins with meaningless appeals such as, "something has to be done quickly to stop this carnage." He is right at least in that. Something must be done. But, have appeals and appeasement ever made the aggressors change their policy? The situation demands more than empty appeals and high sundry rhetoric.

Musharraf is cunningly following the neo-cons' agenda. He argues, the world is "an extremely dangerous place" because of "plastic explosives," and "suicide bombers." He concludes that the world is in such a sorry state because "the perpetrators of the crime...are Muslims."

Compare this biased assessment with the ability and atrocities of those who are neck deep in innocent blood; who have stockpiles of nuclear and biological weapons and who bypassed even the UN to occupy two sovereign states (Iraq and Afghanistan), and who killed at least 150,000 people[21] since 9/11 alone on the basis of lies upon lies. What amounts to a carnage? 3,000 deaths at the hands of unknown perpetrators on 9/11, or more than 128,000 at the hands of known liars? [22] Is it enlightened moderation to plead guilty to crimes of unknown culprits and turn a blind eye to the acts of known extremists, and appeal to victims of their aggression, Muslims, to "quickly stop this carnage"?

No one needs to remind Musharraf that the 20th century's mega-murderers—those states killing in cold blood, aside from warfare, one million or more people—have murdered over 151,000,000 people, almost 30,200 times the 5000 killed by Muslim terrorists, and four times the 38,500,000 battle-dead for all the 20th century's international and civil wars up to 1987. All these killers were not only real carnage-makers but also followers of one or another religion and ideology other than Islam.[23] Which faith are these mega-murderers following? Did anyone think of bringing moderation to their faith?

Then there are the kilo-murderers, or those states that have killed innocents by the tens or hundreds of thousands, the top five of which were the China Warlords (1917-1949), Ataturk's Turkey (1919-1923), the United Kingdom (the 1914-1919 food blockade of the Central Powers and Levant in and after World War I, and the 1940-45 indiscriminate bombing of German cities), Portugal (1926-1982), and the US sponsored Indonesia (1965-87). [24]

The US played a leading role in sponsoring and directly taking part in these carnages. For instance, 450,000 to 500,000 communists and sympathizers were killed by the U.S. backed Indonesian Army and affiliates in a brief period between October 1965 and the end of 1966.

If we go a little back in history, we find the Papal bull of 1458 against "infidel Turks" and the subsequent bulls upon bulls to justify colonialist adventure in order to civilizing people other than "infidel Turks" in Africa, Asia and America. According to Steven T. Newcomb, Director of the Indigenous Law Institute, Pope Alexander VI delivered the Inter Cetera papal bull on May 4, 1493.[25] Accordingly, this document, issued shortly after Columbus' first voyage to the Caribbean, expressed the pope's earnest desire that "barbarous nations be subjugated and brought to the faith itself," "for the spread of the Christian Empire." Earlier, such crusading Vatican bulls called for "perpetual slavery" of Africans, by capturing, vanquishing, and subduing them, and by taking away all their possessions and property.

These papal documents were instrumental in the injustices committed against the peoples of the Americas, Oceania, Africa, and Asia. Such papal bulls directly sanctioned colonization, the slave trade, and bloody campaigns that resulted in the deaths of millions. Scholars have correctly identified the Inter Cetera bull as the historic cornerstone of colonialism worldwide.

The Indigenous Law Institute wrote a letter in 1993 to Pope John Paul II, calling upon him to formally revoke the Inter Cetera bull of 1493,[26] and to thereby explicitly overturn the Church's doctrine of conquest and subjugation. But since the last available information, the Institute received only a stony silence from the Vatican. Did anyone call for "moderating" Christianity despite knowing that none of the Muslims issued a "bull" from a high religious authority in the Muslim world to civilize the barbarians of the West through complete genocide? On the other hand, Samuel Eliot Morrison, a Harvard historian and Columbus biographer, admits "the cruel policy initiated by Columbus and pursued by his successors resulted in a complete genocide"[27]

We hope that those who do not get tired of lecturing Muslims and holding their faith responsible for all the wrongs in the world, would find out how their co-religionists with the papal bulls decimated an estimated population of 80 million at the time Columbus discovered America "to a low of 210,000 in the 1910 census."[28] There victims in these places were not Muslim barbarians for sure, nor were the aggressors motivated by extremist Islam and poisonous interpretation of Islam.

One is forced to ask: What role did Islam or Muslims play in these carnages? Why should the world associate carnage, terror and extremism to Muslims for the death of a fraction of human beings (6,000 at the most)[29] compared to the systematic murder of many millions in the 20th century alone?[30]

Islam does not justify killing civilians. However, for the sake of fairness in argument, one has to compare statistics of the deaths at the hands of Muslims in the last 14 centuries alongside the numbers of systematic death, destruction and misery inflicted by European colonialists and the US to see who needs moderation. The US is the only country in the world to have used nuclear weapons in war; the first to use a chemical weapon since the First World War (Agent Orange); is using depleted uranium to poison thousands of Iraqis and Afghans and perhaps make an entire region dangerous to live in. It has been directly implicated in the murders of national leaders like Allende in Chile. Britain used British and Australian soldiers and Aboriginal civilians in "experiments" by setting off nuclear explosions in the 1950s and then studying the effects on people told to stand within line of sight—surely as bad as anything the Nazis did in their "experiments" on concentration camp victims.

For Musharraf and company, moderation is "a two-pronged strategy" of a) "shunning militancy, extremism" and b) "adopting the path of socio-economic uplift." This appeasement-based strategy does not explain how the so-called "moderate" Islam is different from the Islam as prescribed by the Qur'an and the *Sunnah*. Why should one follow them and not the source? If the "moderates" had simply argued that there is no need to use interpretation of the Qur'an to justify acts of violence against civilians, it would have been reasonable. However, introduction of a new version of Islam in an environment in which definition and expectation of "moderate" Islam and Muslims have been totally confused, makes no sense.

As far the two prongs are concerned, no one loves to live in perpetual violence and never-ending poverty. The pre-requisite for addressing these problems is not embracing some kind of convoluted form of Islam. Let us see how the issue of poverty fits with the self-contradictory concept of "enlightened moderation" at a time when government policies perpetuate poverty.

General Musharraf has issued various laws that weaken Pakistan's economy and clear the way for western hegemony over the country's economy. Musharraf's cabinet approved a package for "corporate farming" under which the multinational companies can now buy as much land as they want, thereby exploiting the agricultural land of Pakistan for their own market objectives, whilst ignoring the domestic needs of Pakistan. Musharraf also accelerated the process of privatization, through a "Privatization Ordinance" that makes it compulsory to spend 90% of the amount obtained from privatization sales on external debts. In this way, Musharraf is ensuring that the foreign companies not only deprive Pakistan of its valuable assets but also the proceeds of the sales are handed over to the global institutions for economic exploitation in the name of debt servicing. With making the Legal Framework Order (LFO)[31] part of constitution, Musharraf has ensured that Pakistan remains dependent on the totalitarians in the West, even after he departs, and the doors of exploiting Pakistan's resources remains open to the multi-national companies of the corporate terrorists.

Part of this economic catastrophe is due to the introduction of the Multi-Fibre Agreement (MFA) by the World Trade Organization (WTO), which has slaughtered the already weakened textile industry. In Faisalabad, which is a major textile production centre, 400,000 jobs have been lost in the textile industry. The MFA under the WTO will destroy a lot more jobs.

Pakistan is a byword for poverty, disease and suffering. In early 2005, outside the Lahore Press Club, for instance, 20 kiln workers lifted their shirts to display savage scars on their bodies. This was the result of their "donation" of a kidney for money in order to pay off the crippling loans to their kiln bosses. A member of the Pakistani Human Rights Commission said: "The very arduous work for a laborer is now harder than ever before." In one Punjabi village, a total of 3,000 people have donated their kidneys. Contrary to the impression given in the Western press,[32] most of these "donations" don't go to rich Westerners but to rich Pakistanis. Their kidneys have been damaged beyond repair because of the poisoning of the water supply – itself a product of the capitalist system. Eighty-three per cent of the water supply in Lahore, for instance, is polluted. There is no salvation for the poor whose kidneys fail; they face a lingering and terrible death.

As Musharraf sheds crocodile tears over the plight of the poor, poverty has gone from bad to worse during his 72 months in office so far. At the same time, capitalism has kept blooming. Even government institutions admit that the results are entirely disastrous for the masses. *The News* reported on March 22, 2005 that according to the State Bank, "the unemployment rate in Sindh and Baluchistan has risen considerably in the 2000-2004 period." In the country as a whole, 7,500 industrial units have shut down; over half a million jobs have been lost, a lot of them in industry, in the ten-year period 1995-2005. In some districts, the unemployment rate is 85 per cent.

It is a "boom" that primarily lines the pockets of the bosses and the landlords. It is based upon a big increase in loans, which the regime has encouraged to stimulate purchasing power, not for the working masses, but for the "new middle class", who speculate in property, buy the latest motorcycles, vans, and electronic goods. This disguises the fact, however, that the economic decline has destroyed the old middle class. In Sindh, for instance, 80 per cent of the population lives on $3.50 a month.[33]

Of the four thousand health units in Punjab, 70 per cent have been closed down. Seventy-four per cent of the population has no healthcare at all. Alongside this, the national question has been enormously aggravated, as evidenced by the escalation of the civil war in Baluchistan. According to Peter Taafe of the London based Committee for Workers International: "Pakistan is a powder keg ready to explode at any time." So much for the one prong of the "enlightened moderation" on poverty.

The pre-requisite for addressing the identified problems is bringing aggression to a halt, leaving the victims of oppression alone; bringing an end to the exploitative political and economic systems and structures, and most importantly making the aggressor pay reparations for the damage done. Is an attractive title to the strategy for effective subservience good enough to fulfill any of these pre-requisites?

As for the second prong, Muslims' alleged obsession with their faith has no role in the miserable situation they are facing. Instead, it is the lack of obsession that keeps Muslims groping in the dark. They don't need any moderation in embracing or practicing Islam. "Enlightened moderation" is a deceptive title. It is totally irrelevant to the proposed strategy, which, in turn, is devoid of common sense and the reality of facts on the ground.

Blindness of the proposed strategy touches its peak when Musharraf adds a series of appeals with regards to "the role to be played by the West," saying the US "must aim at resolutely resolving all political disputes with justice," "resolve the political disputes enumerated above with justice" and "justice must be done and seen to be done." Well said.

The excessive stress on justice, however, shows that the label of moderation is deceptive in the first place. What Musharraf is appealing for is exactly what the so-labeled extremists are demanding. Why is it so that when Musharraf begs for it, it is OK? But if someone else just talks about it, it becomes extremism?

Besides the apologetic tone, what makes Musharraf a moderate in this case is his hypocrisy of saying one thing and doing exactly the other. Sustaining an unjust order and demanding justice from the same doesn't make any sense.

The hypocrisy is further reflected in Musharraf's statement that the "root cause of extremism and militancy lies in political injustice, denial and deprivation." That is true. However, he forgets that he is playing a lead role in perpetuating "political injustice, denial and deprivation." He is so obviously responsible for what he calls "acute sense of deprivation, hopelessness and powerlessness."

Let us agree with Musharraf that "a people suffering from a combination of all these lethal ills are easily available cannon fodder for the propagation of militancy and the perpetration of extremist, terrorist acts." The question, however, is: what is the root cause for these ills? When these ills do not originate from Islam, why then needlessly introduce different versions of Islam, or a strategy with a deceptive title, to address them?

In the same breath, Musharraf admits: "it is not Islam as a religion which preaches or infuses militancy and extremism but the political disputes which led to antagonism in the Muslim masses." Logically, the discussion should end at this point because if Islam doesn't teach militancy and extremism, it is of no use to introduce "moderate" or "liberal," or "progressive" forms of Islam and leaving the dispute to the unjust to resolve. The need is to address the causes that lead to reactionary sentiments, but where is the strategy for that?

Musharraf equates moderation with a "conciliatory approach" and shows that Islam is not in conflict with secularism. Here Musharraf attempts to make his mantra acceptable to the enemies of Islam by making Islam compatible with secularism. Musharraf's doctrine[34] displays a mind-set infected with benighted opportunism. It is a mind-set shaped into believing the much trumpeted allegation of the Western warlords that "the suffering of the innocent" Muslims in the world today is only due to Muslim "militants, extremists and terrorists."[35]

Musharraf had no option but to begin his plea with the

same idea. However, the signs of confusion are obvious in his thoughts. He admits in the later part of his plea that these terms are wrongly labeling Muslims alone. In his opinion, if Muslims alone are responsible and he is making a plea to them, why then say they are "wrongly labeled?"

The mantra of moderation is no more than a weapon equally used by the neo-cons in the West and the dictators and other neo-mods for their personal gains in the Muslim world. Their victims are both the Muslim and non-Muslim masses because they equally reap the consequences of wars, occupations and puppet regimes imposed on the Muslim world for "moderating" Muslims and Islam.

General Musharraf is simply supporting and consolidating the neo-cons' argument that the Muslim World as a whole is devoted to terrorism for which the West needs to "rebuild" and introduce a "civil, democratic Islam."[36] Infected with benighted opportunism, Musharraf and other "moderates" endorse this lie when they lump 1.2 billion Muslims into one monolithic group and argue that "the Muslim world has to shun militancy" and "extremism" for "enlightened moderation."[37]

It is not that benighted opportunism has over-powered the "moderates" to the extent that they do not realize the truth. General Musharraf cautiously concedes: "the West, the US in particular, must aim at resolutely resolving all political disputes with justice." It means:

1. The US and its allies are not dealing with justice and their injustice is the root cause of the problems today, and

2. Whoever stands by the unjust in perpetrating injustice becomes accomplice in the crimes of the unjust.

The Question is, what makes the "moderates" stand by the US shoulder to shoulder in perpetrating injustice when they admit, in Musharraf words: "the root cause of extremism and militancy lies in political injustice, denial and deprivation," not Islam.

Opportunism and denial hold "moderate" Muslims from supporting their words with deeds. Musharraf's sermons about "political injustice" are meaningless as long as he remains committed to perpetuating himself in power and ignores his guilt in continuing to heap political injustice on the nation.

In their attempts to make the leg-less moderation stand, the "moderates" contradict and undermine what they stand for. After giving a historical background, Musharraf proves, in total contradiction to the mantra of moderation that Islam, as a religion, is not one that "preaches or infuses militancy and extremism." To him, it is "the political disputes which led to antagonism in the Muslim masses." If this were so, what was the need for inventing "moderate" Islam and Muslims? Why not just follow Islam and be moderate by default?

By virtue of the above mentioned argument from Musharraf, there is no need for promoting secularism, taking out Qur'anic verses from the school curriculum, proposing "moderation," civilizing Islam and advancing new concepts that have nothing to do with Islam at all. If any moderation is required, it is required of those who are responsible for the root causes of the problem.

Promoting "moderation" that runs against the common beliefs of Islam is just a mockery of Muslims and Islam. Musharraf says Muslims have to "wash off the common belief that Islam is a religion...in conflict with modernization, democracy and secularism." This is the crux of the "moderate" message, which takes the soul out of both moderate Islam and the neo-cons' theory of "moderation", because there is no place for secularism in Islam. It also rejects the forms of governance and modernization that are not bound by the prescribed limits of the Qur'an and the *Sunnah*. However, this does not necessarily mean that Islam in its true sense is against democracy, modernization, education, human rights and so on. If anyone thinks so, he is either a victim of the neo-cons' lies or the neo-mods' benighted opportunism. One only needs to refer to the sources of Islam and the truly Islamic scholarship to see what Islam's position is on these topics

The solution to the world's problems lies in the realization that leaving Muslims alone to live by Islam is the only way forward to peace and security for all. Propping up dictators and promoting misconceptions about Islam will never work.

M. A. Niazi of the *Nation* has summarized up the argument quite well: He writes:

> At one level, a single Muslim state, especially one which implements Islam, is the West's only safe guarantee against what it calls terrorism. If it met the *Shari'ah* requirements, it would be able to control jihad, which has always been seen as a state activity, and those who perforce have to carry on an unprecedented 'private' *Jihad* because of oppression, will be bound to follow the decisions of the Muslim [Islamic] State on whether their struggle constitutes a *Jihad* or not. With a strong military, this state would be able itself to deal with Israel and India, at least to reduce oppression, without seeking succour from the West.[38]

3. What Musharraf implies to offer?

The above discussion is merely the icing on the cake of Musharraf's message of "moderation." It brings us to the real issue: the problem of a few Muslim opportunists, such as Musharraf himself, who are exploiting the morbid dread of Islam in the hearts of Islamophobes by various means. They promote themselves under the cloak of being Muslim where in fact they don't even practice the faith by regurgitating the views of the enemies of Islam in different words. These efforts lead to the Islamophobes' objective of introducing different forms of Islam and different classes of Muslims.

Musharraf's publicly known comments on moderation do not fulfill the standards set by those who introduced the rancid notion of "moderate" Islam. To understand Musharraf's "enlightened moderation," we need to understand expectations of the promoters of "moderate" Muslims and what Musharraf implies to offer to their cause.

Islamophobes' intention behind introducing "moderate" Islam

and Muslims becomes evident when they reject arguments from some leading self-proclaimed "moderates" as "reformist apologetic."[39] On the contrary, persons such as Canadian author and TV personality, Irshad Manji, who are shunned even by the self-proclaimed "moderates," are presented as a "practicing Muslim" and real moderate[40] because they sound more in consonance with the anti-Islam agenda.

The acceptable-to-Islamophobes "moderates," in fact, believe that "an uncritical acceptance of the Qur'an as the final manifesto of God" is one of the "disturbing cornerstones of Islam."[41] So the real moderation in the eyes of the standard-setters for "moderate" Muslims is to reject the Qur'an as the final manifesto of Allah. Are Musharraf and his supporters in the deceptive "enlightened moderation" ready for accepting this kind of standards? If not, they are acceptable only as long as they can sell something of interest to their masters.

There is no limit to moderation in the eyes of their masters, who are busy in undermining Islam. The acceptable "moderates"—the "practicing Muslims" such as Irashad Manji—now call the rest of the self-proclaimed "moderates" as "so-called moderates" and equate them with "fundamentalists" for sharing a "sense of spiritual supremacy."[42]

In order to wade through this confusion, we need to understand that the clear commands for Muslims are to be moderate by default.[43] Being moderate is a prerequisite for being a good Muslim. It is not an identity label for a specific kind of Muslim out there to please and appease others. The most perfect moderates are those who most seriously follow the Qur'an and the *Sunnah*. Accordingly, Muslims cannot be part time or partial Muslims to be considered as moderate by virtue of rejecting part of the Qur'an and accepting part of it (Qur'an 2:85).[44]

Someone might quickly ask: Where do the users of violence come in then, the trainers and dispatchers of 14 year old suicide bombers who claim to be Muslim? The answer to this lies in the reality on the ground in Iraq, for example. How many Muslims volunteered to blow themselves up before the US occupation and how many actually carried out such attacks? Were not they Muslim before the US occupation? Was not their religion providing them any motivation? Were not they oppressed? If or when Islam is referred to when these acts are committed, it is the religion that is being co-opted into the political agenda and used as justification but Islam itself remains blameless.

Islam is a Muslim's identity. It means submission to Allah. It embodies the basic elements of moderation—balance, due proportion, tolerance, justice and equity—because abiding each and tranquility is unthinkable in a situation of extremes. In fact, moderation or balance is the core value, the very soul of Islam.

In the light of specific Qur'anic verses (2:143, 4:171, 25:67, 17:26-27, 20:81, 6:108, 2:178, 17:33, 5:45, 42:40) and numerous others where fairness, justice and balance are extolled and excess is deplored, we can safely say that those who suggest moderating Islam only expose their ignorance of the Divine Message.

The fact is that Islam enjoins its followers to give lessons in moderation to other people. What Muslims need today, therefore, is not lectures in the concept of moderation, but to delve into the treasure trove of guidance that Islam has already bequeathed to them. They also need to have the obvious inequalities and injustices lifted, as discussed previously. The two issues are joined. If so many people didn't live lives of desperation, there would be little opportunity to recruit "terrorists" or "freedom fighters".

To confirm demystification of moderation, we need to see who the visible enemies of Islam consider as "extremists" and "Islamists." The standard-setters for "moderate" Muslims believe that strong belief in the totality of the Qur'an makes Muslims "Islamists," and "extremists."[45] Accordingly, the most partial believers of the Qur'an become the most perfect "moderates" because promoters of the "moderate" Muslims believe they "are absolutely at war with the vision of life that is prescribed to all

Muslims in the Koran,"[46] which, in their view, contains 389 specifically intolerant verses.[47]

This shows that Musharraf's statements might be some kind of intelligent deception to him. But it is, in fact, a foolish self-deception. He titles his adventure as "enlightened moderation" to make it acceptable to the shrewd enemies of Islam. At the same time, he attempts to deceive Muslims by talking about totally irrelevant issues to give the common man an impression that "moderation" is all about good feelings for reconciliation, tolerance and poverty alleviation. The well-known criteria of Islamophobes for "moderate" Muslims clearly shows that this is not what is expected of "moderate" Muslims and their moderation.

Besides what is mentioned above, "moderates" are required to totally reject parts of the Qur'an, such as rejecting the clear commands about inheritance[48] (Qur'an 4:11-14, 4:33, 4:176), court testimony[49] (Qur'an 2:282) and even *Riba*[50]—the charging of interest on financial dealing and transaction (Qur'an 2:275-76, 278-79; 3:130; 4:161; 30:39). The overt Islamophobes publicly say that "the fundamentals of Islam are a threat to us."[51] It clearly shows that Islamophobes do not want the "moderates" they support to follow the fundamentals of Islam according to the Qur'an and the *Sunnah*.

The Qur'an tells Muslims on several occasions not to coerce other people (2:256, 5:92, 24:54, 6:125, 42:48, 76:03, 18:29, 6:106, and 17:07). Accordingly, Muslims must present the message to them in the most cogent and clear way, invite them to the Truth and do their best in conveying the Truth. It is up to people to accept or not to accept the message. Thus intolerance could not be ascribed to a book which excludes compulsion from the sphere of religion altogether, and which is full of verses that exhort believes to exercise restraint, mercy and kindness.

The question is: If Allah gave humanity a choice to believe or not to believe, then why did He punish the people of Prophet Nuh, Lut, Shu'aib, the 'Ad, the Thamud, and Pharaoh and his followers and why did Prophet Mohammed (Peace be up him - PBUH) go to many wars? The very fact that Mohammed (PBUH) fought wars is enough to show that Islam I not a religion of peace alone.

The above mentioned nations were not punished simply because of their disbelief. They were punished because they had become oppressors. They committed aggression against the righteous, and hindered others from coming to the way of Allah. There were many in the world who denied Allah, but Allah did not punish every one, nor did Mohammed (PBUH) go out to slaughter all non-Muslims.

The phenomenon of '*zulm*' (injustice and oppression) in any form and at any point of time is repeatedly and emphatically condemned in the Qur'an. There is no tolerance for *zulm* and no reconciliation with the oppressors as long as they do not renounce their *zulm*. However, this is not justification for acts of violence against civilians in Western countries or non-combatants and visitors from Western countries. There is no scope for transgression of these Divine injunctions in Islam. On the other hand, the condemnation of '*zulm*' or 'wrong' by virtue of its repeated emphasis and the centrality of the terms that define it, has immense significance for building a just social and economic order which characterizes the religion of Islam.

As Professor Kenneth Cragg of Cambridge University has explained in his book, *The Mind of the Qur'an*, that the usage of "the derivatives of the root '*zalama*' verbs, nouns and participles are among the most frequent of all Qur'anic terms... exceeded only by the most central of all words, like Allah, *Rabb* and *Rasul*."

Now compare Kenneth Cragg's explanation of the word *zulm* in the Qur'an with the words and deeds of those at the hands of whom their own people in general and Muslims in particular suffer today. According to Cragg: "The basic sense of '*zalama*' is to do wrong, to treat wrongfully, to deal unjustly, with or without an object. It is the act of falsifying in not according to what is due, whether to things or to people, to truth or to trust. It means distortion and perversity, tyranny and evil will. More frequently 'zulm' denotes wrong against fellow humanity—injustice, deceit, fraud, slander, treachery, calumny, robbery and the rest."[52]

If we start with the lies of Bush and Blair for invading Iraq and go back to search the history of colonialism for the past five hundred years, we will come to the conclusion that the root cause of the present turmoil is nothing but pure zulm of the colonialists of the past and the totalitarians of today on the one hand, and perpetuation of a colonial legacy by their puppets among Muslims on the other. Their misinformation campaigns misled Muslims away from what the Qur'an repeatedly calls "the Straight Path," and their economic tyranny robs them of every possible opportunity to invest in poverty alleviation and other ventures for human development.

In the light of this discussion, the real purpose of fighting for Muslims is to remove injustice and aggression. Muslims are permitted to keep good relations with non-Muslims. Allah says, "Allah does not forbid you that you show kindness and deal justly with those who did not fight you in your religion and did not drive you out from your homes..." (Qur'an 60:8). The objective of allowing Muslims to fight was to establish religious freedom, to stop all religious persecution, to protect the houses of worship of all religions, mosques among them (Qur'an 22:40, 2:193, 8:39, 2:190). In this regard, one can look at the history of Moors' humane treatment of Jews and then their dehumanization at the hands of Spanish successors.

Tolerance, moderation and reconciliation are the mechanism used for upholding human rights, pluralism (including cultural and religious pluralism), and the rule of law. Submission to injustice and tyranny is no tolerance. Islam is moderate between turning your left cheek to him who hits you on the right one, and between paying someone back tenfold. According to the Qur'an: "And those who, when an oppressive wrong is inflicted on them, help and defend themselves. The recompense for an injury is an injury equal thereto (in degree), but if a person forgives and makes a reconciliation, his reward is due from Allah; surely He loves not those who do wrong" (42:39-40). This argument is repeated in another verse: "And if you punish (your enemies), punish them with the like of that with which you were afflicted. But if you endure patiently, verily, it is better for those who are patient. And endure you patiently; your patience is not but from Allah. And grieve not over them and be not distressed because of what they plot" (16:126-127).

There is no such thing as moderate and extremist Islam, justified with either of the two grand misconceptions discussed above. Islam doesn't need any prefixes or suffixes. Islam's moderation lies in its balanced approach towards living individual and collective living. Any attempt at justifying classification of Islam and Muslims amounts to helping the Western warlords in their war on Islam.

4. Stabbing the soul of Pakistan

General Musharraf's supporting agenda of the enemies of Islam under the smart title of "enlightened moderation" is not the first step. He has been stabbing the soul of Pakistan long before that. One of the prominent examples is the constitutional changes to permanently close the doors on the possibility of having an Islamic State in Pakistan.

Musharraf introduced a wide range of changes to the Constitution and launched a campaign to make these permanent features of the constitution for a stable government and sustainable democracy in the country. The question, however, should have been about the ultimate, higher objective—the overall goal. Was "sustainable democracy" impossible without re-writing some of the basic clauses of the Constitution? Or it is that the public was kept in the dark about the overall goal of these amendments?

The fact that Pakistanis ignored was that rewriting the constitution was part of the bigger game: the covert war on Islam under the banner of "war on terrorism" and the overt promotion of "war within Islam" as promoted by major American analysts and organizations.

The first thing to keep in mind is that the Supreme Court of Pakistan authorized the military regime to "amend" the constitution, not rewrite it. A quick count of the proposed changes shows that 10 clauses were to be omitted; 29 articles changed and a total of 97 articles and sub-clauses to be substantially changed or omitted altogether.

Amendment means a partial change; rectification of any error or omission to fulfill the natural evolutionary requirements by adding or deleting something in consonance with the basic structure and strategic system of a constitution. No change in deviation or clash with it can be treated as a legitimate amendment. What the nation ignored are serious violations, which have become necessary for transforming the Constitution into a potent weapon for the war on Islam.

We witnessed a military regime that turned the Constitution upside down when even parliaments elsewhere in the world, which come into being under a constitution, have only limited authority to amend their constitutions. Even such elected bodies do not enjoy the right for its abrogation or metamorphosis as we witnessed at the hands of military men at the top. That was no justification that the Supreme Court had granted permission for amending the Constitution; because the Court had also lost its credibility for the way it played its role since October 12, 1999 in almost all major decisions.

Let's examine how America comes into this affair. The initial reaction of the US towards Musharraf's coup in 1999 was that the US cannot "do business as usual" with a military government. Richard Boucher, the US State Department spokesman, told the world that Musharraf's actions to dissolve the elected assemblies and to appoint himself president "severely undermined Pakistan's constitutional order."[53] Compare these reactions with comments of US analysts, government officials and think-tanks before and after Musharraf's January 12 and July 12, 2002 speeches. A detailed study shows that they knew what Musharraf was to tell the nation well in advance.

One day Musharraf tells the nation that military role in politics is essential and the next week people read headline news: "US supports Army role in civilian set up".[54] The question is, why? The answer is: because the US wants the imposition of a top-down form of transformation of Pakistan in the image of Zionist Christians and neo-cons, which is not possible unless delivered at the barrel of a gun. Daniel Pipes sums up this approach in *Elections Today*: "Muslims must accept that the West has discovered ideas and methods that they must learn, adopt, and apply—that ignoring or rejecting them is a major mistake. Mustafa Kamal, the founder of modern Turkey, understood precisely this and imposed a top-down form of modernization in the 1920s and 1930s. He is the great exception, as is Turkey more broadly."[55]

The morbid dread of "fundamentalists" taking power in Pakistan forces Washington to impose the Turkish model and entrust to the military the responsibility to act like a secular bulwark. Musharraf quickly proved himself to be "the great exception". All he needed were Hosnie Mubarak (military) kind of powers and a Turkish kind of constitution (secular). If Pakistanis could look from a proper perspective, they would have seen that it was as much the issue of including military in the political set up as it was the soul of their Constitution that was under attack with the military-made amendments.

According to section 6 (iii) of the limiting clauses of Supreme Court's May 12, 2000 decision, "no amendment shall be made in the salient features of the Constitution, i.e. independence of judiciary, federalism, parliamentary form of government blended with Islamic provisions." The following analysis shows how the regime violated these limits and how Islam was the main target without making any direct reference to this intention.

The regime conceded under proposal 19(b) that its proposals sought "to change specific provisions of the parliamentary form", which was the first violation of the limiting clause of the Supreme Court's decision. The regime once more admitted under 19(e), that the proposed "changes [would] impact the parliamentary character of the system." Admitting and still going against the Court's decision shows that the regime was determined to impose these changes because it had to. Unfortunately, there was no legal way to take illegal actions. The regime made a circuitous argument under 20(b) that there is "no universal formula of federalism," therefore it may seek to "adjust specific provisions," ignoring that Pakistan's founding generation had agreed to a specific formula, a standard, and the Court's decision warned the regime not to change it's essence with the lame arguments, such as, "there is no universal formula."

After admitting that it was going against the Supreme Court's decision, the regime started stabbing the soul of Pakistan. It attacked the electorate with a reduction in the voter age from 21 to 18 years and the adoption of a joint electorate. The seemingly naïve rewriting of these clauses means a lot. The inclusion of teens in elections means a high percentage of voters would now be madly attracted to glamorized secularization and modernization, thus reducing the chances of anyone securing more votes with calls for enforcing Islamic clauses of the Constitution or enforcement of "draconian" *Shari'ah* as the supreme law of the land. Moreover, we witnessed the misuse of this clause during the referendum held by Musharraf for reinstating himself, where college students were brought in to show an increased turnout.

Removal of the word "Muslim" from Article 51(1) of the Constitution means any number of non-Muslims, or Muslims like Salman Rushdie and Ibn Warraq (who prefers to be called "a former Muslim"), can not only be elected to different assemblies, but also hold the position of Prime Minister or Chief Minister—a clear violation of the spirit of Objectives Resolution—the preamble and part of the Constitution, which states, "sovereignty over the entire Universe belongs to Almighty Allah alone, and the authority to be exercised by the people of Pakistan within the limits prescribed by Him is a sacred trust." Would a non-Muslim Prime Minister care about the limits prescribed by Allah? Someone argued that if the people of Pakistan are truly Muslim, such a person will never be elected. The question arises, if Pakistanis are truly Muslim, why this clause in the first place, which violates the Preamble to the Constitution?

The preamble of the Constitution further states, "the principles of democracy, freedom, equality, tolerance and social justice, as enunciated by Islam, shall be fully observed." Would a non-Muslim Premier or his fellow members in the elected bodies care about the principles enunciated by Islam?

The soul of the Constitution requires the state to "enable" Muslims "to order their lives in the individual and collective spheres in accordance with the teachings and requirements of Islam as set out in the Qur'an and the *Sunnah*." How would a person who does not believe in the "teachings and requirements of Islam as set out in Qur'an and the *Sunnah*" lead Muslims? Article 2 of the Constitution states that Islam shall be the State religion of Pakistan. Does Islam permit a non-Muslim to be the head of the "Islamic" state, or lead a majority of Muslims? Of course, the Anglican version of Christianity is the official religion of Great Britain, yet Disraeli was once Prime Minister. In fact, UK is a professed secular state, whereas in the case of Islam, a country doesn't become Islamic by stating a few pro-Islam articles in the constitution. This issue of what makes a state Islamic is discussed in detail in chapter 2, which will clarify that it is almost impossible to think of a non-Muslim head of state in an Islamic State.

Questions in the preceding paragraphs are essential because Article 41(2) of the Constitution clearly states, "a person shall not be qualified for election as President unless he is a Muslim..."

But there is no such restriction for the Prime Minister. Throwing out the Objectives Resolution and associated Islamic provisions was not possible at this point in time. The regime thus decided to introduce new provisions that would not only render the rest of the provisions ineffective but also pave the way for future "valid" objections for removal of any reference to Islam.

The clause restricting the entitlement of political parties securing less than ten percent of the total votes cast in the election on general seats to any reserved seat, or securing less than 5 per cent seats for any seat in Senate is directed at religious parties, notorious for securing minimum percentages of votes. Reduction in voter's age would further reduce the chances to improve their image as underdogs in the election process.

Reserving a high proportion of seats for women is actually a pretext for an attack on Islam. Interestingly, the increase in women seats goes hand in hand with a decrease in the seats for those who have the highest possible degrees from religious institutions. More than 70% of the population lives in rural areas, where women to men ratio at Primary, Middle and High levels of education is 1:4, 1:5 and 1:9 respectively.[56] With such a low comparative literacy ratio, reserving 22 percent of seats for women is a folly in the name of development, because countries with much higher literacy rates have far less percentage of women seats.

In Japan, with a much more liberal culture and higher literacy rate than ours, between the years 1952 and 1980, the proportion of women in parliament averaged a mere 3%. Since 1980, however, when a proportional representation system was introduced in the Upper House, the number of candidates, as well as women elected, increased significantly, but is still less than 6 per cent. At the Euro-parliamentary elections of 1989, out of 26 members, only one was a woman (4.5%). In the local elections of 1986, out of 303 mayors, there were only six women (1.9%); among 5,697 community presidents only 30 were women (0.52 per cent); in municipal councils, out of 4,999 councilors only 412 were women (8.24%); in community councils, out of 40,402 only 812 were women (2%); and out of 303 presidents of municipal council only 4 were women (1.6%).[57]

Moreover, women representation in the British parliament has been notoriously low, less than 5 percent through the 1970s and only rising to 6.3 percent after the general election of 1987. At national level, the 1990 figures of women in legislation as the percentage of all elected officials in some leading countries are as follows: Canada 13.7%; Great Britain 6.3%; Greece 5.3%; India 5.8%; Japan 5.9%; Mexico 12%; Norway 35%; Poland 14.8%; Spain 7%; U.S. 5.4% and Uganda 14.4 per cent. The question is: why do any of these countries not reserve such a high percentage of seats for women, so that the rest of the world shall consider them "moderate" or to allow women to play a meaningful role in development? The only reason to force us into playing by such rules is to make it easy to inflame the "war within Islam," using women-related issues as bones of contention.

All other Constitution re-writing proposals regarding checks and balances, appointment of Prime Minister, Governors and Chief Ministers and dissolution of assemblies, establishment of NSC etc., were directed at giving the military a permanent role in politics. Musharraf argued in his July 12, 2002 speech that politicians repeatedly came to the military General Head Quarters (GHQ) for consultation and mediation. This doesn't mean that the military should be given a permanent constitutional role, because these politicians have made more visits to the American consulates and Washington than GHQ. Does it mean Washington will be given a permanent constitutional role in Pakistan? The only objective of forcing Pakistan into giving the military a permanent role in civilian government is that as soon as American newspapers start a hue and cry about an elected Prime Minister, like Erbakan in Turkey, the military is constitutionally ready to remove any threat to secularization.

The strangest of all proposals was the Amendment in Article

91(5) under which the National Assembly was expected to sign its own death warrant in case the Prime Minister desired to dissolve the assembly and the President either relieved him or asked the assembly to endorse the PM's advice of its dissolution. Similarly, the proposed "modifications" in article 58 (2) and 101(1) were simply to empower every President as much powerful as General Musharraf is now. What a mockery of the claim to introduce checks. Who is there to check the President and what is going to balance his powers?

Most of the proposals for re-writing the Constitution were directed at neutralizing the Objectives Resolution and paving the way for full-fledged secularization of the country. In the Nusrat Bhutto case, the Supreme Court determined the Objectives Resolution as the basic law of the country and later the high courts also acknowledged this principled stand. Gradually, all courts confirmed this principle, which ultimately formed part of the Constitution with a full bench judgment of the Supreme Court in the Achakzai case. The judgment says: "One thing is beyond dispute that in all the three Constitutions, Objectives Resolution is common and the same, which has been incorporated as preamble in all the three Constitutions including the Constitution of 1973..."

Supreme Court's May 12, 2000 and previous decisions settle in clear terms that any amendment (not re-writing) could only be made by staying within these limits. None of the legal, religious or political forces could deter Musharraf from making all these changes part of the constitution. We will look at this factor in detail in chapter 4. Suffice it to say at this point that as part of the broader, anti-Pakistan move, the military has already stabbed the soul of Pakistan.

5. Conclusion: Undermining Pakistan

The Call of Islam is one which transcends the bounds of country.
It may have lost some of its force as a result of the abolition of the

Caliphate by Mustafa Kamal Pasha, but it still has a very considerable appeal as we witness for example Jinnah's insistence on our giving undertaking that Indian troops should never be employed against any Muslim State, and the solicitude which he has constantly expressed for the Arabs of Palestine. I cannot help thinking that if separate Muslim State did indeed come into existence in India, as now contemplated by the All India Muslim League, the day would come when they might find the temptation to join an Islamic Commonwealth of nations well nigh irresistible.

Secretary of State for India, Lord Zetland,
to the Viceroy of India, Lord Linlithgow, April 24, 1949.

These words from Lord Zetland above reflect the common perception and understanding about Muslims' demand for a separate homeland. The most dangerous aspect of the Musharraf Doctrine is distorting the identity and dream of Pakistan.

Pakistan did not stand for separation per se, it was not conceived as a Muslim ghetto, run by a dictator and living on the sufferance of the rest of world; it was a charter of freedom from the colonial-imperialist world order.

Those were the heydays of imperialism, secularism and territorial nationalism. The demand for a sovereign and independent state which claimed Islam as its *raison d'etre* was meant to be a clean break from imperialist control and imperialist ideologies. Pakistan was meant to be "the greatest Muslim State of the world." As the leader of the movement, Muhammad Ali Jinnah clearly spelled out as their main task to the would-be officers of the future Pakistan army—that was going to be a reality after 11 days on March 23, 1940.

The movement for a separate homeland for Muslims was the result of a decades-long resistance against the British colonial adventures. It was a reaction to the British objective of destroying Muslim power in South Asia. Soon after, a religious reformation, a scientific and economic revolution, simultaneously took place, namely Protestantism, modern science and Capitalism respectively. These *'events'* transformed the British Isles into a 'United

Kingdom' for Empire building. Britain inherited Columbus' objective and colonized *India*. Thereafter, Britain used the resources of its Empire to destroy the Muslim powers in South Asia, Africa and Ottoman Caliphate (Middle East). This culminated in the colonization of Palestine in 1917—its last colony.

Many analysts still believe the aim of the British Empire had nothing to do with Islam. It was a way of making wealth. To the British of the time, indeed for all Europeans, anyone not from Europe were "primitive savages" with no rights. They came to India to plunder, by right of self-perceived superiority. This had nothing to do with religion and they didn't recognize the culture. In fact, keeping the historical grudge of the crusades aside, anyone familiar with the history of South Asia is aware of the reality that the only resistance posed to the British imperialist plans was carried out by Muslims from day one until the British departure in 1947. During this period, the colonialists developed specific hatred towards Muslims and all the strategies for consolidating colonialism revolved around taming Muslims and diluting their religion. The initial crusade against *Jihad*-related verses in the Qur'an was carried by British colonialists. Lord Macaulay carried out specific educational reforms to indoctrinate Muslim youth for taming the resistance posed by Muslims. British three pronged strategy to address Muslim problem was based on a) promoting sectarianism among Muslims, b) promote a regional and linguistic feudal system and c) introduce a British education system.

The movement for Pakistan was unlike all other national freedom movements in the Muslim world, from Morocco in the far west to Indonesia in the far east. The movement was a precursor to the wave of liberation that soon swept the entire Muslim world. Unlike the military regime's resolve to abandon Afghanistan, Kashmir and Palestine, the new and nascent Islamic state of Pakistan found itself duty bound to contribute morally, materially and politically to the freedom of almost every Muslim state. Such was the sense of commitment and enthusiasm to the Islamic cause and the Muslim world in the early years of Pakistan that King Farooq of Egypt is reported to have derisively remarked that it appeared Islam had been revealed now—in Pakistan. In 2002, Musharraf told his nation in a televised address: "We are not responsible for the defence of Islam." The exact words from Musharraf in Urdu are: *"Hum koee Islam ke tekadar tho naheen."*

For the Muslims of the South Asian sub-continent, their solidarity with and their support for the *Ummah* very much pre-dated their own independence. Such solidarity was integral to their very identity and their history. Islam had begun to reach the sub-continent through traders, travellers and religious scholars in the very first century of Islam (7th century of the common era). Muslim political presence had reached parts of the present Pakistani province of Sindh during the Caliph Umar.

One single event which has had a deep and abiding impact on the Muslim psyche in the sub-continent was a mission to rescue some Muslim girls who had been abducted by pirates off the coast of Daibul in the Arabian Sea.

That historical rescue event and the Muhammad Bin Qasim character have had a defining effect on Muslim identity in the sub-continent. Although never part of any *Khilafah* but masters of an empire in their own right, Muslims in the sub-continent have never felt apart from the *Khilafah*. Despite the fact that Muslims of the sub-continent were struggling to break free from British imperialist rule, they stood up to defend the caliphate against imperialist designs and machinations. Women parted with their jewelry and Muslims contributed their might to help defend the Ottoman caliphate.

The commander-in-chief and chairman of the Grand National Assembly, Kemal Pasha, acknowledged the donations with a 'Thank you letter' to the treasurer of the Indian Muslim *Khilafat* Committee, Mr Chotani. It said, "in the victory that has been gained by us, there is an important and honorable share for [Muslims of] India."

However, instead of defending the caliphate for which the donations had been given, Kemal not only deposed the sultan, he also abolished the caliphate, revoked the Islamic *Shari'ah* laws and replaced them with French and Swiss codes. What the Muslims did not know until quite recently was that their donations had been misappropriated by the sole ruling party, the Republican People's Party, to set up a bank, TIB (Turkish Business Bank); and the RPP held 33% shares in it.

Muslims felt sorry for what the Arabs and Turks had done to themselves—"freeing" themselves from each other and becoming pawns in the hands of imperialist powers—yet they did not relent or waver in their commitment to the Islamic Ummah.

Again, while passing the historic Pakistan resolution on 23 March 1940, the All India Muslim League did not forget to reiterate the Muslim stand on the question of Palestine. The Palestine resolution said:

> The All India Muslim League views with great concern the inordinate delay on the part of the British government in coming to a settlement with the Arabs in Palestine, and places on record its considered opinion, in clear and unequivocal language, that no arrangements of a piecemeal character will be made in Palestine which are contrary in spirit and opposed to the pledges given to the Muslim world, and particularly to the Muslims in India, to secure their active assistance in the War of 1914-18. Further the League warns the British government against the danger of taking advantage of the presence of a large British force in the Holy Land to overawe the Arabs and force them into submission.

The preceding All India Muslim League session in 1938 in Patna had similarly declared:

> ...the problem of Palestine is the problem of the Muslims of the whole world, and if the British government fails to do justice to the Arabs and to fulfil the demands of the Muslims of the world, the Indian Muslims will adopt any program, and will be prepared to make any sacrifice that may be decided upon by a Muslim International Conference, at which the Muslims of India are duly represented in order to save the Arabs from British exploitation and Jewish

usurpation.

The commitment to Muslim causes around the world was an integral part of the Pakistan movement. All India Muslim League observed a Muslim Solidarity Day on November 02, 1940 when Jinnah told a huge Friday congregation that it was "our duty to help our Muslims brethren wherever they are" and went on to assure full support for the sovereignty of Afghanistan, Egypt and Turkey and the independence of Iran, Iraq, Syria, Palestine and all other Muslim countries.

The birth of Pakistan did indeed represent actualization of a long held commitment and vision which Muslims in the sub-continent had tenaciously held on to despite the loss of political power in 1857 and the liquidation of the Ottoman caliphate in March 1924. Pakistan was the only country in the world which did not define itself in terms of territorial nationhood; it saw it-self as an integral unit of the *Ummah*, and hoped eventually to remove the colonial disconnection in the Muslim entity.

The secular dictator and his like-minded cohorts are distorting Jinnah's vision of Pakistan, but here is what he clearly spelled out regarding the role of Pakistan:

> Pakistan would be a base where we will be able to train and bring up Muslim intellectuals, educationists, economists, scientists, doctors, engineers, technicians, etc. who will work to bring about Islamic renaissance. After necessary training, they would spread to other parts of the Islamic world to serve their co-religionists and create awakening among them, eventually resulting in the creation of a solid, cohesive bloc - a third bloc - which will be neither communistic nor capitalistic but truly socialistic based on the principles which characterized Caliph Umar's regime.[58]

Jinnah passed away on 11 September 1948, but the foreign policy agenda he bequeathed to his nation was clear and unmis-takable. Instead of helping imperialist powers to invade and oc-cupy other Muslim countries like the Pakistan under Musharraf is doing, Jinnah wanted Pakistan to work for uniting the Muslim world so as to face the perils together and making the Muslim "voice felt in the counsels of the world."[59] That was also in accordance with the task he had given to military officers even before Pakistan had come into existence, namely "to build Pakistan as the greatest Muslim State."

But 58 years after the passing away of Jinnah, it appears the highest ambition of the military rulers of "the greatest Muslim State of the world" was no higher than somehow to please the modern day fascists in Washington, London and Tel Aviv. It is one thing to have good relations with all states. It is quite another thing, however, to sell the independence and sovereignty of Pakistan, and demean and debase yourself in order to secure yourself in power.

As a result of Musharraf's self-centered doctrine, the country which used to be in the forefront of Islamic solidarity is now passing through a crisis of identity and incapable of mounting any serious political, much less military challenge to India's hold over Jammu and Kashmir, Israel's hold over Palestine, Russia's genocide in Chechnya—not to speak of the US occupation of Afghanistan and Iraq. This is a sad state of affairs for Pakistan, and, as a result of Musharraf's doctrine of opportunism, the future of the nation looks bleak.

CHAPTER 2

The Impossibility of Establishing Islam

ALL HOPES for achieving the objective of Pakistan's creation have turned into despair. There is absolutely no hope that Pakistan will ever become what the thousands of people who gave their lives for its creation in 1947 envisaged it to be: a model Islamic State.

Ideologically, Pakistan today stands in the middle of nowhere, notwithstanding the illusive gains of the religious party's alliance (MMA) and Musharraf's claim to practicing "enlightened moderation". Both the Muslims' promise to establish the *Deen*[1] and the secularists' dream to fully secularize Pakistan remain unfulfilled.

Religious parties' leadership has no strategy to show how they would achieve the objective of Pakistan's creation. In the following analysis we will try to find out if the religious political parties are as secularist as the rest of the political parties. A few slogans in the name of Islam mean nothing in the absence of a clear approach, vision and direction toward establishing an Islamic State. Nevertheless, the secularists and "moderates" never get tired of calling them "Islamists".

Religious parties in Pakistan made their strongest showing in the general election held in October 2002, when they secured 11.1 percent of the popular vote and 20 percent of the seats in the lower house of Parliament. This was when the religious parties were supported by the military regime to achieve two objectives:

1. to use them for constitutionalizing dictatorship; and
2. to show promoters of the secular dictatorship that Islamic "fundamentalism" is on the rise.

Musharraf and his "moderate" supporters do not get tired of claiming that since elections in Pakistan, the religious parties have pressed for Taliban-style Islamization in the North West Frontier Province (NWFP) bordering Afghanistan.

The reality is that MMA could not do a fraction of what they are blamed for despite being in the majority. This shows the ploy of using the religious parties for projecting the regime's image as moderate and secular.

Establishing an Islamic State is impossible in a situation where the secularists with and without uniform are in competition with each other to score more points with the supporters in the US. Hussain Haqqani and other self-proclaimed "moderates" try to sell their kind of moderation in their appearance before Jewish Institute for National Security Affairs (JINSA) and Musharraf his own kind of moderation before the Jewish National Congress. It is not that the Jews need lectures in "enlightened moderation," it is only that these "moderate" competitors want to market themselves at the best places that influence US policies.

Competition among "moderates" intensifies with each move on either side. The "moderates" without uniform try to discredit Musharraf's surrender with comments, such as:

> The Musharraf government also remains tolerant of remnants of Afghanistan's Taliban regime, hoping to use them in resuscitating Pakistan's influence in Afghanistan in case the US-installed regime of President Hamid Karzai falters... Since the country's inception,

Pakistan's leaders have played upon religious sentiment as an instrument of strengthening Pakistan's identity. Under ostensibly pro-Western rulers, Islam has been the rallying cry against perceived Indian threats.[2]

The roots of Muslim resistance to injustice in Pakistan lie far deeper than just the inception of the country. The roots lie as deep as the initial colonial adventures in the region. Pakistan's state institutions, especially its national security institutions, such as the military and the intelligence services, have absolutely nothing to do with playing a leading role in building Pakistani national identity on the basis of religion since its emergence as an independent state in August 1947. One has to read history and the one hundred years' Muslim struggle to understand the meaning and objectives of Pakistan. The Pak-Military simply exploited the slogans about Islam and didn't play a meaningful role in facilitating living by Islam for ordinary citizens.

This is not to say that the "Islamist groups" have been sponsored and supported by the state machinery at different times to influence domestic politics and support the military's political dominance. In fact, both civilian and military governments in Pakistan have followed this approach to maintain the façade of taking all necessary steps to consolidate an Islamic State according to the vision of the people before 1947.

It is naive to assume that religious parties have been allies in the Pakistan military's efforts to seek strategic depth in Afghanistan and to put pressure on India for negotiations over the future of Kashmir. If leadership of religious parties could think and plan so strategically, they would have achieved their stated objectives in the fifty-eight years since the creation of Pakistan. The religious parties in Pakistan are hardly different from secular political parties: one day with Benazir Bhutto, the other day with Nawaz Sharif and yet another day strengthening the hands of a military dictator.

To separate Muslims' struggle for a homeland from their desire to do so for peacefully living by Islam in an Islamic state, the "moderates" are promoting the falsehood that it was the "Islamic rhetoric" of the Muslim league that resulted in "almost total identification of Pakistan with Islam in the course of the campaign. The rural Muslim masses were encouraged to develop "a vague feeling that they would all become better Muslims once a Muslim state was established."[3]

This admission not only contradicts the initial contention that Islam came to play in Pakistani politics only after 1947, but also proves that the masses were galvanized only because of Islam, irrespective of whether the leaders of the Muslim League were sincere in their rhetoric or not.

In their confusion, the secularists contradict their statements that Jinnah wanted a Muslim, not an Islamic Pakistan by quoting facts and statements which go against their logic in favor of secularization. For example, Haqqani writes:

> Before extending their support to the Muslim League, some religious leaders demanded assurances from Jinnah that Pakistan would follow Islamic laws. Jinnah offered these assurances, as professor Khalid bin Sayeed notes: In a letter to the Pir of Manki Sharif, the [Muslim] League leader clearly stated in November 1945: 'It is needless to emphasize that the constituent Assembly which would be predominantly Muslim in its composition would be able to enact laws for Muslims, not inconsistent with the Shari'ah laws and the Muslims will no longer be obliged to abide by the un-Islamic laws. . . .' In the League meetings that the Quaid-i-Azam addressed, particularly in the Muslim majority areas, Islam with its symbols and slogans figured very prominently in all his speeches. Addressing the Pathans, he said, 'Do you want Pakistan or not?' (shouts of *Allah-o-Akbar*) (Allah is great). Well, if you want Pakistan, vote for the League candidates. If we fail to realize our duty today you will be reduced to the status of *Sudras* (low castes) and Islam will be vanquished from India. I shall never allow Muslims to be slaves of Hindus. (*Allah-o-Akbar.*)[4]

So, who demanded an Islamic State? Was it one person or the masses? The masses made it possible and they wanted Islam irrespective of the fact that a single person, Jinnah, actually wanted it, and allegedly not presented it that way. In Haqqani's view: "The Quaid-i-Azam was not unaware of the use of religion in this manner by the Muslim League, although on principle he was opposed to mixing religion with politics . . . And yet it is a fact that the people of Pakistan talked in the only idiom they knew. Pakistan was to be the laboratory of Islam, the citadel of Islam."[15]

It is easy to quote a source, saying that several Muslim league leaders from Punjab added religious titles, and religious leaders reduced the argument in favor of creating Pakistan to a simple question of survival of Islam on the South Asian subcontinent. However, this quote goes against the secularists' argument. After taking command in their hand, if the leadership didn't work to establish Islam's just order in Pakistan, whose fault is it? The masses who sacrificed their homes and lives, or the leadership? The answer is: both. The masses were deceived with slogans and empty promises and gradually got stuck in fulfilling their basic needs and taking their eyes off the main objective and the purpose behind the creation of Pakistan.

Today, Pakistan is in the hands of the most powerful man, wearing multiple hats, for the first time in the history of Pakistan. Unfortunately, he and his promoters are determined to turn Pakistan into a publicly declared secular state. Unofficially, it is already a secular state, but the secularists want it to be formally recognized as such. For this purpose both civilian and military "moderates" are promoting the lies that Jinnah expected the new country to be a homeland for Muslims but that he did not expect a role for religion in its governance. If that were the case, Muslims could privately practice Islam in any corner of the world. Why specifically carve out Pakistan? Some secularists go to the extent of claiming that the abstract notion of a Pakistan that would be Muslim but not necessarily Islamic in a strict religious sense is confronted with alternative visions. The question is: whose abstract notion was this and was it presented to the masses during the campaign for the creation of a separate home-land on the basis of two-nation theory?

Pakistan's internal crisis has been deepened beyond any hope of management. The secularists who intensified their struggle in the final years of the 20th century are now encouraged by the commitment of military and civilian "moderates" and the substantial support they receive from the anti-Islam and anti-Pakistan circles abroad.

As far Jinnah, Pakistanis were supposed to have matured as a people in the past fifty-nine years. Fifty-nine years of relying upon what Jinnah wanted or didn't want has brought us nothing except Jesuitical hairsplitting of Jinnah's speeches. Musharraf and his cronies do not need to manufacture quotes from Jinnah's life to fit to the vogue of the day, be it secularism, or privatization, or imposing emergency and martial law. It doesn't matter what one person, Jinnah, has said or thought, because this country has never been his estate to be developed exactly in accordance with his wishes alone. It belongs to the people of Pakistan and what matters most is to see whether it is being run in accordance with the wishes of the masses who sacrificed their lives for it.

In any event, having mocked so many other things, let's not turn Jinnah into a joke and cite him only when it suits our convenience. If he was against clericalism and a priesthood of the sanctimonious, was he in favor of the suppression of democracy which has been Pakistan's favorite pastime since the country's birth? Jinnah denounced clericalism because it has no place in Islam either, and in his mind that represented a danger for the new state. We need to understand the difference between theocracy and living by Islam in an established order. Jinnah never spoke out against dictatorship because the thought never crossed his mind that in the country he was creating democracy would ever wear a widow's weeds. Imagine Jinnah saying that he would be president for five years, as General Musharraf has, regardless of any election.

Of course, Jinnah did not want Pakistan to be a "theocracy," governed by narrow-minded *maulvis*, who are hardly any different from the secular zealots when it comes to defending their personal interests. In that sense, Pakistan has never been a "theocratic state" in the last 58 years. But Jinnah did not want Pakistan to be a Muslim State in name alone either.

Describing Jinnah's vision of an independent state, Carl Posey writes in *Time,* December 23, 1997, that Jinnah "had discovered in the Congress Party's dismissive treatment of the League the one thing worse than British rule: Hindu Raj. Islam, he began to caution his auditors, was in danger...Islamic culture would be diluted to extinction in a Hindu sea." It proves that he was conscious of the Islamic culture and didn't want it to be diluted in a Hindu or secular culture. From this statement one can understand that on Jinnah's culture alone could not be on Jinnah's shrewd mind. He was intelligent enough to know that in many western countries, there is a 'Catholic culture' that is quite different from that of Protestants (or Jews etc.), and yet many Catholics who behave in accordance with this culture decline to practice the religion. Also, we have many countries dedicated to being homelands for people with Islamic culture, without the States being religious. It could be a secular state and still protect and enhance Islamic culture. The USA is generally considered to be a "Christian" country, and yet there is an explicit separation of Church and State.

Christopher Mitchell, who is the director of a documentary on Jinnah's life, clarifies that it was not just culture, but Islam as a religion that played a role in shaping public and Jinnah's opinion. In Mitchell's words: "You can try to apprehend Jinnah's greatness as a mass leader intellectually, but the support which he got was from people... The basis of Jinnah's appeal was the Cry of Islam, and the threat to that." This shows that the Pakistani leadership and masses have moved a lot from the founding vision of the masses, to which even non-Muslims testify.

According to the secularists, Jinnah died within a year of independence, leaving his successors divided, or confused, about whether to take their cue from just one mis-interpreted independence eve call to keep religion out of politics or to build on the religious sentiment that led to the creation of Pakistan. The opportunists are trying to make everyone believe that Islam was only used in "political bargaining for Pakistan."[5] If Jinnah's successors were confused and divided, it means they had no clear idea right from the beginning or they were simply deceiving the masses on the one hand and cheating British and Hindu leaders on the other. This, however, was not the case.

In fact, the fear of losing status in the eyes of former colonialists, who continue to exert influence, forced the power-hungry elite to gradually steer away from identifying Pakistan as Islamic. This attitude culminated in an inferiority complex to the extent that in September 2003, when the Pakistan embassy issued invitations in Washington, the cards read: The "dominion of Pakistan," instead of "Islamic Republic of Pakistan".[6]

The secular elite were willing to embrace Islam and *Jihad* when their modern-day colonial masters wanted them to shed the blood of their gullible co-religionists in Afghanistan. But on the home front, the fear of Islam and running away from the Islamic identity became the new nation-state's hallmark, reinforced over time through "liberal" regimes, such as that of Benazir, or the "enlightened moderate" regime of dictator Musharraf.

Contrary to the claims of Pakistanis, thriving under the influence of Zionists in American think-tanks, it was not the emphasis on Islam as an element of national policy that empowered the new country's religious leaders. Actually, when the secularists turned away from Islam, others felt the need to struggle for the original objective for Pakistan. Of course, there has been a nexus between the leadership of political parties and the country's military establishment. However, if they were joined by "civilian bureaucracy, and intelligence apparatus," as claim the secularists, they would definitely have achieved their objective of transforming Pakistan into an Islamic State. But as we see, Pakistan is not even near an Islamic State.

It shows that Islam was not the objective of the elite in the first place. This can be proved from the self-contradictory write-ups of the Islamophobes-promoted secularists under the banner of "moderates." Hussain Haqqani, for example, writes that there are "three interlinked problems" which "have dogged Pakistan's internal politics over the past fifty years: "part of the state apparatus used religion and religious groups for a political purpose. The extent of the religious groups' influence and the sentiment unleashed by them could not be controlled."[7] It shows, the masses didn't want secularism and they were ready to sacrifice for Islam. The problem is that all the stakeholders—military, and secular and religious politicians—have cheated them. It is very unfortunate that all these stakeholders worked only for self-interest and have brought Pakistan to a stage where it cannot sustain in the present form and shape for too long.

Religious nationalism was never promoted for making the country an Islamic State. It was used for justifying a stay in power, confrontation with India and reserving a huge portion of resources for the military budget. Bolstering Pakistan's self-image as a bastion of Islam without being Islamic has its own consequences. Ultimately, the masses become fed up with hypocrisy on the part of the military, secular and religious leadership's slogans to the extent that they hardly care if they are living in the Islamic Republic of Pakistan or in secular India. They hardly care if the United States, which was used to be persuaded of the value of Pakistan's strategic location and its anticommunist credentials, is now being persuaded to save it from Islam.

In such an aimless situation, the greatest threats to Pakistan's central authority come from groups seeking regional autonomy, ethnic rights, or political inclusion. Hiding behind Islam helped the government hold these tides for all these years. However, now that Islam is the enemy, the government can no longer claim

that a gathering momentum in these movements is either an In-
dian-inspired plan to weaken Pakistan or a communist-inspired
revolution. Running from Islam, either to please the US, or because of the real inner fear of Islam, leaves the military generals
and other opportunist leaders with no state to exploit and parade
themselves as leaders of a country.

The evidence that Islam was the only justification and glue
to put different ethnic groups together in a state named Pakistan lies in the following self-contradictory quote from a secularist. Although its author claims that religion was an easier tool
for mass mobilization, he could hardly mention the alternative in
case religion is officially discarded from the public square.

> Liaqat Ali Khan was not a religious man himself and most members
> of the first constituent assembly were members of the country's
> secular elite. They had clearly been influenced in their decision to
> declare Pakistan an Islamic state by the realization that Pakistanis
> had multiple identities. The experience of language riots by Bengalis
> in East Pakistan had pointed out the difficulty of subsuming ethnic
> identities into a new Pakistani identity. Religion was an easier tool of
> mobilization. Making being Pakistani synonymous with being a good
> Muslim was considered the more attainable goal. Given the reality
> that Islam meant different things to different people, however, the
> development of an ideological state could not be left to the will of
> the people. Institutions of state had to control the process of building
> the new nation. Ensuring the supremacy of these state institutions
> required greater centralization of authority. [8]

If Islam played a cohesive role in binding people with "multiple identities" together, running from it would lead to unraveling
of the cohesiveness it provided. This unraveling is already underway. The alliance of religious political parties and their strength
in the elected assemblies are just meaningless blips in the smooth
transition toward the demise of a country known as Pakistan.

The religious parties' alliance (MMA) is neck deep in the very
mire of godlessness from which it has been promising to liberate
Pakistan. It has rather become the forerunner of a system that
negates both Islam and democracy.

The little leftover hopes of putting the country on the right ideological track were associated with the religious parties. The MMA's success in legitimizing the dictatorship and failure in establishing Islam are clear signs of the validity of calls asking religious leaders not to divide Muslims in numerous religious parties; participate in secular systems for the supremacy of Islam, and turn means—such as elected positions—into ends in themselves.

The leadership of the religious parties claims to have sided with the dictator for the "supremacy of democracy." It neither says, nor can claim, that its actions are for the supremacy of Islam. Establishing one or another form of twisted democracy cannot absolve religious parties and the nation from their real obligation of establishing the *Deen*.[9]

Fifty-nine years is enough time for the Pakistani nation to realize and admit that the course it has taken has landed it in *kufr* (disbelief) rather than Islam. The main folly behind the failure is its committing *shirk*.[10]

The reality is as harsh to digest as it is difficult to deny from where the Pakistani nation stands and dies today. But this is where it stands and dies. It can not deny that the Qur'an has repeatedly admonished those who establish *Hukm*—the system of law and justice—on the basis of 'other than' or 'contrary to' Allah's authority and law.

Neither the secularist Musharraf nor the sleeping nation can deny the fact that Pakistan's legal system is primarily based on the common law of the colonial masters, from whom our forefathers liberated us at great cost and with great hopes. Apart from the cosmetic inclusion of the legal code of *Shari'ah*, English case law remains a primary source of authority in commercial law matters. Legal system is only a part of the *Hukm*—system of law and justice (politico-socio and economic system)

Neither "enlightened moderation", nor the convoluted approach of the religious parties can disprove that the Qur'an unequivocally condemns and accuses those of *Kufr* (disbelief), *Zulm* (injustice and oppression) and *Fisq* (wickedness and enormous sin) who fail to establish law and authority on the basis of the revealed Divine Law. The Pakistani nation has done so despite having the opportunity of self-rule in an independent state for 58 years.

Both rulers and the ruled in Pakistan perfectly fit this Qur'anic description: " .... And whoever fails to judge on the basis of that which Allah revealed has committed *Kufr* (disbelief)." " .... And whoever fails to judge on the basis of that which Allah revealed has committed *Zulm* (injustice and oppression)." " .... And who-ever fails to judge on the basis of that which Allah has revealed, has committed *Fisq* (wickedness and enormous sin)." (Qur'an, 5:44-47)

The secularists under the leadership of Musharraf and the flag bearers of Islam are equally guilty. In exchange for the religious parties' fake opposition and granting constitutional legitimacy to a dictatorship, they could not, for example, ask Musharraf to make the constitutional clause—"no legislation shall be done re-pugnant to the Qur'an and the *Sunnah*"—effective.

In exchange for wholesale changes to Pakistan's Constitution in favor of dictatorship (as described in chapter 1), the religious parties could have asked for a small amendment to make Article 227 of the Constitution part of the Objectives Resolution as arti-cle 2(b) to address the loophole that renders Islamic articles inef-fective. At this point it is necessary to understand the distinction between a secular and an Islamic state.

Muslim or Islamic State

Some of the secularists-turned-moderates in Pakistan have started arguing that the founding fathers of Pakistan were inter-ested in establishing a Muslim, not Islamic state. We need to un-derstand the difference between a Muslim and an Islamic state. Those who consider Pakistan just a Muslim state argue that Paki-stan was not created for Islam, but for the Muslims of the Sub-continent. Islam was never in danger in the pre-partitioned India. As a matter of fact Islam was and probably still is in Deoband, Breilley, Lucknow and other places. Islamic schools in Akora, Okara, Mansoora, Karachi, and Satellite Town Rawalpindi have not been able to attain the stature of their pre-partitioned alma-maters.

To further support their point of view, the secularists add that it was for the improvement of the socio-economic condition of the Muslims of India more than their religious need that Pakistan was created. Accordingly, they considered Pakistan dysfunctional simply because it is an ideological state. In his book, *Between Mosque and Military*, Haqqani concludes: "Pakistan was created in a hurry and without giving detailed thought to various aspects of nation and state building. Perhaps it is time to rectify that mistake by taking a long-term view. Both Pakistan's elite and their US benefactors would have to participate in transforming Pakistan into a functional, rather than ideological, state."

A deeper reading of the secular argument reveals a consistent contradiction due to prevailing confusion between the Muslim and Islamic State. For example, a write up which claims Pakistan was not meant to be Islamic, adds that the founder of Pakistan "had on many an occasion said categorically that Pakistan will be governed in accordance with the injunctions of Islam and Qur'an. Speaking at a broadcast speech from All India Radio Bombay on 13 November 1939, he said: 'All social regeneration and political freedom must finally depend on something that has a deeper meaning in life. And that, if you will allow me to say so, is Islam and Islamic spirit—in the pursuit of truth and cultivation of beliefs we should be guided by our *rational* (emphasis added) interpretation of the Qur'an and our devotion to truth is single minded, we shall in our own measure, achieve our goal.'"[11]

From adding stress on "rational interpretation of the Qur'an" the secularists assume the objective was secularism or just a Muslim Pakistan. The same secularist author goes to un-knowingly contradict his thesis by adding:

> Similarly replying to a correspondent's question in 1946 at New Delhi, as to what type of the constitution Pakistan will have? The Qaid had replied, 'I cannot say as to what type of the constitution Pakistan will have, as it is a matter for the future Constituent Assembly of Pakistan to decide, but we have our 1400 year old constitution – the Qur'an with us to draw from'.[12]

Part of the confusion lies in the acceptance and a simultaneous rejection of Islam. Those who argue that Pakistan was supposed to be simply a Muslim state accept that: a) Qaid, too, "like Iqbal believed that Qur'an could be a complete source of inspiration for the Muslims to help them guide their life according to the true spirit of Islam; and b) Pakistan was created as "a country to be ruled in accordance with the Islamic injunctions for the amelioration of the economically and socially down trodden Muslims of pre-partitioned India." The question is: how can a country be both run according to the Qur'anic injunctions and still remain secular or proclaim to be secular and still use the Qur'an to guide in all walks of life? What is more important to ask is: Is just being a Muslim or secular state enough to justify the continued existence of Pakistan?

Demystification of Islamic State and understanding the reality of secularism is essential to answer questions surrounding this issue and see where Pakistan is heading: towards progress and prosperity or an inevitable demise.

Logically, it doesn't make sense to have just a piece of land for Muslims to live under secularism. Muslims are living under secular systems in Europe, America and elsewhere. What was wrong with living in the Indian sub-continent in one secular state that forced the Muslim masses to demand a separate homeland?

Allama Iqbal, the spiritual founder of Pakistan, answers this question by rejecting secularism in these words:

> As the Prophet establishes God's decrees, he repudiates Caesar's law.
> In his eyes the royal palace is like an old idol-temple; his sense of

honor makes him disobey the order of the other-than-God. He (the man of truth) is the meaning of Gabriel and the Qur'an, and he is the custodian of God's Law.[13]

Iqbal here brings into sharp contrast God's Will and king's will, keeping in mind perhaps the well-known saying of Christ: Render unto Caesar what is Caesar's and render unto God what is God's. Iqbal feels that it is not possible for one to be loyal to God's will and yet to accept and follow the lead of ordinary mundane rulers under the influence and protection of the Pharaohs of this age. This shows that establishing an Islamic state was the core objective behind demanding a separate homeland.

Before we explain the concept of an Islamic State and the extent to which it is different from a Muslim (secular) state, we need to clarify that Iqbal was against secularism or just a Muslim state. For him "Islam is only an effort to realize the spiritual in a human organization."[14] "Iqbal emerged from his European stay as a champion of Islam. His early Indian nationalism seemed to have given way to his newly found Islamic universalism."[15]

Regardless of the anyone's intentions among the founding fathers and founding masses, secularism—which is the core of the modern, progressive Muslim state—has no place in Islam. If we could establish this argument, it would mean the concept of a Muslim state, as opposed to an Islamic state, is absolutely meaningless. In that case, a secular Pakistan's existence and demise become irrelevant. This is particularly true in the case of Pakistan because it was specifically demanded in the name of Islam. It doesn't make any sense to establish a state in the name of Islam and then run it according to the laws and systems which negate the core of Islam.

To establish that secularism has no place in Islam and simply calling it a Muslim state is not good enough to justify the purpose of Pakistan's creation. We need to see how the secular revolutions transformed Euro-Christian civilization, which used to be based on faith in God and in His Sovereignty and Supremacy. Under secularism it no longer recognizes the God of Abraham as Sovereign, nor His Authority and His Law as supreme. The "modern secular state" and the people are now recognized as "sovereign," and that is *Shirk* from an Islamic perspective as explained below. The authority and law of the "modern secular state" are now recognized as 'supreme', and that is *Shirk*! The state has the authority to declare *Halal* (i.e. to declare legal and permissible) that which the God of Abraham has declared to be *Haram* (illegal and prohibited)—and it proceeds to do so—and that is *Shirk*!

Shirk is a very great sin for anyone who proclaims to be a Muslim, regardless of his being "moderate" or "fundamentalist" (5:72).[16] Indeed, according to Islam, it is the greatest of all sins. It is the one sin which Allah declared that He would not forgive: *"Surely Allah does not* (or will not) *forgive Shirk. But He* (can) *forgive everything else to whomsoever He wishes. And whoever commits Shirk has committed an awesome sin"*. (Qur'an 4:48)

The common perception among the Muslim masses is that only the worship of idols is *Shirk*. Of course, that is the most overt form of *Shirk*. This form of *Shirk* has largely disappeared from the world today. Instead, there are other forms of *Shirk* that are clearly described in the *Qur'an*. Pharaoh, for example, declared to Moses: *"I am your Lord-God the Most High"*, and he declared to the Chiefs of his people: *"Oh Chiefs! No God do I know for you but myself ...."* That was *Shirk*! The worship of Pharaoh by the Egyptian people required them to submit to his authority as the supreme authority in the land of Egypt, and to recognize his law as the supreme law in the land of Egypt. That, also, was *Shirk*!

The *Qur'an* has repeatedly admonished those who establish *Hukm*, i.e., the system of law and justice, on the basis of "other than" or "contrary to" Allah's authority and Allah's law. However, when the divine guidance reaches a people (such as Jews, Christians, Muslims), and they accept that guidance, then the situation is quite different. If such people have an opportunity to establish their control over territory and they then fail to establish law and authority on the basis of the revealed Divine Law, then the *Qur'an* unequivocally condemns them and holds them responsible for committing *Kufr* (disbelief), *Zulm* (injustice) and *Fisq* (wickedness and grave sin):

" .... And whoever fails to judge on the basis of that which Allah revealed has committed *Kufr* (disbelief)."

" .... And whoever fails to judge on the basis of that which Allah revealed has committed *Zulm* (injustice and oppression)."

" .... And whoever fails to judge on the basis of that which Allah has revealed, has committed *Fisq* (wickedness and enormous sin)." (Qur'an, 5:44-47)

Since the declaration by Pharaoh and its concrete application in the land of Egypt were acts of *Shirk*, it followed therefrom that the same declaration by the modern secular state was also an act of *Shirk*! Since Allah declared that: *"Whoever fails to judge on the basis of that which Allah revealed has committed Kufr* (disbelief), *Zulm* (injustice and oppression) *and Fisq* (wickedness and enormous sin)", and the modern secular state has done precisely that, it followed therefrom that Jews, Christians, Muslims etc, who establish the secular state after having received the Divine Law through the Torah, Psalms, Gospel and *Qur'an*, would be guilty of having committed *Kufr*, *Zulm* and *Fisq*!

If a Jew, Christian, or Muslim, were to cast a vote in a national election in a modern secular state, that vote would imply that he considered that party he voted for to be fit to govern over him. And if that party as government committed or commits *Shirk*, *Kufr*, *Zulm* and *Fisq*, then the implication would be that the Jew, Christian, or Muslim, would follow his Party and his Government into *Shirk, Kufr, Zulm* and *Fisq*! The Qur'an has also denounced as *Shirk* the act of making *Halal* whatever Allah had made *Haram* (and vice-versa). Thus revelation came down from the God of

Abraham in which He denounced Jews and Christians of such a monstrous sin. The Qur'an clearly states that they *"were not ordered other than to worship and serve one God. Glory is to Him. He is far and above the Shirk which they commit."*[17]

Those who claim that the mere inclusion of "The Objective Resolution," passed by the Constituent Assembly of Pakistan in March, 1949, in the Constitution should be good enough because it says No law should be repugnant to the Qur'an and the *Sunnah."* However, we need to assess and system and laws on the basis of these clear injunctions of the Qur'an to the humanity.

We must judge our words and deeds and compare then to the Jews and Christians of the past. Pakistanis have put their intentions according the injunctions of the Qur'an in the Constitution. It shows their knowledge as well as realization of their responsibility. However, they are acting against this by making *Haram* as *Halal,* such as in the case of interest (*Riba*), with the justification that we cannot survive without it. When the Jews acted in this way, David and Jesus cursed them:

> "Curses were pronounced on those among Banu Israel who rejected Faith, by the tongue of David and of Jesus, the son of Mary, because they disobeyed and persisted in excesses. They did not enforce the prohibition of that which was sinful and evil which they committed: evil indeed were the deeds which they did." (Qur'an, 5:78-9)

According to the Qur'an, it is the height of hypocrisy for a people to declare that they worship Allah and to then proceed to legalize that which He had made illegal, and to prohibit that which He had made permissible.[18] Can we deny that the Supreme Court of Pakistan has been a tool in the hands of the rulers for continuing interest (*Riba*) *Haram*? Can we deny that David and Jesus cursed the Jews for acting exactly in this way?

If it were an act of *Shirk* when Priests and Rabbis made *Halal* that which Allah declared to be *Haram*, then it would also be an act of *Shirk* when a government does the same thing now. And if it earned the curses of Prophets at that time, it would do the same now.

Now the usual method of approach for studying this subject is to weigh the 'pros' and 'cons' of participation by believers in the electoral politics of the modern secular state. The defenders of the secular state wax eloquently about its merits. Some argue: "If we do not participate in electoral politics then we will have no political representation—no one to struggle for our rights." At a more serious level of thought another argument is raised: "Participation in electoral politics is the necessary condition for any successful struggle to change the godless political system." The matter of *Shirk* is addressed by way of a subterfuge: "We will participate in elections but will do so on the basis of a public stand that we do not accept the secular constitution and the secular state which it preserves. This escape clause will protect us from *Shirk*."

In fact, participation in electoral politics in a secular state *ipso facto* signifies acceptance of the secular character of the state. The secular state makes the same declaration that Pharaoh made to Moses. That declaration is: The state is sovereign. Its authority is supreme. Its law is supreme. That is *Shirk*. Period! When people vote in elections in a secular state they thereby accept the claim of the state to be sovereign. They accept its claim to supreme authority, and they accept its law to be the supreme law. When believers vote in such elections, therefore, they cannot escape from committing *Shirk*.

Secondly, when believers vote in elections in a secular state they have to vote for a political party. If that party, as government, declared to be *Halal* what the God of Abraham made *Haram*, or enforced laws as such, then that government committed *Shirk*. Around the world today governments and parliaments of secular states have already declared *Halal* nearly everything that Allah declared to be *Haram*. When believers cast their votes for such political parties and governments that have already committed *Shirk upon Shirk*, such votes would imply acceptance of such people as fit to govern over them. Thus believers follow them into *Shirk, Kufr, Zulm and Fisq*!

Thirdly, this method constitutes a violation and an abandonment of the *Sunnah* of Prophet Mohammed (PBUH). Political parties and governments around the world today are comprised of those who disdainfully persist in declaring *Halal* that which Allah declared to be *Haram*. When a people disdainfully persist in *Haram,* they pay a dreadful price. It is as plain as daylight that the modern secular world is already paying precisely that price. What is it?

> "....and then, when they disdainfully persisted in doing what they had been forbidden to do, We said to them (i.e., We ordained for them) Be as apes despicable!" (Qur'an, 7:166)

What this implies is that they would now live like apes, so incapable of exercising any restraint over their gross appetites and passions that, by the 'End Time', they would be committing sexual intercourse in public like donkeys.

The modern secular state, including Pakistan, legalized the lending of money on interest *(Riba).* An ever-increasing number of modern secular states have already legalized gambling (and lottery), the consumption and sale of intoxicants (e.g. alcohol) and pork, the use of paper money that constantly loses value, abortion, homosexuality, adultery and fornication.

Around the world today most modern secular states no longer recognize Allah's Law that a son must inherit twice as much as a daughter. They declare such a law to be discriminatory against women, and they establish their own laws that, they claim, are more just than Allah's Law. It is a pre-condition for the "moderate Muslims" to repudiate the relevant verses of the Qur'an in this regard as we discussed under the Musharraf doctrine earlier. Islamic laws are attacked and criticized before even understanding the wisdom behind them. They are looked at with a surface understanding with no attempt to see the reason behind them.

The modern secular state has prohibited a man from marrying more than one woman at a time since they claim that such a practice would be discriminatory against women. Rather they have made it mandatory for a man to have no more than one wife at a time. They claim, this removes the injustice against women that is present in Allah's Law. But a man can have as many girl friends and have sexual relations with as many women as he may like and even be admired for his virility. Similarly, he can have as many out of wedlock children as he may wish. This alternative has resulted in a revolution that is making a mockery of marriage itself.

The defining characteristic of the religion of Abraham is that there is no place whatsoever for *Kufr* (disbelief) and *Shirk* (corruption of, or rejection of the worship of One True God) in it. Yet the secular political system of the new essentially godless civilization is based on *Kufr* and *Shirk*.

How then do Pakistanis explain their acceptance of a modern secular state, established in the name of Islam? How then do we explain participation of political parties, established in the name of Islam, in the secular system that goes to the Supreme Court to allow *Riba*-based financial systems to exist and throw away unanimously passed resolutions from a provincial assembly, which the secular system fears will "Islamize" the system? And how do we explain the acceptance by Pakistanis secular state and secular law as a valid substitute for an Islamic State? Perhaps this is the right moment for us to explain what the *Khilafah* was and why Musharraf, an enthusiastic promoter of Ataturk's secular model, believes that it is impossible to establish *Khilafah* in this age.

The Islamic *Khilafah* was precisely such a conception of a state and political system that recognized Allah's Sovereignty, Supreme Authority and Law, and enforced *Haram* as *Haram* and *Halal* as *Halal*. The absence of modern technological advances in that age doesn't mean anything to change the reality or make recognition of Allah's Sovereignty impossible in this age. The *Khilafah* emerged in consequence of precisely that divine imperative demanding obedience of Allah, His Messenger, and *"those in author-ity amongst the Muslims."* Regardless of the title, a polity established in the name of Islam, demands no more and accepts no less than these basics:

> "Oh you who believe, obey Allah, and obey the Messenger, and (obey) those from amongst yourselves who are in (positions of) authority …." (Qur'an, 4:59)

Islam refused to recognize divided loyalties – that one could deliver supreme loyalty to the state and yet, also deliver supreme loyalty to Allah. The two worlds (the worlds of religion and of politics) were not to be separated from each other since the Qur'an proclaimed, "Allah is the First and the Last, the Manifest and the Hidden." (Qur'an, 57:3). Supreme loyalty must be deliv-ered to Allah, not to the state, since the Qur'an asked the believ-ers to proclaim:

> "Say: Verily my prayer, and my service of sacrifice, and my very living and my very dying are all for Allah the Lord of all the world.... " (Qur'an, 6:162)

Europe destroyed that Islamic model of a state and political system when the now defunct Ottoman *Khilafah* was targeted and destroyed. Europe went on to ensure that the Islamic *Khilafah* could never be restored. There are a number of reasons that ex-plain why Europe targeted and destroyed the Islamic *Khilafah*. The first was to facilitate the achievement of the goal of liberat-ing and returning the Jews to the Holy Land. The second was to make possible the universal embrace of *Shirk* of the new Euro-pean model of a secular state. When the remnants of the *Khilafah* were destroyed, the modern secular State of Turkey replaced it; and the secular State of Saudi Arabia in the Arabian heartland. Following this, Indian Muslims were exquisitely deceived into embracing the secular Republic of Pakistan. Thirdly, the *Khilafah* had to be destroyed because it obstructed the realization of the ultimate goal in the new godless European agenda.

The secular state could not have won acceptance amongst a Christian and Jewish people, or amongst Muslims, had it not camouflaged its *Kufr* and *Shirk* with certain obvious merits. The modern secular state emerged in Europe in response to a dominant and oppressive Euro-Christian theocracy, and in order to challenge the 'temporal' power of the Euro-Christian Church. It challenged the Church when it proclaimed a fresh and exciting new gospel of complete and unfettered intellectual and religious freedom and human rights for all, and religious tolerance of all. It also established the political conditions that preserved peaceful coexistence amongst different religions within the same territory. It thus put an end to all the bloody religious warfare that had plagued Europe for so many centuries.

In fact, the concept of "Nation State" is contrary to Islam. It certainly divides Muslims over loyalties and anything that divides Muslims has to be avoided. The basis of unity is *Deen*, not state in Islam (Qur'an 21:92, 23:52-53). Islam does not classify on the basis of regions, states or mere places of birth. A place of birth and family or race is beyond one's control and individual choice. Therefore, there is no logic in dividing the world on the basis of one's place of birth or color. The only valid reason for drawing a line on the map is the way of life, ideology and civilization. Submitting to a state erected on godless standards and sacrificing everything on the defense of such a state has no place in Islam. All the efforts are focused on limiting Islam within a nation, which can be called as nationalization of Islam. Muslims are divided into 57 states and every nation has its own "Islamic" perspective on the same local and global issues. For example, the Saudi Islam considered arrival of the US forces in the Middle East before the Gulf War necessary and perfectly legitimate. Whereas Islam of Iraqi, Yemeni and Jordanian religious scholars had a totally different view. Interestingly, in the nation-states of Saudi Arabia and Egypt, for example, Fatwas of religious scholars are astonishingly 99% in accordance with the state policies. These are not mere coincidences. These are the direct results of Muslims embracing the concept of secular state.

Secular state skillfully bribed its way into the bellies and the hearts of mankind through its inventive creativity. It discovered or produced most of that which has been joyfully embraced by Muslims along with the rest of mankind, regardless of religious beliefs, as an indispensable necessity of modern life. Whenever anyone embraced modernity with all its wondrous inventions one also embraced the secular state and the secular way of life. That was no mean achievement!

In reality, these obvious merits of the secular state did not change that basic foundation of *Kufr* and *Shirk*. Indeed the modern secular state slowly began to reveal its real hidden agenda of rivalry when it began to wage a relentless war on the religious way of life. Indeed religion slowly became a receding force in the new essentially godless secular world.

The democracy of the modern secular state turned out to be a sugarcoated pill of poison. The 'political' democracy worked in such a way as to sustain a usurious system of economic oppression and exploitation of the masses based on *Riba*. Economic oppression was oft-times supplemented by racial and ethnic oppression. The impoverished masses could never wrest real political power from the rich predatory elite, and hence could never have the power with which to end economic oppression. The new gospel of the modern secular society was that *the rich shall inherit the earth*. And that is precisely what has happened.

The new Europe proceeded to use its invincible military power and awesome powers of deception to dominate and brainwash non-European humanity. The new godless political philosophy with its godless conception of a sovereign state, exploitative economic system, and corruptive culture, eventually embraced all the rest of the world. That, too, was no mean achievement!

Western colonial rule was now imposed upon the rest of mankind, including the Muslims, and through this means the new godless political system, based on *Kufr* and *Shirk,* was deceptively and subtly introduced. Thus the ominous prophecy of Prophet Muhammad (PBUH) was fulfilled! He prophesied that his community (of Muslims) would imitate and follow Jews and Christians to such an extent that even if they were to go down into a lizard's hole, his community would do the same!

The result was that the world of Jews, Christians and Muslims entered into a collective trial of all trials *(fitnah)* and failed miserably in obeying the command of Allah when He ordered:

> "Follow what has been sent down unto you by your Lord-God, and follow no Master other than Him. How seldom do you keep this in mind!" (Qur'an, 7:3)

The new modern secular state devised a system of electoral politics for constituting parliament and government, and sometimes for electing judges. Citizens of the secular state, regardless of their religious beliefs, voted in democratic elections. They were obliged to submit to its authority and be obedient to it. If the elections were to produce a government dominated by idol-worshipping Hindus who were openly hostile to those who worshipped the God of Abraham, or a government which declared to be *Halal* (permissible) everything which Allah Most High had declared to be *Haram*, then the principle of democratic elections required that Jews, Christians, Muslims etc., who were citizens of that secular state, recognize that government as their lawful government, submit to its authority, and be obedient to it.

There is nothing in the revealed scriptures (Torah, Gospel, *and Qur'an*) or the *Sunnah* (example or way of life) of the Prophets that can be used to justify Jews, Christians, Muslims, etc., participating in such elections in which they freely vote for such a government as lawful to govern over them. On the contrary there is very clear condemnation of such conduct!

Muslims in South Asia asked for an opportunity to live in an Islamic State. They struggled to restore the sovereignty of Allah in the political system—to recognize His Authority as Supreme Authority—and to struggle to recognize His Law as the Supreme Law. They succeeded in achieving a piece of land but failed to recognize and establish God's Law and Sovereignty. Pakistanis could not uphold whatever Allah made *Halal* as *Halal*. They could not condemn those who commit *Shirk*, *Kufr*, *Zulm* and *Fisq*, then believers should condemn such conduct, oppose it, struggle against it, and turn to Allah and ask Him to separate them from such people.[19]

The secularists' argue that Jinnah wanted a secular state so that religious minorities may have equal rights. This shows their lack of knowledge about the message of Islam. There is a plural model of a state in which Muslims would share control over a territory with non-Muslims on the basis of political equality and through a constitutional agreement that would allow Muslims to recognize the sovereignty of Allah and the supremacy of His Authority and Law over 'them'. Prophet Muhammad (PBUH) established that 'plural' model of state in the city-State of Madina wherein Muslims, Jews and pagan Arabs shared control over territory, and over the state, on the basis of political equality. Muslims in Madina were not supposed to live by un-Islamic laws and values, nor was Islam imposed on non-Muslims.

Mankind has the freedom of choice to accept or to reject the religion of Abraham. However, once the religion is accepted, believers do not have the freedom to choose between either a government following the Law of God, or a government which consider everything *Halal* as *Haram* and vice versa. Thus Allah has commanded believers to "obey Allah and obey the Messenger."[20]

When they no longer have the freedom to establish their own government anywhere, and they have to live under non-believing rule, believers in the religion of Abraham 'submit' to that rule until such time as they can once again choose fellow-believers to rule over them. But 'submission' to such non-believing rule cannot involve their participation in *establishing* that non-believing government. Believers will submit to such rule on the condition of religious freedom, i.e., that nothing is forced upon them that violates the Law of Allah. While such a government will not be 'their' government, they can advise and assist the government in all that is true, good and virtuous, while warning, resisting and abstaining from all that is false, evil and harmful.

It is in the very nature of the modern secular state that it would never allow elections to be used to transform it into a different model of a state—such as a state that would recognize the Sovereignty of Allah and the supremacy of His Authority and His Law. Electoral politics was meant to sub-serve the godless secular state. Pakistan is no exception. The irony is that despite clear Constitutional clauses, *Haram* has been imposed and secular law has been enforced. There is no guarantee that any number of seats in the elected assemblies could ever give those Muslims, who believe that Allah's Will and Law should be supreme, a chance to transforms the system.

When the Muslims of Algeria used 'electoral politics' to seek to restore the religion of Abraham in Algeria and won 85% of the votes in the national elections, the godless world all came together to ruthlessly punish that 85% of the electorate which dared to seek to transform the godless secular foundation of the state.

In the light of this discussion, there is nothing such as a Muslim state. The very fact that a people calling themselves Muslims means that they must submit to the orders of Allah and his Messenger (PBUH). A Muslim entity has to be either Islamic or non-Islamic (secular). Pakistan's experience shows that despite slogans and various initiatives, the state remains a secular state and the way the US, UK and others are ganging up against the very idea of an Islamic State, there is no hope that Pakistan's would get an opportunity by itself to protect themselves from *Shirk* by disconnecting from the secular state. They should also respond to it by arguing that the 'plural' model of a state established by Prophet

Muhammad (PBUH) is a superior model of a state when compared with the modern godless secular state.

Pakistan's unique position

Secularists argue that the founders of Pakistan intended a Muslim state. However, a major reason for partition was to avoid civil war. In that, the establishment of Pakistan has been successful. Muslims were moved to one place, Hindus etc. were moved to another, and as a result the killing was reduced. This is surely a good thing, even if the end result is a Pakistan that has changed from the original intention of the masses. Other countries also change and evolve. Charlemagne's "Holy Roman Empire" was neither Roman nor Holy, and resulted eventually in the Hapsburg Empire that was centered in Vienna, and had nothing to do with religion. But it lasted successfully for some hundreds of years. Accordingly, "Pakistan is not an Islamic country as the founding masses intended" is a legitimate complaint, but does it necessarily imply that 'Pakistan has no reason for existence' or 'this has failed'?

Of course, it does because of the unique circumstances in which Pakistan was established. Despite the overwhelming odds, the only galvanizing force that brought it into being was Islam; neither culture, nor ethnicity, not even language or geography. The loss of faith in that objective has cost the nation half of the country in 1971 and continues to weaken the rest with every passing day. There is absolutely no other justification at all for separating this piece of land in South Asia, calling it Pakistan, or keeping people of different cultures and ethnic backgrounds together for so long. If a secular state was the objective, a single independent state of India made more sense than two separate entities, which drained their resources on arms build-up and wars. We will return to this issue in the conclusion to see how different groups have already started challenging Pakistan's existence and legitimacy of the 1947 partition in South Asia.

Suffice it to add here that the first faltering step of the nation was a division into different religious parties without a clear strategy for establishing Islam. Some of the basic arguments of the religious leaders for participating in the secular system are: "without participation, Pakistanis will have no political representation," of "participation is necessary for changing the godless political system."

Pakistan is not an Islamic State by virtue of its title or a couple of dead constitutional clauses. The existence of *Hadood* laws or restriction on propagation of Qadyani (Ahmadi) views neither makes Pakistan Islamic nor exonerates its secular practices within a system that is secular to the core.

Participation in Pakistan's electoral politics *ipso facto* signifies acceptance of the secular character of the state. As discussed above, Pakistanis are facing a grave situation when looked from the perspective that they are indulging in multiple forms of *shirk*.

The interest-based institutions, lotteries, prize bonds, saving certificates, raffle tickets, and prevailing landlordism in Pakistan are just a few examples of how the government has already declared *Halal* nearly everything that Allah has clearly declared to be *Haram*. Casting votes for all parties and government that have already committed many acts of *Shirk*, implying the voters' following them are also committing *Shirk*, *Kufr*, *Zulm* and *Fisq*.

The right course was to match words with deeds, to act as a single force; launching campaigns for abolishing un-Islamic systems—starting with reviving the dead clauses of the Constitution and finishing with compelling the government into developing systems, ways and means for making the Qur'an and the *Sunnah* supreme. Pakistanis were supposed to be Islamic and not merely to seem so. How can Muslims run away from being Islamic? Pakistanis could "talk the talk," but they failed to "walk the walk."

The result is that Pakistan's becoming an Islamic State has become totally impossible without a miracle. Islam can never be imposed from the top. Acceptance for living by Islam must grow out of the people's longing for Islam at the very grassroots. People at the grassroots levels, however, are fed up with religious parties, their substance-less slogans about establishing an Islamic system, and a majority is not even ready to listen to anything about Islam from these groups.

One might argue that there are still many dedicated followers of the religious parties who are struggling to turn Pakistan into an Islamic State. The question is: would they achieve their objective if they are supposed to go North but their leaders are taking them towards the South? This is the situation for those who are affiliated with religious parties in Pakistan. That's why Islamic Pakistan will remain a dream unfulfilled.

Pakistanis used to call for an alliance of religious parties. Now that they have seen and experienced it in Pakistan in the form of MMA, the case has become stronger to say good-bye to religious parties once and for all.

The myths, such as *Shari'ah* is inhuman, Islamic governments are repressive and their totalitarian nature would undermine the existence of Western societies, have deepened beyond imagination. Muslim "moderates" play a leading role in consolidating such misconceptions. It is just a matter of time until individual or groups, working for the establishment of an Islamic state, will be declared terrorist and subsequently banned. Very soon the powerful media will blur the distinction between the sectarian groups carrying out such bloody attacks and the religious parties claiming be working for Islamization of society in a peaceful manner.

Islam is one, but the number of parties out there, claiming to establish it, are countless. It clearly shows the either each one has a different approach or everyone is struggling for its personal interest, which they would lose in case there is just one party, engaged in establishing the *Deen* (the way of life of Islam). As a direct result of several religious parties all claiming to work for the establishment of the Islamic state—misunderstanding about *Shari'ah* has increased to the extent that it seems impossible to make two Muslims agree on a particular form of *Shari'ah*. Many Pakistanis are unaware of their individual and collective responsibilities and subsequently feel that they are responsible only for their individual acts on the Day of Judgment and the concept of an Islamic state is redundant and irrelevant.

Since Pakistanis are not fully aware of their responsibilities, they lack the sense of obligation to understand Islam. It further leads to their lack of awareness about the core issues as well as the difficulty in differentiating between right and wrong. Incomplete, unplanned and above all self-centered attempts at implementing Islam have further worsened the situation. The most common fear due to the presence of multiple Islamic parties and the untutored mind of the common man is that in an Islamic State, someone will decide if men should keep a beard, wear a particular brand of clothes and be forced to as many different thoughts as there are parties.

It is thus true that Islam is a challenge to the corrupt form of democracy and oppression in the name of liberation but the present day Muslims are definitely not. The present state of affairs will continue as long as the common men in the street in Pakistan do not seriously undertake the challenge they are facing. But that is not going to happen in the near future. Dictatorship will remain unchallenged as long as Pakistanis do not understand that Islam does not offer a myopic world view.

The energies of religious parties are wasted in trying in vain to throw out Musharraf rather than correcting the system in which many Musharrafs to come would have no option but to stay on the same course. For that, the basics were supposed to be correctly aligned. Unfortunately, the countless parties working for enforcing *Shari'ah* could not convey the basic message that *Shari'ah* serves the Islamic system. It is part of the whole. In the prevailing un-Islamic system in Pakistan and elsewhere, *Shari'ah* alone can do no good; rather it would strengthen the corrupt system and harm the image of Islam. *Shari'ah* is not the burning issue, the system is. *Shari'ah* is not the challenge, establishing Islamic governance mechanism as a whole is. That is, however, impossible with multiple religious parties. With limited public support and the ever increasing confusion, it has now become totally impossible.

Integration of Islam and injustice (Qur'an 5:44-47)) is impossible. Pakistanis have utterly failed in taking this basic lesson the easiest way. Now Afghanistan- and Iraq-like invasions, occupations and subsequent systematic humiliation is in store for them to let them forget about their petty interests and form the much needed single party to "enjoin the right and forbid the evil" (Qur'an 3:110). Such a revolution is as inevitable as the demise of Pakistan in its present lost state. This revolution had to come. Pakistanis, however, have lost the opportunity to do it without a drubbing by the U.S. and its Allies. If the flag bearers of "moderate" and Mulla extremes in Pakistan did not bring down their personal stakes with their own hands, India's Pritvi, or Israeli F-15s and Pakistani Abu Ghraib will do it for them at a great cost. Iraqis and Afghans are paying the price for their lethargy and losing great opportunities to live by Islam today. Pakistanis will pay the price for their morbid dread of Islam tomorrow.

CHAPTER 3

Restoring Democracy Impossible

W HAT'S IN a name? Plenty when it comes to ruling a country by brute force.

Leaders with recognized titles, such as President or Prime Minister, sell better than leaders with frightening, dictator-type titles. Two years after General Musharraf had ousted Pakistan's legitimate prime minister in a coup, *The Economist* summed up world opinion of him with damning brevity as, "a useless dictator."

Three years later, on November 16, 2002, he turned himself into an "elected president" without removing his military uniform and without any endorsement from the parliament, thus becoming the "legitimate" president of Pakistan and visiting the UN, Downing Street, and the White House frequently.

The day he Musharraf-passed Pakistan's Constitution and appointed himself President, 324 opportunistic Pakistanis swore, as members of the National Assembly, to remain subordinate to five more years of his military control. They heralded the dawn of a military-tailored democracy in Pakistan. Soon the nation had an impotent, spineless parliament, steered only by the presidency.

All the rest is rhetoric and misleading slogans about democracy, some for local, and the rest for foreign, consumption.

Interestingly, the elected members of the National Assembly fooled not only the nation, but also themselves, into believing that they were taking their oath under the 1973 Constitution as it existed before the 1999 coup. Musharraf had, however, made them take their oath under a constitution that incorporated the controversial Legal Framework Order (LFO) decreed by the junta.

Gullible Pakistanis faced blaring news headlines about "the dawn of democracy in Pakistan" when General Musharraf, however, had in fact just empowered himself to sack future prime ministers, to dissolve the parliament, and to set up the overseeing of a National Security Council to keep the armed forces in the governance mechanism permanently.

Pakistanis, thus, started living under a "democratic" set-up in which their civilian leaders had accepted the supremacy of the armed forces in all decision-making simply because they were too focused on wheeling and dealing for different positions in the future set-up.

The all-empowered general-cum-president had what had previously been the prime ministerial powers to appoint the armed forces' chiefs and provincial governors, who in turn were empowered to sack provincial chief ministers and dissolve provincial assemblies with dictatorial assent from the president.

The restoration of the National Assembly and the labeling of the dictator as Elected President didn't change the reality that Musharraf was still no different from Saddam Hussein, Hosnie Mubarak, Bashar-ul-Asad, or any other dictators who win their single-candidate elections or referendums with margins of no less than 95% of the vote.

The new assemblies proved no different from the assemblies gathered under General Zia ul Haq to endorse his brand of democracy. The objective in both cases was only to silence the politicians and hide the junta behind the shield of being properly elected and inducted into the government.

This was done under the auspices of the same General who told the nation shortly after coming to power that he will "not allow the people to be taken back to the era of sham democracy." Four years later, the people realized that Musharraf has truly kept his word. He did not allow anyone to take people back to the era of sham democracy. He did it himself.

Musharraf followed a cunning course that led to making democracy impossible for Pakistan for the foreseeable future. The constitution didn't legitimize his actions, so he de-legitimized the constitution. He did it by virtue of holding it in abeyance. In the meanwhile, instead of mending his ways, he rewrote the constitution in a way to legitimize both his actions and the "sacred" document. It might sound odd and impossible but not for someone backed up by absolute power from within and a superpower from outside.

The former sham Pakistani democracies now look far better by comparison, particularly when seen from the perspective that the crusaders of democracy fully approve and support the life of a people under the systematic and legalized dictatorship.

The doubters must begin with the Parliament's approved package of "amendments" to Pakistan's Constitution. It "legitimizes all the actions and deeds of General Musharraf since he seized power in a military coup four years ago."[1] One has to actually see what are "all the actions and deeds" on the part of Musharraf which have been constitutionally endorsed.

People hardly doubt when a BBC correspondent tells them that Musharraf's "biggest critics" have provided the "constitutional legitimacy he so badly needed." No one asks if only the religious parties' alliance is the real force behind granting legitimacy to Musharraf's unconstitutional deeds, and if he is really now a constitutionally legitimate president. Some people argue that these moves did not close the doors for people's democracy in Pakistan forever because Bush also "won" through fraud in 2000. Such an argument ignores the situation in Pakistan, which is different from the US, where even if Bush "won" through fraud, he did not make any constitutional changes.

We need to look at who is actually behind bestowing the "constitutional" legitimacy on Musharraf. Internally, it is now an open secret as to who brought the so-called critics belonging to MMA to this bargaining position and how everything unconstitutional before the coup is now perfectly legitimate in the corrupted Constitution, rewritten with brute force.

The language of brute force is evident from the wordings of the new version of the Constitution. It reads: "The Proclamation of Emergency of October 14, 1999, all President's Orders, Ordinances, Chief Executive's Orders... shall not be called in question in any court or forum on any ground whatsoever."

A constitution is nothing more than what we put in it. Any clause inserted under the label of amendment can never be legitimate if it makes its way only through a series of extra-constitutional measures against the will of the people.

No one can tell that today's General is sitting at the top with a fraction of the public support which he had on October 12, 1999. By the same token, he occupies the top slot not because of any legitimacy but simply for having far more powers than he had on the eve of the coup—thanks both to the half-dead nation and the promoters of tyranny in Washington and London.

Up to 9/11, Musharraf could not say he would be able to stay in power until 2003. Today his stay until 2008 is perfectly ensured, not to speak of the guaranteed extensions like many of the dictators most favored by the US. He has formed the government party and he has bought the opposition. Who can beat him now?

General Musharraf's authority to dismiss Pakistan's national and provincial assemblies is legitimized and despite all the tall claims to democracy, he can do so now without first consulting the Supreme Court.[2]

Furthermore, Musharraf has now formed the National Security Council that has directly involved the armed forces in the "civilian" government's formal decision-making process.

In fact, the constitutional amendments have given not only Musharraf all these abilities, but also any future government will have these elements of tyranny available to it to ride roughshod over the public will. We, however, need not let our short memories hold us from asking: who did this rewriting of the constitution and for what purpose? And: who approved these amendment and under what circumstances?

Let us not forget that the 1999 coup was widely condemned. The US President urged for a quick return to "civilian democratic rule."[3] The US State Department spokesman said: "We believe as we have stated before and let me reiterated very strongly today that Pakistan's constitution should be respected in the spirit as well as its letter." He further confirmed that Nawaz Sharif "had the constitutional authority to remove the military officers.[4] The UK Foreign Secretary stressed that the General should respect the "civilian constitution."[5]

Note the reverence for "constitution" and "civilian" in these messages of condemnation. Germany called for respect of the constitution. EU president, Finland, said: "The EU can in no circumstances approve extra-constitutional and non-democratic means."[6]

The European Union canceled plans to sign a trade and cooperation agreement with Pakistan the very next day after the coup and Commonwealth leaders at their Durban summit decided a month later to suspend Pakistan from the group.

From the beginning, Musharraf was in the hunt for un-constitutional means to legitimize his rule. In the very first press conference on November 1, 1999 he hinted at holding a referendum to make amendments to the Constitution.

Four months later, the regime decided to restore Article 58(2)

B of the Constitution to give Musharraf powers to dissolve the national assembly and the government. In June 2001, the dictator dissolved the parliament and named himself president to replace the figurehead president, Rafiq Tarar.

The US, European Union and Commonwealth once more criticized Musharraf's unconstitutional decisions. On August 10, 2001 the Lahore High Court also observed that the coup leader had no extra powers as president.

The next month, however, came with many glad tidings for Musharraf. Just 12 days after 9/11, Washington lifted sanctions against Pakistan. Constitution and democracy went up in smoke as Powell descended on Islamabad 35 days after 9/11 and Musharraf was offered an $800 million immediate cash grant on October 20, 2001.

The German Chancellor forgot all German calls for respecting the constitution. He did not hesitate to proudly embrace Musharraf on October 28, 2001. Rumsfeld was in Islamabad on November 4 and Musharraf was in London four days later. What a change of fortunes for the dictator.

Less than a week after Rumsfeld's visit, the once unacceptable dictator was addressing the UN General Assembly. And exactly two months after 9/11, Bush—the chief crusader for democracy—stood shoulder to shoulder with Musharraf on November 11, promising him up to $1 billion, and talks on Kashmir.

Less than a month later, the IMF executive body agreed to lend Pakistan $1.3 billion. Afterward, there appeared no bumps and turns on the highway to Musharraf's legitimacy. If Blair was in Islamabad on January 07, 2002; Kofi Annan followed on 24th; Musharraf dashed to White House on February 13 and emperor Akihito of Japan lauded him in March. It was a never ending honeymoon for the dictator and an ideal environment for the rubber stamp cabinet and the National Security Council to approve holding of a referendum for extending the dictatorial rule.

Six days after declaring victory in a referendum widely criticized as unconstitutional and fraught with irregularities, Musharraf focused on permanently inducting the army into the future civilian setup. Constitutional amendments were next to come out of Musharraf's Pandora's box.

In August 2002, Musharraf granted himself further sweeping new powers for which he was widely accused of perpetuating dictatorship. The champions of democracy turned a blind eye to Musharraf's taking several measures prior to the October 2002 elections to ensure his long-term survival and influence the election outcome.

The major embarrassment in the referendum misled many to believe that Musharraf would be less inclined to interfere in the future election process. However, political developments indicated this was not to be the case.

This summary of unconstitutional steps shows that a seemingly constitutional vote in the end does not legitimize all the means adopted by the dictator in the last four years before the vote on the rewritten Constitution.

This shows the extent of US interference and Western manipulation of democracy in countries such as Pakistan. The victims of sham democracy have absolutely no idea as to how to bring an end to a dictatorship that went constitutional with their own vote because all elements of a perpetual tyranny are not embedded in the newly rewritten Constitution. Can these changes be undone? If yes, how many decades would it need to undo the changes which dictator Musharraf has made in the last six years? If they are to be undone, would the forces, which imposed these changes now, be upset and resist these changes? Or is it that we now have to permanently live with these changes and just do the voting exercises to merely changes faces in the tyrannical system?

Of course, that is the situation in modern "democracies." In the US, people can choose between a Republican billionaires' President and a Democratic billionaires' President. In Australia, the policies of the two main parties are almost indistinguishable, and favor big business. However, the situation in Pakistan is worse in the sense that either the military dictator will stay at the topmost position from now on, or he will stay behind the scene, influencing every aspect of life in the country. At the same time the outside powers will stay behind the military chief to keep him as a puppet-in-chief for serving their interests.

While voting in the 2002 elections, very few Pakistanis knew that most of the apparently anti- Musharraf candidates were also propped up by the most powerful government agency, the ISI. The result is granting constitutional legitimacy to tyranny with the people's vote by the people's representative. This is how Pakistanis dug two graves: one for democracy in Pakistan and the other for Pakistan with their own hands.

A hopeless future

The US's overwhelming trust in strong men to serve its interests has resulted in the military emerging as the sole powerful institution for usurping power and exploiting everything in the name of democracy in Pakistan. Democratic institutions have remained weak due to self-serving politicians whose primary concerns have been to remain in power, regardless of the interests of the people they represent and irrespective of who is at the topmost position in the country. They hardly care about the system and the Constitution. Their debates on these issues remain debates for the sake of debate. They have manipulated various democratic institutions, including the Constitution, to perpetuate their rule.

The military cooperated with Washington and these self-serving politicians to further their vested interests and the military as an institution got strengthened at the cost of democracy. If Washington says, "go for *Jihad*," the military is all for *Jihad*, establishing madrassas and training centers and running all types of covert operations. If the US says, "take a U-turn on *Jihad*, the military" sweeps the country to remove any reference to *Jihad* in any school book, other than the Qur'an itself.

The army-defined democracy is leading the country to face utter disaster. The dictator-defined security parameters are leading the country into spending enormous amounts on defense at the cost of socio-economic development at a time when Musharraf has surrendered almost everything to the US, India and Israel. Who needs expensive defense with policies of unprecedented concessions like these? In fact, the tyrannical character of the Pakistani regime emanates from the self-insecurity syndrome. This directly puts Pakistan at stake and undermines Pakistan's polity, which cannot be defended with bombs and guns. The absence of true democracy and greater provincial autonomy are leading to the growing dissatisfaction of various ethno-linguistic groups. This, in turn, makes the state more vulnerable.

Pakistan was a security-centric state, but now the regime's insecurity has overshadowed the state's insecurity. As a result, the role of the opposition has disappeared altogether. Any opposition to the regime now amounts to terrorism and a threat to global security. Instead of emphasizing change through democratic means, the opportunistic political parties have never hesitated to ask the army to intervene. Now they have made the military part of the political setup and there is no going back.

The civil society has become more marginalized. Even if it is active, it is active in the sectors that consolidate cultural imperialism and the concepts of "moderate" Islam for further divisions in the society. The press is hesitant to criticize the government. Despite utter desperation, high inflation and unemployment and a total lack of opportunities, apparently no reactionary force seems ready to emerge to counter this injustice perpetrated from the top in various ways. All these factors have stunted the growth of democracy and there is no hope or any factor that could lead us to hope that democracy will revive and flourish in Pakistan in the foreseeable future.

Democracy is itself a failed concept and ineffective governance mechanism. Here we will not indulge in discussion about democracy. We would look at it from the perspective that if democracy is the best system of governance that enables the participation of the masses, why have the Pakistanis been so reluctant to be critical of the military takeover? Even the break-up of Pakistan under military rule has not eroded the confidence of the people in the army or in its ability to provide efficient administration. One needs to ask why the people and the leaders have behaved as they did. To understand that democracy is impossible in Pakistan, it is important to analyze how the concept of the security state has turned into a security regime and a culture of tyranny.

"Security Regime" Predominance over the Survival of Pakistan

Over the years Pakistan gave overwhelming emphasis to the military aspect of security. But this has not been so for the last four years. Under Musharraf, things have turned upside down. The situation has moved far away from the time when the perceived threat from India put Pakistan on high alert. The insecurity parameter defined after a war with India soon after independence has long vanished with Musharraf's concessions to India before any meaningful dialogue on the Kashmir issue which has taken the lives of thousands of Indian, Kashmiris and Pakistanis.

The military was needed to act like a strong and cohesive institution to exercise control over the newly emerged state saddled with the enormous task of rehabilitation of the uprooted Muslims and reigning in political opportunism. The same military has become a liability for the country. By taking Islam out of the equation, this institution is not only confusing the state's identity (ethnic vs. religious vs. linguistic and tribal identities) but also it has to redo its motto from "*Eeman* (faith), *Taqwa* (fear of Allah) and *Jihad fee sabeelillah* (struggle in the way of Allah") to "Faith in Washington, Fear of the Pentagon and Struggle in the way of the US."

The events of 9/11 and Musharraf's opportunism have changed everything. With the dominance of the army, defense undoubtedly was a priority area for Pakistan: the country had to be protected even at the cost of democracy. Its foreign policy orientation and its defense policy were geared toward the single dominant factor of counter-balancing India. The unfortunate pattern of resource allocation to defense persists since independence.[7] The situation has came to such a point that despite Musharraf's submitting to the will of all the enemies of Pakistan, it is neither feasible to reduce the defense budget nor is it possible to further cut down the meager allocations for development and economic assistance provided to the provinces. The military and the weak political leadership are perpetuating each other's vested mutual interests through a method of cooptation at the top, while the masses suffer at the grassroots level.

In the most corrupt military dominated political culture, the armed forces have become sacrosanct in the politics of Pakistan. There is no doubt that Pakistan still needs a credible military deterrence. However, in the changed environment, this force is now working to serve the interest of the enemies of Islam and Pakistan. The military strength is now used to keep the regime in power and the nation subdued, lest it rise up against the indirect occupation of Pakistan. Over the years, defense-related measures escaped in-depth political scrutiny and debate under the falsely exaggerated cover of national security. Now the situation has worsened beyond that. In the absence of the system of parliamentary committees and honest press, the army's sense of exclusivity has further strengthened. It considers itself above the law and parliamentary scrutiny. All major decisions, such as the secret talks to normalize relations with Israel and paving the way for recognition of Israel, have taken place without any consultation at all.

Of course, the emphasis on the security paradigm over socio-economic issues has paralyzed the functioning of the state apparatus in the past. Under Musharraf, the shift from state's security to the regime's security has worsened the situation. It is not that the defense forces are irrelevant to the threats that Pakistan confronted, but that such endeavors have distorted the balance of power between the state and civil society in the past, and the shift in focus from state to the regime's security has led to the exploitation of the military power to the extent of undermining the survival of Pakistan.

The regime's fear of losing power within Pakistan replaced the fear of India and became a ruling passion in the regime's internal and foreign policy since September 11, 2001. The military assumed importance due to the absence of open and credible political challenges at home. Political leaders sold their consciences and preferred to run elections, take oath under a military-written Constitution and then blindly approve all those changes to the Constitution without considering the consequences for the country. Interestingly, the so-called elected Punjab Assembly passed a resolution demanding Musharraf to retain the offices of the Chief of the Army Staff and the President, even after the December 31, 2004 deadline fixed by the 17th Amendment called on him to relinquish one of these posts.[8] These members were "elected" for dealing with provincial issues, not for demanding continuation of a dictatorship on behalf of the country.

It used to be the Indo-Pakistan conflict over Jammu and Kashmir that justified the assertive role of the military in civilian affairs. Now, it is the US war on terrorism and the military's determination to transform Pakistan into a modern, secular state that helps the military exaggerate the threat perceptions from the enemies within in order to justify its role in politics and power.

The regime's security concerns and the army's vested interests made democracy its first victim. There is no constructive political opposition in the absence of a real political setup in a society characterized by feudalism. Mostly feudal, Pakistani society has nurtured and is still willing to sustain a system wherein the interests of the land-owner class are protected. For example the same feudal lord, Aftab Khan Sherpao, who was running for Benazir Bhutto's People Party and served as the Chief Minister of NWFP, made a deal with the junta and was elected again by the same voters to become the Interior Minister. Unfortunately, he is just one example of many more like him. Since a limited "power elite" enjoyed the fruits of freedom, the masses had little stake in the political system in the absence of real political participation. For them, there is hardly any difference between democracy and dictatorship. Thus, democracy in Pakistan became elitist, and largely a medium for self-aggrandizement of the feudal elements, which are part of the political parties, the military, and the bureaucratic structure.

Although the military is being blamed for the death of democracy in Pakistan, it is evident from history that there has never been a serious movement for the sake of democracy. In Pakistan, even the most popular leaders such as Zulfiqar Ali Bhutto lacked a real commitment to democracy. Political parties, on the other hand, never tried to develop a democratic culture. Benazir became a Chairperson of the party for life. The leaders of other parties have also behaved in the most arbitrarily dictatorial manner. General Zia's regime mutilated democratic institutions. Provincial autonomy is still considered a threat to the centralized character of the regime. Musharraf has merely put the final nails in the coffin of democracy in Pakistan.

There is no hope that politicians would overcome their feudal character and political opportunism, and they would end their cooperation with the military dictatorship.

There is no hope that Opposition parties in the future will wait to fight an election to bring about necessary democratic changes and will not play second fiddle to the military.

There is no hope that the changes made by the present junta to the constitution can be easily undone and the military taken out of the political process and institutions.

There is no hope that any political party may penetrate the independent power base of the feudal politicians in their constituency. Regardless of party affiliations, or even by running independently, many of them will continue to win by mobilizing caste, tribe, and other relevant social networks.

There is no hope that political parties will be able to develop a political culture which would not hinder the emergence of the second line of leadership. The break-up of the political parties, allegedly by the military, would continue to reflect the fragile party structure and the democratic credentials of the politicians.

There is no hope that there can be any change in the dynastic organizational structure of the main political parties. Without grassroots support, these parties keep attracting the feudal lords with vested interests.

There is no hope that the opposition would be strengthened with the annulment of the fourteenth amendment, which makes it mandatory for the legislators to follow the party whip while voting in Parliament. A legislator can disobey only at the cost of his seat in the National Assembly.

There is no hope that in the near future the gap between the elite and the poor will reduce considerably and a strong middle class might emerge. Instead, the feudal societal structure will get strengthened with the passage of time and increased poverty, inflation, unemployment and lack of opportunities will be the result.

There is no hope that Pakistan Television (PTV) will free itself from the state monopoly and the press relinquishes its self-adopted restrictions to tell the truth. The media mafia and their presstitutes will continue to toe the regime's line and keep calling a dictator the president of Pakistan.

Keeping the unimaginable funding opportunities and addiction of the NGO sector to these funds, there is no hope that civil society can put Pakistan on the right track toward fulfilling the objective of its creation. Instead, the emergence of liberal and

"moderate" sections in civil society will consolidate cultural imperialism and promote the agenda of anti-Islam and anti-Pakistan
elements with increased enthusiasm.

There is no hope that the intelligence agencies will stop inter-
fering in the political process that contributed immensely to the
weakening of democracy. ISI will continue to be used by both
the military and the civilian government to serve their own interests.

There is no hope that the judiciary will not remain the victim of the whims and fancies of military dictators and will not
face interference from democratically elected leaders. There is no
hope that the Supreme Court will stop legitimizing dictatorships
based in the "doctrine of necessity". There is no hope that judges of the superior courts would refuse any of the future General's orders to take a fresh oath of office under the Provisional
Constitution Order (PCO).[9] If they do refuse, there is no hope
that they will be spared and not treated like the chief justice of
the Supreme Court, along with five colleagues, who resigned and
the government cordoned off his house, not allowing anybody to
leave until the oath-taking ceremony.[10]

There is no hope that the government will not tap the phones
of the superior court judges and the executive will not intervene
in the functioning of the judiciary to undermine its independence
and status as an essential pillar of a functioning democracy.

There is no hope for an independent and democratic government coming to power in Pakistan. Even if it does, there is no
hope that such an elected government will not create obstacles to
the accountability of rulers, using purportedly democratic institutions for purposes that are not wholly democratic. There is no
hope that a future elected and independent government will not
establish military courts in accordance with article 245, against
the directives of the Supreme Court to create a parallel judicial
system.[11]

There is no hope that politicians will overcome their moral

bankruptcy, allowing Pakistan to evolve into a society where individuals will not overshadow institutions and a democratic political system will not be relentlessly preached but really practiced.

There is absolutely no hope whatsoever that the Pakistani army will allow itself to be marginalized from mainstream politics. Apart from external threats, the ambit of the army's security parameter has extended to internal threats also. Since there is no hope that an epitaph on military intervention can be written, there is a strong possibility that Pakistan may not remain as it stands today.

In such a hopeless environment, it is hard to predict that Pakistan will survive without an independent, representative self rule, under the tyrannical regimes with an unjust order[12] and absolute mismanagement for ever to come.

CHAPTER 4

The Height of Collective Helplessness

Musharraf's silence over the growing demands for his resignation shows that it is not for the Pakistanis or their elected representatives to decide whether they want him or not. Musharraf has not left much room for them to say no to him.

This helplessness before Musharraf began when, soon after 9/11, news headlines started reading in Pakistan: "Musharraf not to quit." The self-appointed President then made it amply clear in 2002 that he had no intentions of standing down because he thought he had "a role to play in bringing democracy to Pakistan."

This was the role for which Musharraf had to stay in uniform; publicly promise to remove it and then renege on his promise because the role could not be played without his military uniform. This was the democracy for which he had to pay the cost of the nation's independence and the *raison d'être* of Pakistan.

The role that Musharraf played brought the nation to a situation where it is facing a sold-out army, sold out politicians and the most corrupt and aimless political parties ever. The masses see no alternative at all other than witnessing the military and civilian dictators replacing each other at the top, unless they take to the streets in protest.

This lack of alternatives has sapped the public will to protest and rise up in rebellion against the oppression they have to live with on a seemingly indefinite basis. This helplessness has seeped gradually into their veins over the last fifty-eight years. However, the reign of Musharraf's dictatorship has further sapped the left-over energies in the masses because it made them lose the direction and faith in other available alternatives.

The following facts show the sequence of Musharraf's increasing highhandedness and the corresponding increase in helplessness of the masses. Finally, where the nation stands today, forcing Musharraf to resign would be a gift for him in view of the crimes he has committed by violating the Constitution and Supreme Court rulings. At the same time, even his departure will not solve all of Pakistan problems because some of the destructive seeds he has sown are yet to germinate into horrible consequences. These realities further intensify the helplessness Pakistan faces today.

Pakistan's slide on the slippery slope towards this helplessness started on October 17, 1999, when Musharraf proclaimed himself chief executive of Pakistan in his speech to the nation. The nation helplessly watched Musharraf state that the army planned to stay in charge only so long as was "absolutely necessary to pave the way for true democracy." The helpless nation, however, has no standard for measuring the "absolute necessity" except Musharraf's wish to continue.

Everyone then helplessly watched the beginning of Musharraf's crimes against the Constitution, beginning with easing out President Mohammed Rafiq Tarar through an executive decree and having himself sworn in as President under the Provisional Constitutional Order (PCO).

Earlier, dictators of his league had also proclaimed themselves presidents, but by doing so, they had not violated the Constitution. This is because they had abrogated or suspended the Constitution, proclaimed Martial Law and obtained the endorsement of a compliant judiciary for their action under the so-called doctrine of necessity.

In his anxiety to show himself as a different dictator, Musharraf did not replace the Constitution with Martial Law and kept in force the fundamental features of the 1973 Constitution such as those relating to the election and removal of the President, the National Assembly, the Senate, and the judiciary.

The Supreme Court, while endorsing his seizure of power under the doctrine of necessity, had at the same time ruled that he could not change the basic features of the Constitution. The list of Musharraf's crimes extended to violation of both the Constitution and the Supreme Court judgment by removing Mr. Tarar in a manner and for reasons not provided for in the Constitution, by proclaiming himself President and by dissolving the Senate which, under the Constitution, is a permanent body not subject to dissolution.

The referendum decision came against the backdrop of his succumbing to American threats and unconditional cooperation without trying to find out what alignment with the US would entail. In other words, Musharraf sold Pakistan cheaply, rendering vital services to the American cause without getting much in return except taking the pulse of the nation and finding the extent of opposition he could face for making independent decisions on crucial issues related to sovereignty and independence of Pakistan. He realized that if the public is not fully numb, it could be silenced with brute force.

The nation then faced the farce of a referendum. Most people humbly participated in the national drama at the cost of public funds. Teachers, municipal workers and other government servants could hardly refuse to attend Musharraf's rallies. Private transport was forcibly hijacked for the same purpose. The

General announced a huge victory on the evening of April 30th, 2002 without any constitutional backing. And the nation with its so-called leaders had no option but to live with the results.

Then came the time for the mother of all violations from Musharraf which was the climax of the nation's helplessness. Musharraf is not the first soldier to attempt prolonging his rule through constitutional changes. Other dictators, however, put on the pretence of securing the "consent of the people" by getting them ratified by the chosen "National Assembly" of the day. Musharraf does not believe in such niceties. At the historic press briefing on August 21, 2002 he said: "I hereby make it part of the Constitution under the powers vested in me by the Supreme Court and it is now the Constitution."

When a reporter reminded Musharraf that under the Constitution Parliament alone had the right to amend the Constitution and the Supreme Court could not be expected to give him powers that it did not have, he said: "Let those who disagree go to court." The question, however, is: Which court was he referring to? The courts with intimidated judiciary and judges who accepted to take oath under Musharraf's Provisional Constitution Order (PCO)?

Exposure of the Judiciary's helplessness began on January 26, 2000 when he issued an order requiring all Supreme Court and High Court judges to take an oath that would bind them to uphold his proclamation of emergency and the PCO.

According to a Human Rights Watch report, on the evening of January 25, the chief justice of Pakistan's Supreme Court, Saeeduzzaman Siddiqui, was summoned to Musharraf's offices. Musharraf asked Siddiqui to take an oath of loyalty under the newly promulgated PCO, but Siddiqui refused, saying that it was impossible for him take a fresh oath because he had already been sworn in.[1] Later that night, Interior Minister, retired General Moin-ud-Din Haider, accompanied by two active-duty generals, went to Siddiqui's residence and asked him to reconsider his decision, but Siddiqui again declined. At 6:00 a.m. on January 26, an army colonel arrived at Siddiqui's residence and told him that he should not go to the Supreme Court that day. The area around his house was subsequently cordoned off and no one was allowed to enter or leave his residence. Along with Chief Justice Siddiqui, five other judges of the Supreme Court were forced to resign when they refused to take the oath, as were nine provincial High Court judges.[2] Interior Minister Haider told Human Rights Watch that four of the provincial judges were not invited to take the oath "as a means of getting corrupt judges to leave."[3] These crimes effectively immunized officials of the military regime from prosecution.

Fifteen judges, including the chief justice of the Supreme Court, were removed for refusal to take the oath. Four months later, a reconstituted, quiescent Supreme Court validated the coup and set a three-year time frame for the restoration of democracy. The court also gave the military regime authority to unilaterally amend the constitution. The dictator asked those who disagreed with him to refer to this court against the unauthorized and illegal constitutional amendments.

Helplessness of the opportunist politicians is evident from the fact that after putting dummy assemblies in place, Musharraf made members of both the National and Provincial Assemblies take an oath under a constitution that included the Legal Frame Work Order (LFO) and incorporated an Article (Article 270 A). This article states that all decrees by the military junta since October 12, 1999 "are affirmed and will be adopted and declared, notwithstanding any judgment of any court, to have been validly made by competent authority and notwithstanding anything contained in the Constitution shall not be called into question in any court on any ground whatsoever." Hence by making the LFO part of the constitution, all the orders issued by Musharraf have become a permanent part of the constitution. And even after Musharraf removes his uniform or his regime ends, the institutions of the state will be bound constitutionally to continue implementing American inspired policies.

They are clearly indeed American approved policies. After officially announcing the end of the war against Afghanistan, America expanded its "war on terrorism" to Pakistan, so as to tame Pakistan according to its new policy toward Muslims and Islam. In order to ensure the success of the American plan, Musharraf issued various ordinances and orders. America herself gives testimony of this. The US Congressional Research Service referred to remarks by the US State Department Spokesman, Phillip Reeker, in its August 22, 2002 report and stated, "In response to Musharraf's imposition of constitutional revision, the United States indicated that full US support for Musharraf would continue, even if some of the changes could make it more difficult to build strong, democratic institutions in Pakistan." Furthermore, on October 10, 2002 in Washington, US Assistant Secretary of State for South Asia, Christina Rocca, stated, "We are committed to helping Pakistan modernize and strengthen its law enforcement capabilities." Making LFO part of the Constitution was part of the US designs to make Pakistan strictly pursue the path that she has chosen for it. Both religious and secular political parties together helped the army make LFO part of the Constitution. Musharraf promulgated 292 laws in the first three years, the majority of them in 2002 after 9/11. In addition, 67 ordinances were promulgated after October 12, 2002, when the military ruler had lost all kinds of legitimacy. All these ordinances were of far reaching consequences, and, unfortunately, all these are part of the LFO.[4]

The General didn't put a gun to their head. The politicians simply found themselves helpless because in their blind pursuit for power and self-interest, they could not see any other alternative at all. That was the end of the world for them. LFO clearly says that no suits, prosecution or other legal proceedings will stand in any court against any authority or any person for or on account of or in respect of any order made since October 12, 1999. This is the height of dictatorship. And it shows that even after the departure of Musharraf, these opportunist politicians cannot undo whatever had been done with their signatures of approval on it. They have tied their own hands and the hands of the nation. They deserve to be equally prosecuted with the Musharraf who has undermined the very existence of Pakistan. Most interestingly, the politicians were not acting under duress. Musharraf did not obtain their signature under the barrel of a gun. Therefore, there is no hope that if the threat of force from Musharraf were removed, they might be willing to revoke previous agreements.

Musharraf justifies all his actions by claiming "democracy has different principles in different societies" or "we are tailoring a new democracy for Pakistan." He then goes back and claims, "I don't want to share power"—"I just want to monitor." What kind of monitoring is it that requires putting all powers of the land in the hands of one person?

The state of utter helplessness is due to the lack of a real alternative. This lack of alternative, in turn, is because of US interests. Looking at the phenomenon at play in most Muslim countries would help us understand the situation in Pakistan, where both democracy and dictatorships are promoted at different times in order to save American interest. There is no Pakistani who would believe that our forefathers made extraordinary sacrifices only to live again in a secular state, under the same British law and systems, and make foreign and domestic policy subservient to the whims and wishes of other masters in Washington and keep calling it the Islamic Republic of Pakistan. Who would believe that Pakistan was demanded and established for *a reason*, and still consider exchanging its sovereignty for handful of foreign exchange reserves as the meaning of life in a "democratic" Pakistan?

Democracy alone was not the objective. Pakistanis could have enjoyed democracy anywhere in the world, including under British rule or with Hindus in an undivided India. The *raison d'être* of Pakistan is, however, of little concern for Musharraf and his political cronies with ambitions for power. They forget that democracy is not an end in itself. It is merely a means to a greater end, which is good self-governance without selling a nation's sovereignty, diluting its identity and butchering its people to please its masters abroad.

Like Egypt, Afghanistan and Iraq, Pakistan is facing a serious deadlock with nowhere to go. The words and deeds of Western governments since the 1999 *coup d'état* have clearly shown their lack of concern for democracy. Their real concern has been to have a pro-western government, irrespective of its title. They know that there is no need for Musharraf to stay indefinitely if the system he proposes for "sustainable democracy" is sound for serving their interests, and the imposed constitutional changes should ensure its continuity.

Musharraf serves a purpose other than establishing democracy. The story started way back in 1999. Many image-building stories appeared on the pattern of an Associated Press headline, "Coup Leader-Iron Will, Sharp Mind." Just 16 days into the coup, Bill Clinton publicly called for a "restoration of democracy" while privately rushing to make use of Brownback-2, the presidential waiver authority attached to the new defense bill, to ease US sanctions on Pakistan. Clinton lifted all restrictions that he could considering that Section 508 of the Foreign Assistance Act supersedes Brownback and expressly forbids aid to countries where elected governments have been replaced by military regimes.

Today, Musharraf has dumped the nation in the slough of despondence and helplessness, and brought himself to a position where he gets glowing stories in the Western media about progress on human rights, modernization, and women's rights, along with the occasional criticism to keep him going. This royal treatment is in return for his surrendering Pakistan's objective, sovereignty and independence, and maybe nuclear deterrence as well. Tens of millions in American aid has been provided for undermining religious institutions, permanently inducting the military in politics and watering down the state's identity-related clauses in the Constitution.

Anyone with even a cursory understanding of American priorities understands that the Bush Administration believes that a substantive role for the Army in Pakistan's national life is necessary. It suits American interests in the war on Islamic movements with the objective of hindering them from establishing an alternative model of Islamic governance anywhere in the world. As a result of the measures taken to achieve this objective, if Pakistan's survival is threatened, that is an added advantage to Washington.

There is no savior for Pakistanis. Even religious parties have exploited the sympathies of the masses in the name of Islam. They have adopted the same godless system which has now clearly proved to be against anything that is remotely associated with Islam. Continuing *Riba*-based (interest based) business through the Supreme Court in 2002 and thwarting the initiative of the NWFP government for introducing some pro-Islam initiatives in 2005 clearly proves that there is no way the religious political parties would ever achieve what they highlight as their agenda.

With the forces behind the scenes in London and Washington interested primarily in Musharraf's campaign for reducing any chances of an Islamic revival, the restoration of democracy has clearly become a non-issue. Democracy has ceased to be a reality. Forces behind the establishments in London and Washington hold the real power. The public is not informed about the major decisions they reached with the dictator. The room for maneuvering is getting more and more restricted for Muslim states by agreements made about people who have never been consulted or informed.

One can make the same argument for other places as well. For example, Australia has no dictator. There are fair and open elections. However, one can say almost the same things. The decisions taken by the government of the day suit the USA, not Australia. The media are owned by a few billionaire power brokers, so that public opinion can be manipulated at will. Economics is used to bribe, intimidate and blackmail ordinary people. The details are different, the effects similar. And even in the US, Bush is not the real power. Most analysts believe, he is there to serve his masters. That is where the problems of Pakistan begin. Whoever are Bush's not-so-hidden masters, they have a serious grudge against Islam. Their unfolding agenda explains it all. In such a situation, all hopes of a representative, pro-Pakistan democracy fade away.

The helpless nation will continue to vote in election after sham election, but their votes have been deprived of all meaning. Pakistanis vote for opportunist leaders, who like the current dictator at the top, are in charge of practically nothing other than promoting their self-interests.

Externally, Pakistan has become totally defenseless against foreign interventions but internally the regime has become more powerful, intrusive and repressive in total contrast to the helplessness of the masses. Internal repression helps Musharraf keep a check on every action that could lead to mass mobilization against the regime. A nation is really helpless whose hope for democracy rests with a coup leader and where "defenders of Islam" are still clueless about the way they need to proceed to achieve their stated objectives. In this complex situation, Musharraf is a leading factor in expediting and ensuring the demise of Pakistan.

The reason for hopelessness

As mentioned earlier, one of the basic reasons for the extreme hopelessness in Pakistan is the lack of an alternative to what is before the nation in the form of Musharraf's dictatorship. The nation cannot think of the form of government, political actors and their policies after the departure of Musharraf from the scene. Seeing no meaningful change in the daily routine, suffering and disorder, the common man has limited himself to the struggle for making both ends meet. These factors lead us to the real reason behind the prevailing hopelessness. It is the nation's collective blindness.

Their blindness doesn't make the nation see the alternative. This blindness is the common ailment from dictator Musharraf at the top to the toiling laborer and farmer at the bottom. We proudly call this the 21st century. However, from the perspective of human behavior and moral decency, we may be living in the darkest period of human history with the most closed minds ever possible. Pakistanis are no exception. They are part of the humanity groping in the dark with wide open eyes, thinking they are the most enlightened and civilized human beings of all ages, not knowing their folly and misguidance.

Being the direct target of a propaganda campaign, Pakistanis are the victims of lies and misconceptions from the West. Part of the nation's blindness is due to its grand misconception that the unprecedented technological and scientific advancements are signs of human intellectual enlightenment. Therefore, whatever comes from Washington and London is enlightened and needs to be accepted as such. This mentality translates into the people's purchasing behavior also. Shopping at St-Michael stores or eating a Big Mac is a sign of high status. They fail to see such actions are destroying the nation.

The reason for the nation's living with jaundiced eyes is simple. If Pakistanis cannot reach the truth with all the available means of communication, research and education; if they cannot see an alternative; if they have surrendered to tyranny because they don't think there could be an alternative to the problem as well, we are far worse off than those who lived through the dark ages of the past and failed to reach the reality without these facilities.

We can easily draw parallels between the present and any dark age of the past. However, the easiest and most comprehensible parallels are with the latest Dark Age that was hardly 14 to15 hundred years ago at the time of Prophet Mohammed (PBUH).

For assessing the dark minds of our age, all one needs is to pick up any article, news-report or documentary produced by the "mainstream" media about Islam in the US, or the statements of the self-proclaimed moderates among Muslims and compare these with the beliefs, views, perception and particularly the reaction to the message of Truth in the dark ages in the 7th century.

The oft repeated argument is that we are living in the 21st century. As such, we cannot go back to 7th century to live by Islam the way people in 7th century used to live. Gen. John Abizaid, whom the *Washington Post* Editor, David Ignatius, could not elevate any more than he did in his December 26, 2004 column, is like any of the doomed commanders in history – busy dreaming of conquering the world and achieving the impossible for their masters. General Abizaid has been clearly telling the world that his forces are out there to crush those who "try to re-create what they imagine was the pure and perfect Islamic government of the era of the prophet Muhammad."

Presenting views of the 21st century crusaders, Abizaid told the *Washington Post's* David Ignatius that invading and occupying Iraq and Afghanistan are just "the early stages" of a "long war" against the "loose network of like-minded individuals who use 21st century-technology to spread their vision of a 7th-century paradise."

Joining this chorus, a "moderate" Muslim General, Pervez Musharraf, told BBC on September 11, 2003:

> So I would say that there's no chance of going back to *Khilafat* really. *Khilafat* requires certain environment in a country. It demands a lot from the nation, from the government. It demands that everyone, the entire country - its masses, its people - should have social justice. They must have at least the minimum requirements that are required of life, they must not be wanting in food, shelter at the minimum.

So these have not been fulfilled by any of the Islamic states, I would say, for all its population. [Not fulfilled anywhere on earth, sadly.] So therefore imposing the *Khilafat* when the entire environment has not been created for it, is totally a Utopian idea. We cannot go back to *Khilafat* unless we've created a certain environment. And now we are living in the 21st Century, after all what was *Khilafat*? *Khilafat* ensured social justice and equality, freedom to the people. And now in this 21st Century through a democratic dispensation you can achieve the same goals, you are moving towards what the caliphs did in the earlier part of the Muslim era. So therefore I think there is no such thing as going back in the 21st Century - the environment is not at all available to go back to *Khilafat*. [5]

The 21st century mantra is the root cause of our blindness and hopelessness. We are five years into the 21st century and it has shown us the most despicable and barbaric nature that human beings can display. The butchery in Iraq, Afghanistan and Palestine, and the tortures in Guantanamo and Abu Ghraib are just the visible example of man's inhumanity to man in this so-called enlightened age.

It would be naive to assume that it is a two-sided issue. For example, Palestinians and Israelis are equally savage, and both feel self-justified. The attacks against civilians by terrorists are just as bad. If we do an in-depth analysis, in each conflict, those who claim to be more enlightened have a lion's share in atrocities committed against humanity. And the savagery is not limited to issues involving Muslims alone. There are the various wars of genocide in Africa. Not long ago, they were being fought in the Balkans, and there is Ireland, and the various crimes committed by the Indonesian and Chinese governments.

It shows us that the moon is not that far away. Even if human beings conquer the sun and all the stars in our galaxy, still their basic human nature will remain the same. For that reason, Allah has given us the ability not only to conquer the universe but ourselves as well. For this reason, human beings have been declared the best of all creations (*Ashraful Makhlooqat*).[6] This conquering itself is not possible without the manual (the Qur'an) provided by the Creator.

When we talk about the 21st century, we look at the previous ages as the Dark Ages of human history and assume that we are passing through the most enlightened age. To some of us, those who have invented rockets and reached the moon are living the most enlightened life. They never stop impressing upon others with examples of Boeing planes taking us non-stop from California to Dubai and our ability to fax and e-mail our friends while on board. But this has nothing to do with the enlightenment of its inventors or the blindness of those who call for establishing the *Deen*—the just order of Islam and living by the Qur'an.

To understand the reality that we are living in the darkest age of human history, we would have to zoom out of the minor details of what the most enlightened people are doing all over the world; the way they have butchered more than 128,000 people in Iraq based upon "a pack of lies"; the way they have established concentration camps around the world and the way their Congress has recently approved that they can indefinitely detain human beings in those camps even if there is no evidence of their involvement in any wrongdoing. Similarly, the US Patriot Act grossly violates the US Constitution, and severely impacts on the freedom and dignity of American citizens.[7]

The enlightened mind of the 21st century is as much afraid of the message of the Qur'an as it was at the time of its revelation 1400 years ago. What General Abizaid and General Musharraf are telling the world today is exactly what it has been hearing since 7th century—611 after the time of Jesus (AS) to be exact. The intellectuals, religious and tribal leaders, and even common man said the same thing: We are not against Mohammed (PBUH) and his friends; we are against what he preaches and him calling it the word of God. Compare this with the words of Sam Harris, a member of the enlightened community of the 21st century: "we are absolutely at war with the vision of life that is prescribed to all Muslims in the Koran."[8]

In the 7th century, Arab society had many superstitious and groundless beliefs. These early Arabs believed in legends inherited from past generations. They supposed that mountains supported the sky above. They believed that the world was flat; burying daughters alive was an honorable deed and living life in licentious ways was the ultimate goal of existence.

Mohammed (PBUH) was just one person challenging the status quo of a people, who would fight for forty years on the slight provocation that a camel belonging to the guest of one tribe had strayed into the grazing land belonging to another tribe and both sides had fought till they lost 70,000 lives in all; threatening the extinction of both the tribes. These well established people felt threatened by the words of a single, unarmed, powerless individual – Prophet Mohammed (PBUH).

Today we see a number of anti-Islam preachers of hate spreading fear of the religion and the Qur'an on some baseless grounds. For example, Sam Harris says: "The only reason Muslim fundamentalism is a threat to us is because the fundamentals of Islam are a threat to us." Unfortunately, he is not alone, whose words can be ignored as personal opinion. Of course, the general attitude is: Islam is one of the great religions on a par with Christianity, and people are entitled to worship God in that way, as long as they don't force others to do so, and as long as they don't attack us in the name of their religion. But there are numerous preachers of hate with increasing influence at the street level, where a Westmoreland County Church in Philadelphia displayed a sign, reading: "You must remember, Islam is the enemy,"[9] and a sign posted in front of Danieltown Baptist Church read: "The Koran needs to be flushed."[10] At the macro-level, statements and policies of Bush, Blair and their associates are good enough to expose the insecurity they feel from the core message of Islam, which is, of course, not irrational and indiscriminate violence against non-believers as they present. No amount of "poisonous interpretations" can make it so. These are just ruses to hide the negative implications of the unjust aggressions launched on the bases of lies, chicanery and deceit.

Some Muslims also have the same attitude toward Islam and its fundamentals. Think of the hue and cry when something associated to Islam is introduced. Remember Muslims protesting in the streets in Canada and elsewhere when the government approved to introduce *Shari'ah* based arbitration? The leading anti-*Shari'ah* activists are from Pakistan and they claim to be Muslims. We must keep in mind that Arab society was against the message of Prophet Mohammed (PBUH) even when the Qur'an was not fully revealed. Nor was there an army of companions with Mohammed (PBUH) engaged in any *Jihad*.

In the 21st century, the same fear of Islam remains in the hearts of Muslims as well as non-Muslims. Same Harris and his fellow enlightened members of the 21st century community are afraid of the Qur'an. One can come up with countless items of evidence to prove this point. One of these is the launching a fake Qur'an, with 47 chapters eliminated, under the title: *The True Furqan*. This shows the morbid dread of the Qur'an and fear of Muslims' living by its guidance. People in Arabia reacted the same way, when the Qur'an was revealed to them fourteen hundred years ago.

Sam Harris writes: "This is not to say that we are at war with all Muslims, but we are absolutely at war with the vision of life that is prescribed to all Muslims in the Koran." Harris is just a spokesperson of a poisoned and darkened mindset of the 21st century. His message is no different from what the *New York Times* told us in its lead editorial of November 14, 2003. This is what the *Newsweek* has been doing with publishing Qur'an-bashing articles such as "Challenging the Qur'an" (*Newsweek*, July 28, 2003). This is what Musharraf is telling us indirectly when he says, *"Khilafat* requires a certain environment in a country." If it demands "a lot from the nation, from the government," it doesn't mean we should discard the idea because we do not intend to do "a lot." If it "demands that everyone, the entire country - its masses, its people - should have social justice," there is nothing wrong with striving for that. In fact, there is absolutely no justification at all for discarding living by the Qur'an for Muslims but still we reject it. How many signs do we need to show that the basic human nature remains the same, whether our traveling is on the back of camels or flying in rockets?

Musharraf claims that "imposing the *Khilafat* when the entire environment has not been created for it," is totally a Utopian idea. We cannot go back to *Khilafat* unless we've created a certain environment." No one has asked for imposing the *Khilafah*. Some people are struggling to make the environment conducive for it. However, it is absolutely impossible in a state where the government models itself on Ataturk's Turkey and runs to the Supreme Court to throw away anything that may facilitate the creation of an environment where living by Islam would become possible. Musharraf agrees that *Khilafah* "ensured social justice and equality, freedom to the people," however, he believes that instead of living by the Qur'an, in the "21st Century through a democratic dispensation you can achieve the same goals." The absurdity of Musharraf's argument comes to the fore when one compares the encompassing message and way of life of Islam with modern day democracy as a tiny fraction of Islam's teachings. It is beyond all logic and reason to expect that living by Islam and its real practice will become possible through "democratic dispensation." The US and UK, the leading champions of democracy and secularism, could not demonstrate a fraction of the just order demonstrated by the 7th century *Khilafah*. In fact there is no connection between a secular democracy and establishing the just order of Islam from the individual to collective life in a society.

People with dark minds were feeling the same way 1400 years ago. They reacted the same way. To them their unjust order was just. They didn't want to live by Islam. General Musharraf, General Abizaid, Sam Harris and others in the *Newsweek* and *New York Times*-like recognized sources of "mainstream" media only confirm the thinking of the dark minds in the 21ˢᵗ century. The general feelings among the elite in Pakistan are the reflection of the same thinking that living by Islam in totality is impossible in the "modern age." From there on our blindness begins and we hardly see any alternative to help us get rid of the local tyranny, at least, which has intensified since 9/11.

One may argue that people who disagree with Islam do not necessarily have 'dark minds'. They may be acting from the purest motives and be genuinely good people, who happen to have a different understanding. To counter this mindset, comparison is given from the 7ᵗʰ century, where a people thought that the Qur'an is nothing but myths, stories and full of barbarity. They thought themselves good people, with an established civilization with the purest of motives. Nevertheless, history shows the difference between their world order and the order later on established by Prophet Mohammed (PBUH). A comparison of that order is a proof of the dark minds, which refused to accept light.

From the killing fields in Iraq and Afghanistan to Islam Karimov's justifying slaughter of innocent civilians in the name of avoiding the establishment of *Khilafah*, every moment we witness the dark mind of 21ˢᵗ century on display. Compare what has been happening in Iraq and Afghanistan since Bush declared "mission accomplished" in Iraq with what the Prophet of Islam taught in an age of barbarism. He humanized the battlefield with strict instructions not to cheat, not to break trust, not to mutilate, not to kill a child or woman or an old man, not to hew down a date palm nor burn it, not to cut a fruit tree, not to molest any person engaged in worship.[11]

Remember the way Saddam was treated after his capture with the way Prophet of Islam treated his bitterest enemies 1400 years ago? At the conquest of Mecca, he stood at the zenith of his power. The city which had refused to listen to his mission, which had tortured him and his followers, which had fought him, that city now lay at his feet. That was a display not only by Mohammed (PBUH) but also all his companions. Bush says the inhuman torture and unbelievable humiliation and human degradation carried out by his troops is done only by a few "bad apples." Why were there not a few bad apples at the time of Mohammed's (PBUH) conquest of Mecca? The reason is: They had conquered themselves and, thus, were able to conquer the hearts and minds of others.

The result of the early Muslims' hard work is before our eyes. The self-proclaimed enlightened minds of the 21st century could hardly conquer any mind and soul despite spending billions of dollars, the use of superior technology and what they consider to be superior moral and ethical values.

To address our blindness and helplessness, we were supposed to stop the mantra of the 21st century because this is no argument at all. However, we found it hard to get rid of this misconception that occupies our mind both knowingly and unknowingly.

We can even go a little further back in history before the age of Prophet Mohammed (PBUH) to understand that the technological superiority must not blind us to the reality and lead us to the conclusion that there is no option but to live the way Washington demands us to live. There is no doubt that technologically we have come a long way from the age of Pharaohs' chariots to the age of Bush's Air Force One. The centers of powers have, undoubtedly, moved from the United States of Egypt (1500 BC) to the United States of America (21st century).[12] But human nature and the way it behaves in the darkest periods remained unchanged even for the last thirty five centuries.

Styles of subjugation, ways of deception and means of oppressing the weak are all part of human nature and they have now become more sophisticated than ever. That's why enlightenment of minds has nothing to do with technological innovations. It is all related to human behavior and attitudes.

In the much vaunted 21st century, supine opportunists are

still willing to submit to all the lies, chicanery and deceit from the mighty, whether the mighty is sitting in Washington or his minions are considered mighty in their respective spheres in Islamabad, Kabul, Baghdad, Cairo and elsewhere. This is not something new. The opportunists have always been submitting to different tyrannies all along. Most of them have always been blind and under the impression that there is no way out. This, however, doesn't turn tyranny into enlightenment.

Let us accept that most Muslims who believe in the totality of the Qur'an and hence not considered as "moderates" are stubborn, dumb, dull, bigots, conservative and averse to moderation. However, we need to look at the mental state of those Americans, who are setting the standards for Muslim moderation and lecture Muslims in enlightenment, and to whom the "moderates" look for help in attaining "enlightened moderation." Most of them are still trying to let the rest of the public believe that Saddam was connected to 9/11; he had weapons of mass destruction and was a threat to US security. Their victims, the masses, are in a shocking state of mind. For example, a poll taken by Princeton Survey Research Associates showed that 50% of the American people believed that most of the 9/11 hijackers were Iraqis.[13]

The highest figure showing mass blindness was 75 percent Americans, approving the way Bush was dealing with Iraq in late April 2003. In late June 2003, more than 6 in 10 said Bush's decision to go to war was justified even if the United States does not find weapons of mass destruction in Iraq. The worst is yet to come. Most Americans happily approved the use of force when Bush declared in mid June 2003 that the United States "will not tolerate" nuclear weapons in Iran. According to a Washington Post-ABC News poll, by 56 percent to 38 percent, the public endorsed the use of the military to block Iran from developing nuclear arms.[14] Like Pakistanis, both Americans and British, too, think they don't have any alternative and they elected Bush and Blair again, despite their lies and deceptions for justifying the barbaric invasions and occupations of Iraq and Afghanistan.

Muslims are constantly reminded that the world has gone beyond the moon and they are still stuck in the medieval text and struggling with the help of 21st century technology to spread their vision of the 7th century paradise.[15] Let us move one step further in understanding that technological advancement is totally irrelevant to enlightenment and self-actualization, or our perfection as human beings. Self-actualization is the focus of Islam, not building empires. This is an issue which seems immediately obvious to anyone other than the professional Islam-bashers.

In the 21st century, women can go bare-breasted in most enlightened states,[16] but they cannot put a scarf on their head (schools and some work places in Turkey and France for example) or display the 10 commandments because the former does not violate state religion or enlightenment, whereas the latter acts do assert a religious belief system—a threat. So much for the enlightenment of the 21st century!

Women have a choice to go out in public topless or not,[17] but they are choice-less when it comes to headscarves[18] because of its threat to the state's religion: secularism. Does it not sound like a Mulla Umar-like theocracy à la Islamic Emirate of Afghanistan that we do not get tired condemning day in and day out, or a communist state à la Soviet Union? The only difference is of the religion proclaimed and practiced by the Taliban and the religion and practice of the "enlightened" secular "moderates."

This shows that human behavior has not changed a single bit in the course of human history. Despite confronting the obvious disaster, Pharaoh refused to change his ways. Such a resolve to stay on the same course remains the hallmark of present day enlightened Pharaohs.

Some of us never stop regurgitating the 21st century mantra in their struggle to avoid even a discussion about an Islamic alternative despite witnessing the horrible face of the exposed tyranny at home and abroad. So far, it has been hidden by the banners of human rights and slogans of freedom and democracy.

These minds which accepted the communist ideology to be only way out for humanity's survival, are now singing the songs of liberalism and enlightened moderation in Pakistan today. They can hardly realize that the US zeal for domination is a product of the same tyrannical system called "our civilization" and "our way of life" by the tyrants in every Dark Age. The system is based on core prehistoric precepts: violent wars and dehumanizing occupations.

The so-called post-modern religion of tolerance and pluralism is exposed to be nothing more than the perfection of Pharaohs' doctrine of tyranny. Many around the world still torture themselves over whether the promoters of war on Iraq and Afghanistan are just a minuscule minority of "neo-cons." The facts show neo-cons ideology is turning into a mindset which it is the product of the most depraved mentality and totally imbalanced technological advancement and spiritual bankruptcy.

Like the percentages given above, Americans are so often assured that they live as a great civilization, which remained under threat from communism and is now under threat from the Muslim radicals who hate their "way of life" and 9/11 was one of the attempts to take away "their freedoms." The dim-witted among us, now led by Musharraf type personalities, have taken them to be the leaders of enlightenment in the 21st century because besides grandiose proclamations of being civilized, they have achieved unprecedented technological advancement as well.

When civilization had come to Egypt, it seemed more eternal than most of us see in the US of the present age. It was, of course, designed, like the pyramids, for all time. Who could consider Moses, challenging the roots of Egyptian civilization, as an enlightened person at that time? Perhaps only those, who were considered as "fools" by the progressives of that age.

Pharaoh imagined a state in which no further governmental or social change was possible or even conceivable against their will.

So are our "enlightened moderates" who believe the *Deen* can be established through "democratic dispensation." They are followers of the "sincere" American "scholars," who present the "end of history" theories, promise the Americans the joys of the established order that can never again change and will be immutable forever in *saecula saeculorum*—or, at the least, "Till the sun grows cold, And the stars are old." All those are portrayed as primitive terrorists, Mullas and enemies of this "democratic" order who believe in the way of life as prescribed in the Qur'an – which of course is not against technological advancement or innovation. The only difference is that human excellence and moral development take precedence over technological development in the message of Islam. Without moral excellence, technological advancement alone led to a world of Pharaoh in the past and the world of Bush in present age.

Fourteen hundred years do not invalidate the message of the Qur'an and the actual objective of the struggle for an independent Pakistan. When someone calls others to live by the Qur'an in their individual lives and run the state affairs according to the Qur'an, he only repeats the words of Allah in the Qur'an. It has nothing to do with his being primitive or conservative. His sitting in a rocket or landing on the moon does not nullify his call to humanity to follow the Qur'an. His using 21st or 121st century technology does not invalidate his struggle for establishing Islam's way of life and living by the laws of Allah – that is what the Creator of the universe demands and this is what our forefathers promised in exchange for freedom from the yoke of colonialism and occupation.

If a people, who simply landed on the moon and possess the ability to wipe out humanity with the destructive weapons they have developed, have the right to butcher more than 128,000 people in Iraq to make them live by a system—a way of life—which it considers is right; Muslims have every right to demand self-determination and living by Islam. Musharraf and company will only be justified in criticizing calls to come to the Qur'an as primitive and out of date if they do not believe in the Qur'an and Allah. If that is the case, let them declare it. Otherwise as the symptoms suggest, their hypocrisy—of claiming to be Muslims, believing in the Qur'an and the *Sunnah*, and then running away from Islam—has brought the whole nation to a stage where their blindness make them suffer under multiple tyrannies.

There is absolutely no hope that majority of Pakistanis may see and sincerely struggle for the real objective of their existence to come out of the slough of despondence and helplessness. It would need a serious drubbing, just the way the Iraqis and the Afghans are getting at the moment, to awake them, but by then, it would be too late and they might not have Pakistan available for making it an Islamic model. It would be a totally different ball game and a different struggle in the totally changed geo-political realities.

Pakistan is a tremendous opportunity lost by the Muslims of South Asia due to collective blindness, which they may never regain.

CHAPTER 5

Military Occupation Prevails

If Musharraf stepped down or was removed, he would be replaced by a colleague or peer who is unlikely to be enthusiastic about radical Islam. Musharraf's successor would be replaced in turn by still another general with a similar semi-secular outlook. The army may use Islamic extremists and may not be able to reconstruct and build a normal Pakistani society, but for the foreseeable future, it is most capable of blocking anyone else from coming to power.[1]

The US troops had to physically fight and invade Afghanistan and Iraq to make occupation possible. Israel is still paying in blood for its occupation of Palestine. The Soviet Union had to leave Afghanistan with a bloody nose. Pakistan is the only country that is occupied by its own armed forces on behalf of the United States of America.

Literally defined, occupation means the act or process of holding or possessing a place. Most commonly, occupation is believed to be the result of invasion, conquest, and control of a nation or territory by foreign armed forces. In the real world, we witness that an effective occupation doesn't need involvement of foreign armed forces. There is nothing very complicated or mysterious about understanding the difference between direct and indirect occupation. The aggressor always has some objectives behind occupation. It makes perfect sense that there is no need for military invasion and physical occupation if those objectives are achieved through indirect means.

As a matter of fact, most of the British Empire was not ruled by those from the British Isles, managing direct military occupations. There were regions left in the hands of older rulers or else manufactured rulers who did the bidding of their paymasters. In India, almost half the landmass remained in the hands of Native Princes. China and South America remained nominally independent, and the British foisted monarchs on Jordan and Iraq from the Arabian Hashemite family.

Just after the British secured Iraq in the 1920s, a Foreign Office memorandum put the case for indirect colonialism squarely:

> What we want is some administration with Arab institutions which we can safely leave while pulling the strings ourselves; something that won't cost very much but under which our economic and political interests will be secure.[2]

This is the task of sheikhs, kings and generals in Kuwait, Saudi Arabia, Bahrain, Qatar, United Arab Emirates, Oman and Pakistan, who have became de facto protectorates and virtual colonies (indirect occupation) while maintaining nominal sovereignty under American political, economic and military coercion (direct imperialism). Functionally, indirect occupations have become a symbiotic combination between direct imperialism and indirect colonialism.

Indirect occupation has been the most effective tool of the totalitarians. Effective occupation requires a form of governance with which the occupied people would comply willingly, rather than coercively. This imperative led to the indigenization of the colonial state through the adoption of the system of indirect rule, in places like Cameroon in the early 20th century.

With a few exceptions, almost all Muslim states in the Middle East and South Asia are either physically occupied or indirectly colonized by the US. These have become colonies and lost the status of countries because the concept of an occupied country is not applicable here. France, for example, was an occupied country during WW II, but Hitler did not aim at changing France's religion, domestic and national structures, or partition it into cantons.

To the contrary, the US is restructuring the directly occupied Iraq and Afghanistan, and the indirectly occupied Pakistan and other Muslim states in all sectors in order to conquer them—this is colonization, paraded as freedom and sovereignty.

The concept of sovereignty and freedom in the eyes of Condoleezza Rice's and George Bush shortly after the "handover" to Allawi.[3]

Before discussing the occupation of Pakistan at length, we need to discuss as an example of how occupation (both direct and indirect) have been justified in the past and how Muslim "moderates" are now spreading falsehood in order to conceal the present state of affairs under the indirect US occupation in Pakistan and prepare a mindset for accepting such occupation.

In the history of mankind, there has never been a shortage of individuals like Brutus, Jagat Seth, Umichand, Rai Durlabh, Mir

Jafar and Quisling[4] to make occupations a success. The smell of money and power roused them to sell their country. Mir Jafar and others collaborated with Lord Clive to bring about the fall of Nawabi rule in Bengal at the Battle of Plassey in 1757. This opened the door for subsequent British to colonize all of India.

These facts are an open secret. However, the modern day "moderates" are trying to re-write history and prove that these collaborators-in-occupation were pragmatic individuals. The objective is to justify their assistance in continuation of the US occupation of their countries. Hussain Haqqani's June 2, 2004 article in the Nation is an excellent example of the self-proclaimed moderates' irrational exuberance coupled to unconscionable avarice for credit from the hands that rock their cradle.

Just like many others, who are justifying Musharraf's surrender to Bush's threats, Haqqani justifies the actions of Mir Jafar in these words:

> This historically incorrect account matches the version of events in Pakistani textbooks, which convince junior school students that the British defeat of Nawab SirajudDaula of Bengal in the battle of Plassey in 1757 was made possible only by the defection of another Muslim Nawab, Mir Jafar of Murshidabad. That the British might have had superior armaments and strategy, and that Jafar's decision to support the British might have been the result of their military superiority rather than the other way round is not held out as an option.[5]

What weight does repetition of "might have" carry in the above statement, when the British admits superiority of their weapons and buying out of Mir Jafar? A very simple search of the relevant facts shatters this theory for appeasement. Nikhil Dighe, an Indian web site, states:

> The battle was won even before it was fought. Robert Clive, the plucky representative of the East India Company employed persuasive diplomacy and offered Mir Jafar, a general of Bengal's Nawab Siraj-ud-daullah, the Nawabship after the war, in return for staying away from combat. Clive also bought over the chief financier of the Nawab

called Jagat Seth. Clive had 3,000 troops and Siraj-ud-daullah 50,000. But this seemingly disproportionate array of forces was neutralized by the fact that Mir Jafar's forces of about 16,000 - which included cavalry and heavy guns - did not participate. [6]

It seems if the British were so overwhelmingly "superior," there would be no need to "persuade" Mir Jafar to help them. This refutes Haqqani's revisionist narrative. Even Jawaharlal Nehru, in The Discovery of India (1946), describes Clive as having won the battle "by promoting treason and forgery."[7] A Hindu Professor, Vinay Lal, at UCLA writes: "Mir Jafar was induced to throw in his lot with Clive, and by far the greater number of the Nawab's soldiers were bribed to throw away their weapons, surrender prematurely, and even turn their arms against their own army."

The impartial Hindu writers are more truthful than Muslim opportunists who think the masses hostility towards the US intervention in Pakistan's affairs is just because of the nation's brainwashing through incorrect historical accounts? References from the British and Indian sources show that history is not written by "Jihadists" or a religiously motivated Pakistani establishment. In fact, the secularists want to re-write history against the words of those who were actually part of these historical events. With regard to the "superior" weaponry of the British, Sir Robert Clive writes in one of his letters:

> We soon entered into engagements with Meer Jafar to put the crown on his head. All necessary preparations being completed with the utmost secrecy, the army, consisting of about one thousand Europeans and two thousand sepoys, with eight pieces of cannon, marched from Chandernagore on the 13th and arrived on the 18th at Cutwa Fort.... At daybreak we discovered the Nabob's army moving towards us, consisting, as we since found, of about fifteen thousand horse and thirty-five thousand foot, with upwards of forty pieces of cannon.[8]

Such pragmatic "moderates" of the past made the task of indirect occupiers easier. In the post-colonial period of neo-imperialism, their demand has not tapered down an iota. With modernity, the demand for raw materials from the former colonies and the push to sell surplus "modern" products has grown as much as the demand to assimilate in the Western civilization and diluting Islam to the extent that it has no influence in the collective life because it "incites" resistance against aggression and injustice. Initially, the former masters required new sell-outs to leverage the process of buying and selling. So, they created the likes of Batista,[9] Reza Shah,[10] Suharto,[11] Noriega,[12] Papa Doc[13] and Mobutu[14] in their former colonies. These individuals were supposed to license the perpetual bondage of their nations at the altar of the Capitalist West.

The times have changed. Now, the perpetual bondage is as much necessary for resources and pipelines as much it is for defeating an ideology. It has made the task of indirect occupation somewhat more complex and less translucent than the good, old days. It requires not only persons like Musharraf but also a group of native "intellectuals," trained in the American think-tanks to make the indirect occupations appear less transparent. The beauty of Musharraf is that he is not only commander-in-chief of a strong army but also far ahead from the native "intellectuals." Together they are to propagate the benevolent "civilizing," "modernizing" and "moderating" mission of the United States and its allies.

The more Musharraf tightens his grip to consolidate the occupation, the better it serves American purposes because the state has already started cracking in his grip, leaving many analysts to wonder if it will survive at all.

Despite General Zia's serving the US interest in the region with an unprecedented devotion, no one realized that Pakistan was doing the US bidding because on the home front General Zia portrayed that he was promoting nothing but Islam. The war in Afghanistan for the US was also part of that Islamic portrayal. No one can guess how Zia would have played his mantra of Islamization if he happened to be ruling Pakistan after 9/11.

All we know is that Pakistan has been the strategic cat's-paw for the United States ever since the days of CENTO and SEATO, but it was never occupied. The picture of Pak-US military-to-military and civilian-to-military relations in the post 9/11 period are different and stand out in stark contrast, inviting in depth analysis to look into the ways in which Musharraf surrendered Pakistan's independence and its implications on the long term survival of Pakistan.

It is important to note that even at the height of the Pak-US strategic relationship, none of the previous dictators or civilian government provided access to US military personnel and the CIA to Pakistan's military facilities, dumps and bases on the present scale. The US military presence in Pakistan today is in the thousands, located at strategic Pakistani military bases around the country. Most importantly, the American military presence is not the result of a general consensus in Pakistan after public debate and approval. It is the result of one man's surrender at the top, obviously under dire American coercive pressures and threats, but also blatant political opportunism in the same fashion as Mir Jafar before him.

It is hyperbole to portray Musharraf's decision to allow US bases in Pakistan as a courageous, de Gaulle–like gesture. De Gaulle was a military person, and had led one side in a civil war, but he was never a dictator. He was a 'Regent', and highly popular. Instead, Musharraf can be compared to another military dictator: Hungary's Adm. Nikolaus Horthy de Nagybanya, who attempted to defect from his alliance with Adolf Hitler and switch his support to the Allies. Initially, when the Red Army was well into Rumania, he negotiated a private peace with the Soviet Union. Horthy failed in his gamble, whereas Musharraf has been apparently successful (so far). But that success should not diminish the significance of the historical analogy. Horthy and Musharraf were simply switching to the winning side, well aware that the alternative would bring about their own political destruction.[15]

There was no conversion of the masses to alien values or forces on native lands in either case. Like most of his predecessors, Musharraf knew that Islamabad's ties with Washington were dictated by specific political-military interests and lacked any deep ideological roots. When US officials were hailing Pak-US cooperation in providing support to Afghan Mujahideen, Pakistani leaders seemed to have no illusions about their relationship with Washington. Unlike Musharraf, they knew that after a short marriage of convenience, the two would eventually have to deal with the reality of their diverging core national interests and values.

During a December 6, 1982 meeting in Washington, General Zia told the Secretary of State George Shultz in clear terms that the two countries were a "union of unequal" and "incompatible" in terms of culture, geography, and national power, even though they had strong common interests.[16] The cautionary remarks Zia made probably apply more to the current Pak-US relationship, in which Musharraf is the more enthusiastic partner, surrendering everything for prolonging his stay, including promoting views and values of Islamophobes under the banner of "enlightened moderation" in an attempt to convert the public to alien values.

Of course, a client state can secure support and increase its leverage over the US by accentuating common strategic interests. However, in the case of Pakistan, the regime was not supposed to cross all limits in conceding Pakistan's sovereignty. The erosion of Pakistan's independence has led to continuing political uncertainty and instability, leading to the weakening of the fragile governing system. Existence of US bases in Pakistan and the continued use of Pakistan military on the direction from the Abizaid central command centre in the region have tarnished Pakistan's image even in Washington and contributed to the volatility of the bilateral relationship. Presenting Pakistan as a dog in a *Washington Times* cartoon is a reflection of how Pakistan is being viewed by those for whom Musharraf has put the very existence of the country at stake.

Cold War rhetoric aside, Pakistan and the US not only lack common historical and cultural ties, they are not operating on the same strategic wavelength. After 9/11, the Bush administration decided not only to target Pakistan's strategic and ideological ally in Kabul, but also to destroy the entire education system for the fear of resistance against its double standards, injustice, state terrorism and above all indirect occupation of Pakistan.

Musharraf has made Pakistan a big loser after September 11 with the misconception that it had no option except bending backwards to the US demands. His mantra: Pakistan had no option. It either had to join the US aggression or invite Bush's wrath. Had Musharraf hesitated, the Americans would have clobbered Pakistan's military and 'strategic' assets and allowed India to attack. By siding with Bush, Pakistan has been saved from American anger and its own extremists. It has also been able to break out of its isolation and rejoin the international mainstream.

No one cares to answer a simple question. What would Pakistan have lost if it had chosen to negotiate the fine print of our cooperation with the US? Even America's European allies—with the exception, of course, of Britain—took some time to make up their minds before rushing in with offers of help. Would Pakistan have been declared international terrorists if the spineless Musharraf had negotiated with some toughness instead of being dazzled by the sudden attention he started getting? Now that the euphoria has gone, what do Musharraf and his minions have to show for his caving in? Musharraf got his exclusive dinners with Bush and Blair and accolades from Zionist groups and Islamophobes. Beyond that, what did he get?

From a systemic perspective, 9/11 helped Washington establish its military presence in Pakistan and also re-establish the "red lines" that had disappeared after the collapse of the Soviet superpower, impelling Washington to restrain its Pakistani client state. The key factor in all these developments is Musharraf. The situation could be totally different under a civilian government or a General who was not keen in self-promotion at the cost of the survival of Pakistan.

General Zia played a key role for the US for 11 years, starting with assassinating Zulfiqar Ali Bhutto, who tore up official letters from Washington in public rallies,[17] and going all the way to waging a full scale Jihad movement against the Soviet occupation of Afghanistan. The public still can hardly see if General Zia actually undermined Pakistan's interest for the sake of the United States. A majority is under the impression that Pakistan grew strong during that period. The US got rid of him in August 1988 after the beginning of the Soviets Soviet Union's withdrawal from Afghanistan in May 1988.

Whether Pakistan was occupied by the Pakistan army for the US during Zia's regime might be a difficult question. What is clear without any doubt is the fact that it served the US to the utmost extent possible. The painful reality of Pakistan's occupation by its own military forces for the US came to fore during the reign of Musharraf. Pakistanis were under the impression that the US couldn't take away the soul of Pakistan's army in the manner as discussed below.

One cannot imagine how meaningless all the displayed Qur'anic verses might look like in Pakistan's military bases, when our forces leave for or return after killing their brothers in faith and destroying their homes in Israel-style raids. One cannot imagine the shallowness of their *Takbeer* (Slogan, saying Allah is Great) before pulling triggers on their brothers in faith and dynamiting the homes of fellow Pakistanis in Wanna and other places in Waziristan, for example. Of course, Israeli forces are using the same tactics in the occupied territories but they are facing a people which they consider as sub-human.[18]

Many Pakistanis are under the misconception that the hounded people are terrorists. In this regard, we have to keep two things in mind. First: There is no "us": the hounds, and there is no "them": the hounded. The direct victims alone are not targets.

We together are the target. Secondly, who are they—Taliban, Arabs, Chechens, or the tribal "rebels"? At least, the Pakistan military did not consider the Taliban as terrorists until October 7, 2001. The ISI was feeding and training them all along and standing shoulder to shoulder with them until then.

Arabs were not terrorists as long as they were fighting to liberate Muslim lands from the occupation of the archenemy of the United States, the Soviet Union. As soon as the Arabs thought of liberating their own homelands from the US influence, they became the targeted terrorists.

When Musharraf declared in late September 2001 that the "Taliban's days are numbered," the wise could read the writing on the wall. In fact, it was Pakistan's years that are numbered. Since then the countdown is underway. The planning for undermining Pakistan is as old as the US government's search for an appropriate excuse, such as the bloody drama of 9/11. Long before Musharraf's coup, in March 1999 the then US Assistant Secretary of State for South Asia, Karl Inderfurth, boldly declared that the US doesn't want Pakistan army to become a "Taliban-like force." He proposed "Western style training" for the army to pave the way for its secularization. A quick look at the events and developments since then suggest that the mission Inderfurth started is right on target.

The US needed Pakistan armed forces to do the job of local occupation. The US started its campaign against Pakistan's military as a result of the reports by its spying US military commanders, who could not swallow, for example, the 99 attributes of Allah written on every twist and turn towards the Special Service Group (SSG) Centre at Chirat. They couldn't digest the motto of Pakistan armed forces: *Iman, Taqwa, Jihad fi-saheelillah* (Faith, fear of Allah and Jihad in the way of Allah) inscribed everywhere in the military facilities. Today, *Taqwa* has been effectively replaced by "the fear of Uncle Sam" and *Jihad* by "struggle in the way of the US."

As the news pours in about the death of Pakistani soldiers and civilians in their operation of raining down death and destruction on the voiceless people in the tribal belt, we cannot imagine how relieved the concerned quarters feel in the US, Israel and India who felt the Pakistan army as a thorn in their side for quite some time. Its operations since 9/11 have surely transformed it into a soothing balm for them.

Acting for the first time against one's conscience is difficult. It then gradually becomes easier to the point to seem normal. Under the command of Musharraf, the Pakistani army has joined the first battle of a long "war on terrorism" without any serious consideration of the reality other than the position of Musharraf in the eyes of his masters. It could not see that it has fallen on the wrong side of the battlefield. Al-Qaeda was a no-name group of not more than a couple of hundred Arab dissidents living in exile, who have either been killed or captured since then. The US zeal to eliminate the Muslim's will to resisting its domination and living by Islam has now transformed the so-labelled Al-Qaeda into a movement, which includes both Muslims and non-Muslims resisting the tyrannical world order envisaged by neo-cons and Christian-Zionists. In short, instead of crushing any kind of Islamic resistance movement, US actions have actually sent a wave of anger and resentment throughout the Muslim and non-Muslim world and, as a result, the world is much less safer place under Bush and the neo-cons who craft his policies.

The resistance grows as the lies and real motives behind the "war on terrorism" are exposed. Pakistan's army, with the blood of its fellow Muslims on its hands and already acting against its motto, will never hesitate to repeat the carnage outside the tribal belt as anyone against the tyrannical global order is now an Al-Qaeda terrorist and any political dissent is labelled as "Islamic extremism."

Pakistan army, which the US, India and Israel feared as the only nuclear arms laced with an "Islamic fundamentalist-minded" army, is now ready to make fellow Muslims swim in their own blood. Joint efforts of these three states to dismantle Pakistan's military might have remained fruitless until the arrival of Musharraf on the scene. However, he alone has done what all the three powers together could never do, i.e., gradually eroding justification for the very existence of Pakistan army and eliminating the sources of its inspiration: *Iman, Taqwa, Jihad fee sabeelillah*.

The story, however, is not limited to Musharraf. He materialized what others could only dream of. At home, the enemies within kept on trying to pave the way for the US to make Pakistan army yet another horrible example after rubbing the Iraqi nose in the Middle East sand in 1991. By declaring it the "new fascists" and "a threat to the world peace and security," Benazir Bhutto went too far in her campaign to malign the Pakistani army.[19] She blamed the military for giving "a disproportionate voice to religious fanatics" and alleged that it is "dedicated to the export of religious extremism through Afghanistan to the shores of Europe." In her interview with the Guardian, Benazir Bhutto said the Pakistani army is "infected by extremism." The world does not see that "infection" anymore. Musharraf has done that job better than any candidate, offering his services to the US, could do.

Earlier the US Congressional sources told *Dawn* that the picture presented by the former ISI chief, Ziauddin, before the intelligence committee was so grim and scary that many members supported the public statement issued by the US warning against a military coup in Pakistan.

It shows the October 12, 1999 coup was on the cards long before, because a civilian government could not further the US and the IMF agenda as the military government could. It was only a matter of timing and the suitability of coup leadership. Some US sources were reported as saying the US was not worried about an army coup but "fundamentalist Islamic radicals in the Pakistan army."[20]

Thus emerged a new consensus in Washington to weaken Pakistan's military through promoting secular elements to power in Islamabad. The Observer proposed such a strategy of controlling the "specter of Islamic fundamentalism" in its report titled "Fundamentalism across Asia" (February 18, 1997). It proposed to utilize the might of local armies against the "blessings of the resident governments" to fundamentalists.

Preparing local armed forces as secular bulwarks became part of a coherent policy framework toward Islam, which according to the Director of James A. Baker III Institute at Rice University, Edward P. Djerejian, has "become a compelling need as foreign policy challenges erupt involving an 'arc of crisis' extending from the Balkans, the Caucasus, North Africa, Middle East, Central and South Asia,.... Afghanistan and Kashmir. Everywhere the rallying cry of Muslim fighters – 'Allhu Akbar' – is heard in a complex web of violent conflict."[21]

Under the leadership of Musharraf, the Pakistani army played into the hands of forces determined to ruin it. Pakistan's military might have an upper hand in promoting and imposing the US agenda in the region. However, sustaining this ephemeral success will have serious consequences in the long run. With the passage of time, the kind of operations which Pakistan's military undertook in the tribal areas in the North West Frontier Province will become inevitable elsewhere in Pakistan as well and in the ensuing chaos Pakistan military, as we known it, may not remain intact in its present form.

The future of military occupation

Any Pakistani with an average knowledge of the history and politics know that what the Pakistani army has done to Pakistan is no less than what an outside power would have done. It is not only the matter of violence against civilians, it is also the usurpation of power and resources. The US army in Iraq has been fed and trained at the cost of American resources and it is rightly or wrongly fighting for America. In the case of Pakistan, the GDP grows at a rate around 3% against a target of more than 6%, reflecting low productivity in almost all sectors of the economy. Despite that, Pakistan's defense spending remained one of the largest components of total government expenditures since independence. Although sizeable variation in defense expenditure to GDP ratio has been witnessed over the past five decades and the ratio declined significantly toward the end of the 20th century, the absolute size of defense expenditure is considered still very high and Pakistan's development outlay remains stagnated.[22]

What tips the scale is the same military's turning around and serving the interests of the United States and its allies. The occupied nation is thus doomed thrice: It is the nation's sons in the army; it is the nation's resources invested in their training and logistics, and it's the nation which becomes victim of its occupation for the US and its allies. All if these human and material resources could be used to making the country strong and working towards the purpose of its establishment. The opposite, however, is the case and the country is on a downward spiral. This cannot be blamed on external sources alone, and much of the blame must fall squarely on the Pakistan's leaders and those who willingly follow them for the sake of personal gain.

The line between independence and occupation of Pakistan by its own armed forces is getting finer with each passing day. The cost of weakness on the part of the military leadership is now confirmed as an occupation without a military conquest. Pakistan has, unfortunately, become the first victim of this new kind of occupation—a model of a "failed state" perfectly controlled from outside with curtailed sovereignty and limited freedoms.

Despite the regime's wholehearted sacrifice of all the principles of justice and the norms of independent states, American analysts, such as Leon T. Hadar of the Cato Institute, consider Pakistan "with its dictatorship and failed economy" a "reluctant partner" and a "potential long term adversary."[23] Therefore, instead of friendship or partnership on the pattern of India-US relations, occupation is a must and here the Pakistani nation is: fully occupied. Like any other occupied territory, dictatorship is in full swing in Pakistan. Hundreds of people, pointed out by the intelligence of occupation forces, are routinely rounded up in order to placate Washington.

Illegal detentions and extraditions are on the rise. Many non-government organizations with any link to Muslim countries, or Arabic words in their titles, have been closed down. FBI and CIA agents have declared open season on Pakistan.[24] Pakistan cannot move its own troops without prior permission from Washington. And we witness desperate suicide attacks on occupation forces—Pakistani armed forces—like attacks on occupation forces in Iraq and Afghanistan.

Pakistan's military acting as an occupation force is not as simple as saying: If Pakistan is occupied, and the occupying power decides to remove Musharraf, will Pakistan army remove him? Or, if tomorrow General Musharraf orders the army to attack all US forces in the country, will he be obeyed? If the answers are 'yes' and 'no' respectively, then it is an occupation army. However, if the army stays loyal to its leader, then it is not occupying Pakistan.

The naivety of the above argument lies in the assumption that Pakistan's occupation by Pak-army means that the army has surrendered to the US will en masse. The US has become a demi-god. If Musharraf submits to this demi-god, he gets the check to keep the army with its huge expenditure alive. If he refuses to submit, the life-line gets severed both from Washington and the IMF. Thus the army has not surrendered en masse. This is not possible. Pakistan's occupation by it military took place according to the US well-known strategy of buying out the strongman at the top. Having the commander in chief in the pocket is good enough to make the gullible mass of the armed forces obey orders as per military discipline. If they could attack and kill their brothers in faith on the orders of their commander in chief, how would they spare the Americans on his orders? The beauty of this occupation lies in the use of a 5 million men strong army in the interest of Washington at the cost of protecting one strongman.

The extent of this strongman's dependence on the demi-god lies in the fact that there are no signs of independence at all. Pakistan cannot prepare its budgets without an approval from international lending agencies. The same must be true for other third world countries, including those in Latin America, which are not Muslim. However, the difference lies in finding out if these impoverished countries have other options. Pakistan's consuming every possible penny into its defense budget would have made sense if it were utilized for defending the country's integrity, sovereignty and independence. Why impoverish a people and make them dependent on the capitalist lenders, when the same defense dollars are spent for the interests of the US against its people and against Pakistan's independence?

One can guess the state of Pakistan's independence from the fact that it cannot conduct any investigation without the assistance of the FBI and other external agencies. It is an open secret that Pakistani agencies cannot operate any longer, except in co-ordination with the FBI. Pakistan has to detain almost every person from the Middle East as a potential terrorist and it's the US agencies to decide their fate. The morbid dread of Al-Qaeda is being used to crack down on religion and to further reduce our freedoms as citizens of an independent state. There is no open discussion on any aspect of the ever-intensifying occupation. Dependent states used to be called as client states. However, Pakistan has crossed that state by virtue of the military commander-in-chief's fully committing lives and resources of his country to serving the interests of the United States. Hardly a single day passes by without Pakistani regime making a slavish act or comment. Things get really interesting when there is hardly any difference between the statements issued from Kabul by the Karzai's municipality and from Islamabad by the Musharraf's regime. Both are receiving almost equal Foreign Military Financing and both are serving their American masters well.[25]

Thus, Pakistan will have accumulated a total of $821 million in FMF support between 2002 (when FMF was resumed) and 2005. Additionally, military training funds are on the rise- from zero in 2001 to a $2 million request for 2006.[26]

President Bush took the relationship with Pakistan military one step further in June 2004, naming Pakistan a "Major Non-NATO Ally." This designation, accorded to only a handful of nations, makes Pakistan eligible for previously unavailable weapons like depleted uranium munitions, and new funding sources like U.S. government-backed loans to build up its military capabilities.[27]

Even if all this aid is for defeating Al-Qaeda, one may ask: who needs F-16 to beat Al-Qaeda? At the end of March 2005, Bush, however, reversed 15 years of policy begun under his father by offering F-16 fighter planes to Islamabad. Initially, Pakistan planned on buying two dozen of the Lockheed Martin manufactured planes, but Bush administration officials note there would be no limits on how many could eventually be purchased.[28] Pakistan's economy is not strong enough to allow Musharraf to purchase the $35 million per copy fighter planes, and so the deal will be accompanied by about $3 billion in military aid.[29]

The importance of a strong local military for occupation can be judged from the patterns of US assistance to Afghanistan. The Karzai regime asked for $27.5 billion in aid over seven years, keeping the develop aspect of the country in mind. So far, the war-torn nation has received just $4.5 billion and, according to the UK's Independent, "much of the $2.2 billion earmarked for 2004 was diverted into military projects and emergency relief from long term development."[30]

U.S. aid to Afghanistan in 2005 totals more than $929 million, more than 80% of which is earmarked for the military and police. This comes on top of a similarly skewed 2004 budget of $1.7 billion, where only 10% went to development assistance and child survival and health. Taken on top of a $589 million appropriation for 2003, U.S. assistance for Afghanistan tops out at $3.2 billion and counting, with the lion's share going to the military.[31]

One of the few differences between the direct Iraqi occupation and indirect Pakistani occupation is that in Iraq, the US is in the process of training an army that would replace its forces and in Pakistan it has got a pre-trained army, which can go to any length under a pro-US strong-command-in-chief to ensure American interests. As far the butchery in Iraq and the concentration camps, no need has arisen for that in Pakistan so far.

Pakistan is ensuring American "strategic interests" in everything it does, from implementation of American directions on religious institutions to spying on citizens and banning everything that may promote the spiritual message of Islam. The government officials work round the clock to ensure interpretation of Pakistan's occupation as crisis management. It is rather becoming a cause of the future crisis.

Just like Palestinian authorities in occupied Palestine, the US can force our government to routinely violate basic standards of decency in human behavior as expressed in international human rights law without anyone raising an eyebrow. It can now arrest, indefinitely detain, torture and even kill anyone under the pretext of destroying the Al-Qaeda network.

Al-Qaeda's threat has been blown out of proportion to intensify occupation of what senior British diplomat Robert Cooper calls failed states in the post-modern era.[32] The main characteristics of such occupations described by Cooper are: the breaking down of the distinction between domestic and foreign affairs of the occupied states; "mutual" interference in domestic affairs and "mutual" surveillance (the word "mutual" is used to deceive the weak as Pakistan cannot even imagine interference in the domestic affairs of the US, let alone surveillance); and the growing irrelevance of borders when it comes to safeguarding the interest of the strong.

In 21st century occupations, there are no security threats in the traditional sense; that is to say, the powerful do not consider invading the weak. Going to war is rather a sign of policy failure. Mr. Cooper elaborates:

> The challenge to the post-modern world is to get used to the idea of double standards. Among ourselves, we operate on the basis of laws and open cooperative security. But when dealing with more old-fashioned kinds of states outside the post-modern continent of Europe, we need to revert to the rougher methods of an earlier era of force, pre-emptive attack, deception, whatever is necessary to deal with those who still live in the nineteenth century world of every state for itself. Among ourselves, we keep the law but when we are operating in the jungle, we must also use the laws of the jungle.[33]

So the laws of the jungle are being applied in occupied states like Pakistan and Afghanistan. To remove any leftover doubts about Pakistan being a failed state, news reports from the New York Times and the Washington Post are pouring in, alleging that Al-Qaeda is regrouping in Pakistan and that ISI supports the Taliban and Kashmiri "insurgents." As a "pre-modern" state, Pakistan is thus considered as weak enough "even to secure its home territory... but it can provide a base for non-state actors who may represent a danger to the post-modern world." An occupation of Pakistan is thus justified and Musharraf calls for further US assistance after each desperate attack on his life.

This new form of occupation is acceptable to a world of human rights and cosmopolitan values. In western eyes it is an occupation that "aims to bring order and organization but which rests today on the voluntary principle of people like Musharraf's coming forward and offering the services.

Freedom comes with a heavy price tag, which Generals like Musharraf are hardly able to pay. Under British occupation, Benjamin Franklin observed in 1755 that those "who would give up essential liberty to purchase a little temporary safety deserve neither liberty nor safety." Musharraf abandoned the rule of law, principles of justice and hard won independence simply because America was angry and Musharraf feared an attack on Pakistan.

The US could remove the Taliban from power, but it could not diminish their influence in Afghanistan. In total contrast, Pakistan's strategic depth totally disappeared due to the most effective-ever occupation of the modern age. Pakistan's sovereignty has not only been compromised but also totally diminished when it comes to acting under American influence. Now, American forces are stationed at various centers in Pakistan indefinitely.[34]

One can argue that there are American bases in Australia too, by treaty, and there are Australians who strongly object. But as long as the government allows them, it is not an occupation. Of course, that is not. The US and Australia are allies against "common enemies," whereas Pakistan is one of the perceived enemies. The religion of its people is considered to be the source of terrorism. The country itself is considered to be harboring terrorists despite all the cooperation it has extended. One has to keep all these factors in mind before looking at the scope and implications of the US military bases in Pakistan. On December 13, 2004, the *New York Times* reported that the CIA has set up covert bases in the tribal areas in Pakistan, which the Pakistani regime instantly denied.[35] Earlier, the *Washington Post* confirmed bases at three locations in Pakistan,[36] whereas the US Central Command published a watered-down version of Pakistan's assistance on its website, which shows how Musharraf's regime put the interests of the US ahead of the interest of its own people and exposed millions of innocent Afghans to the US onslaught.[37]

The geo-strategic position of Pakistan could not help ordinary Pakistanis as much as it helped the Pakistan army and other elites. It is this strategic position which made Pakistan prone to military dictatorships. Again, it is this position, which ultimately landed Pakistan as an Anglo-American client State with greatly diminished sovereignty.[38]

From the American perspective, US military bases in Pakistan are necessary to keep an eye on "fundamentalist forces" taking control of sensitive locations, the ISI and some "cells" in the military that may get out of control and act like "rogue" institutions.[39] Musharraf's strategy of appeasement has miserably failed. From day one, Washington didn't pay any attention to his calls, such as those for a halt to bombing in Ramadan, or not to let the Northern Alliance take full control in Kabul.

Instead, the Bush administration decided to continue pursuing the war on Afghanistan during Ramadan and gave a green light to Northern Alliance forces to occupy Kabul. Musharraf again tried to reduce losses by demanding that Kabul be "demilitarized" and the Northern Alliance forces "must not" hold it.[40] Pakistan couldn't play a role in the formation of a new government in Kabul and today Islamabad is totally sidelined from whatever good or bad is happening in Afghanistan. Instead, it gets regular condemnation from the Afghan and US authorities for supporting the Taliban from Pakistani territory.

Despite the Pakistani regime's friendly gestures, the puppet regime in Afghanistan looks down upon Islamabad. Included in the virulent anti-Pakistan statements are those from the then-Afghan-American US ambassador to Afghanistan, Zalmay Khalizad, blaming Pakistan for protecting America's enemies. Khalizad, a member of the inner circle that surrounded Bush in the early days of his presidency, vehemently said that the Taliban leader Mullah Omar and Osama were somewhere in Pakistan. His claim that the Taliban and al-Qaeda militants had infiltrated from Pakistan, in an organized manner, was termed as baseless and irresponsible by Pakistan.

Besides having no meaningful relations with Afghanistan, occupied Pakistan has become one of the strategic losers in the international system that has evolved since 9/11. Yet the US has continued to portray Islamabad as a "friend," and has provided economic and military assistance on the basis of promises to unconditionally support its "war on terrorism." US military bases are the strings attached to this humiliating assistance. In April 2005, the well known Israeli-based web site Debka revealed that Musharraf had agreed to US intelligence agencies' need for a presence on Pakistani territory for gathering intelligence on Iran's nuclear installations and in case of a decision to mount a military operation against Tehran. According to *Debka-weekly-Net:* "There are strong intimations that Musharraf has already agreed to assist America in this eventuality."[41]

The Iran factor makes sense when looked from the perspective that the US bases in Saudi Arabia or Kuwait were there to defend these countries against Iraq. In the case of Pakistan, Afghanistan is fully occupied with a CIA man on the throne in Kabul and American forces dug in military bases throughout the country and central Asia. There is no justification for a continued US military presence in Pakistan because unlike the pre-Afghanistan-occupation, the Allied forces do not need any additional support from US bases in Pakistan. Musharraf's regime has recently allowed Washington to set up four air bases inside Pakistan to help operations inside Afghanistan despite the fact that the presence of US troops in operations with Pakistani soldiers has raised the level of fierce resistance in tribal areas.[42] This shows that the target is not Afghanistan (alone) and that the plan is to milk Musharraf to the last drop.

Most Pakistanis, who have turned a blind eye to the presence of US forces in Pakistan, must not ignore the reality that they are there to stay indefinitely. They are there to ensure that, unlike the 1980s, Pakistan does not get a blank check from the US to combat terrorism and spend it on building up forces that may threaten US adventures in the region.[43]

The conflicting national interests of Washington and Islamabad became obvious during 2002. The US openly rejected Pakistan's position vis-à-vis Kashmir. Pakistan's nuclear program became the prime target of the US government. The US establishment-backed analysts declared Pakistan "the most dangerous place on earth."[44] Permanent induction of armed forced in Pakistan's governance mechanism was fully supported by the US and opportunist political leaders gladly helped the military to constitutionalize military's role. Furthermore, the US has a clear interest in establishing strong ties with India.[45] Pakistan, on the other hand, is increasingly considered as a "potential long-term adversary."[46]

At a time when American policy makers were planning for a gradual disengagement from Pakistan, Musharraf hosted American bases on Pakistani soil. Even some of the US policy makers rejected the idea of continuing American military bases in the existing political environment of Pakistan, which could lead to an escalation of violence and a perfect ruse for imposing a war on Pakistan.[47] Musharraf thought the reward for his cooperation would be growing diplomatic, economic, and cultural ties without any strings attached for domination, but he is not reaping rewards that he thought he would.

Why will military occupation continue?

Pakistan's occupation by its own military will continue in one form or another until it breathes its last, for the simple reason that the nation itself is half dead. A substantial part of a nation dies the day its people start dying for others against their will. The soul of a nation is fatally wounded the day its armed forces start leading it in a battle against its *raison d'être*. Eliminate a nation's purpose, and you extinguish its spark of life. The country that acquiesces in evil can hardly hope to enjoy the benefits of goodness. No one draws freedom or life from a land of oppression and death.

The half-dead Pakistani nation is silently dragging the cross of Bush Junior's crusade to its own Golgotha. On the military front, the nation helplessly watches PTV News which keeps calling army men, who die for America, as "martyrs." On the legal front, the nation didn't say a word in protest when under the influence of the dictator its Supreme Court staged a successful coup de main on clear Qur'anic injunctions and claimed that the nation's survival lies in going against the Qur'an for its banking system.

Pakistanis are helplessly reading reports about their army going on a rampage against its own people—a clear evidence of dictatorship in the service of the United States. Stalin killed more Russians than Hitler. Hitler killed many Germans who were not Jews, merely anti-Nazi. Saddam killed many Iraqis. This is a pattern of dictators. An authoritarian regime cannot allow dissent. The infuriated army commanders in Pakistan herd people out and blast their houses by artillery and mortar fire to revenge the killings of their fellow aggressors. It seems the story of another West Bank or Gaza strip: another factory of desperate "suicide bombers" in the making.[48] No one asks, what is this army fighting for, or what is the meaning of Pakistan's existence?

The *Statesman* reports that in search of Al-Qaeda men "army and law enforcement agencies are capturing every bearded person who has some contact with religious people or mosques' affairs."[49] A tribal elder of Wanna, South Waziristan, told Baluchistan Post that it seems as if "the Army is not operating in its own country rather it is fighting a war in a hostile country." Just to please Bush and company, an occupied nation is at war with itself on military, intellectual, legal and social fronts. This is what Thomas Friedman of the *New York Times* calls a "war within Islam," and this is for what spokesman of the State Department very proudly thanks Musharraf. Interestingly, the victims have nothing to do with the regime. They are no opponents of the dictatorial regime, let alone potential opponents. Therefore, the violence cannot be explained on that basis either.

Like the absolutely absent definition of "terrorism" in the "war on terrorism," there is no definition of Al-Qaeda membership. Any alien who lived in Afghanistan during the Taliban era is a sure candidate to be considered as a member of the "Al-Qaeda network." Similarly, opposition members—particularly those belonging to Islamic parties - who oppose policies of the US-supported regimes, such as Karzai, Mubarak and Musharraf, are now set to be labeled as supporters of the "Al-Qaeda network." Like communist enemies of the Cold War era, the "Al-Qaeda network" will never come to an end until Washington clearly declares victory in its 21st century crusade. Until then, every bearded Muslim, as the Statesman report says, is a potential Al-Qaeda member. Before the US declares a victory, it will have to bury many a half-dead nation along with their dictators.

A nation half-dead doesn't mean that it will die. There is an equal opportunity for it to recover and resist. But, do we see any ray of hope for Pakistan? Are there any signs of recovery? There is no sign that American demands on the Pakistani regime will come to an end. Every time it is successful in extracting concessions from Musharraf and making him surrender Pakistan's principles and freedoms, its appetite will grow for power along with his will to keep ruling. Both Musharraf and Bush began in a humble way because of the humiliation associated with the military coup and allegation of fraud respectively; but one ended by sweeping the world into his vision and the other is struggling to transform Pakistan in the image of Islamophobes in the US.

Bush's associates now pronounce with confidence their judgment upon every subject from the choice of rulers in the Muslim world to the governmental limits within which the Mosque can function. Their impudence is the measure of the Pakistani nation's futility. Their self-expression is purchased by the suppression of Pakistanis' right to self-expression and self-rule. Like many other Muslim nations, Pakistanis too run to meet their chains because every individual Pakistani is too afraid to venture out of the little private corner in which he is buried. He does not seem to know that the power to insist upon his freedom lies in his own hands. He is powerless because he is unconscious of his power. This unconsciousness will help the military prolong

its occupation until it leads the country into total chaos and ultimate tragedy.

Pakistanis are damned to live under perpetual dictatorship not
only because they opted to submit to Musharraf, but also because
they have forgotten that the government is the employee of the
people, and that like any employee, the government is required
to obey orders, not to give them.

Pakistanis are destined to live under military occupation until
the end because they have forgotten that as the employers of the
government, they have the right to decide what their employees
can do and more importantly, what they cannot.

Pakistanis are damned because they have forgotten who is really supposed to be in charge. Everyone is begging Musharraf to
remove his uniform to be acceptable, forgetting that Musharraf
with or without uniform will remain the same: commander-in-
chief of the 21st century Einsatzgruppen, which were mobile
paramilitary units established to liquidate the perceived enemies
to the Third Reich such as Jews, Romany, and political opera-
tives of the Communist party. Pakistan's military, under dictator
Musharraf has taken over the same role for the US—the Fourth
Reich—murdering, capturing, destroying homes and even taking
hostage the families of people perceived as enemies.

The worst part of the story is that Nazi Einsatzgruppen were
killing people they considered their enemies. Pakistan's transformed army, the 21st century mercenary Einsatzgruppen, has
turned on its own officers and its own people because the Fourth
Reich considers them as evil.

Pakistanis forget that Musharraf alone is not the problem because he alone is not the nation, as was the case of any dictator
of the past. Hitler alone could not kill millions of Jews or invade
country after country for planting false evidence, overpowering
their populations with a combination of vicious air strikes and
then installing corrupt and cruel puppet leaders. It takes both the
dictator and the nation to pave the way towards their demise.

Gorbachev alone could not disintegrate the Soviet Union. It was done by all citizens of the former Soviet Union who were afraid to question the system and ideology they were subjected to from day one. That is the state of Pakistanis today.

Pakistanis seem to have become neutral and tamed. Same was the problem with Jews before the holocaust. Michael Berenbaum, editor of Witness to the Holocaust, points out: "Most often, they [Jews] remained neutral, neither helping the killer nor offering solace to the victim. Yet neutrality helped the killer, never his victim."[50] Not only Pakistanis in general have adopted this attitude but also all the so-called elected leaders in the "elected" Houses seem to be in a contest of neutrality on the core issues facing the nation. Furthermore, Musharraf is trying to let Pakistanis believe that because of his surrender they are safe.

Pakistan is in the ambivalent position of having an army that can neither govern nor allow civilians to rule. Whether the army has the conceptual ability to plan a strategy of incremental change that would fundamentally reform Pakistan's ailing institutions is also questionable. It is not in a position to end the invisible occupation it has brought upon Pakistan due to self-centered vision of the military leadership. All failing states have weak armies; Pakistan's army is strong enough to prevent state failure for some time to come but not courageous enough to stand for the objective of Pakistan or imaginative enough to transform it into a model Islamic State, which are the only pragmatic ways for its sustainability and the main parameters for defense.

A truly independent, Islamic Republic of Pakistan is unlikely to emerge until the military and politicians set aside their personal interests and broker some kind of grand accord in the interest of Pakistan. In the invisible conflict of the army vs. Pakistan, if Pakistan does not get dissolved, it will definitely continue as a state that hovers on the edge of true independence and sovereignty for a long time to come. In the final analysis, we would come to know that Pakistan was not at war with India or someone else, but its own armed forces. And the forces that Pakistan nurtured at the cost of 80% of its limited resources proved to be the facilitators of occupation.

It is absolutely impossible that Pakistan's army will end its occupation of Pakistan for the US, because the Army and their flunkies, the politicians, are totally corrupt. Pakistan's politicians are selected, groomed and put into office by the army. They are later kicked out by the army once they have passed their usefulness, or become assertive. Benazir Bhutto was allowed to take office in 1988 only after she accepted the army's demands that her government would have no say in the matters of national defense and foreign affairs. Nawaz Sharif was removed and exiled when he began asserting his authority vis-à-vis the Generals who made him prime minister in the first place.

The military will keep occupied Pakistan alive on handouts from Washington. There is no viable infrastructure to make the country economically strong and the mantra of "enlightened moderation" is not going to make miracles for Musharraf. Pakistani Generals are known to be very rich. It is impossible to document the extent of the wealth of the Generals. Once in a while a long list appears citing serving and retired military officers in the position of power through out the country to show the dominance of the armed forces on every aspect of Pakistani life, but it hardly reaches the general public and, even if it does, it is accepted as part of life in occupied Pakistan (See Annex at the end).

Pakistan's defense budget has never been audited. Anyone who questions the Generals' wealth and power faces all kinds of hardship. In 1999, weeks after the Army took over, some members of the suspended parliament made statements against the Army; they were then kidnapped and brutally beaten.[51]

In 2003, a member of the Punjab Assembly, Sanaullah, taunted the generals over their fabulous wealth. He disappeared for several days. When he returned he had a shaven head, disfigured face and multiple fractures. The news of ISI involvement was all over the world. Sanaullah also tried to bring some Generals to justice, but no one would listen to him for fear of the army. Imagine the fear of the army in the heart of a common man. In the 1980s Time published an article giving a brief account of the wealth of Pakistan's generals, but that issue was banned in Pakistan.

However, once in a while muted, almost negligible protest, is made about the richest generals in the world. For example The Friday Times of Lahore once quoted a former bureaucrat to that effect: ...ex-Inspector General police Rao Rashid said that four Pakistani generals were counted among the world's eight richest generals during the Zia era. He added that in those days the big generals and politicians were involved in heroin smuggling.[52]

According to the Canadian Centre for Policy Alternatives published a report—"A US-financed Military Dictatorship: Pakistan has Long, Bloody History as the US Terrorist Arm (June 2002)— Pakistani generals "were deeply involved" in drug trade and three of them were counted amongst the twelve richest generals in the world.[53] The report adds: "Washington's instrument has been the Pakistan army, which U.S. officials have called 'the greatest single stabilizing force in the country.' Its major "military" campaigns have been launched against its own unarmed people."

The military occupation of Pakistan will continue as long as the US is the Pakistani's Army's main supporter. If the United States or the IMF stopped pouring money into Pakistan, the government there would not be able to pay its 500,000 troops and maintain the status quo of having an upper hand in every decision from local to the provincial, national and international level. Civilians are always looked down upon and military officers are specially trained to keep the contemptuous "civilians" at arms length. Military officers are specifically instructed during their initial period of training to even avoid public transport so as to keep a distance from the occupied, oppressed general public.

CHAPTER 6

Zionist Influence Intensifies

IN A CITATION at a dinner hosted by the American Jewish Congress (AJC), Senator Tom Lantos said the Congress had noted Musharraf as "a man of vision" and "an indispensable leader," who has emerged as "the quintessential Muslim leader of moderation, decency, reason, and acceptance of pluralism."[1]

Earlier Musharraf was given a standing ovation and big round of applause as he stepped into the conference room for the dinner-meeting with leaders of the American Jewish Congress.

Musharraf said he gave a military salute to the audience because he could not "imagine that a Muslim and that too a Pakistani and more than that a man in uniform would ever get such a warm reception and such an applause from the Jewish community."[2]

How naïve of the General who pretended as if he could not understand the reason behind glowing tributes and comments such as: "President Musharraf's decision to be with us tonight is an act of individual courage, leadership and vision."[3]

All Muslim opportunists realize the importance of the Zionist influence on American political leaders.[4] To please their masters in Washington, Muslim opportunists have resorted to making themselves acceptable to the Jewish lobby in the US. These opportunists understand each other's motives very well. Hussain Haqqani, a fellow at the Washington-based Carnegie Endowment for International Peace, has been mingling with Zionist organizations since his arrival in the US. He has been lecturing the Board of Directors of Jewish Institute for National Security Affairs (JINSA) for quite some time on the same themes as Musharraf did lately.[5]

Haqqani doubts Musharraf's intentions. He says, "what remains to be seen is whether the move is aimed only at garnering further US support or is it actually based on a desire for genuine change."[6] The military and civilian opportunists didn't come into being just recently. These are the product of the comprehensive moves by Hindu fundamentalists, Zionists and Christian Zionists since the inception of Pakistan. Such opportunists have been thriving under the combined influence of these forces since then. The civilian opportunists seem to be the strongest opponents of the military role, but when it comes to Pakistan's policy toward Israel, both sound exactly the same.

For example consider Hussain Haqqani's article, published in the *Nation* Pakistan, on July 23, 2003 and compare his ideas with General Musharraf's statements and approach since then.[7]

Both the military and civilian "moderates" believe, Israel is "a reality and it might be in Pakistan's interest to overcome ideology to recognize reality."

Both suggest, Pakistan can "wait a little longer to be part of its collective recognition by the Arab-Islamic world."

Both see religious elements "enforcing ideological paradigms on an unwilling Pakistani populace."

Both conclude, "Pakistan's options for success and development would certainly be better as a functional democratic state, which retains its Islamic ethos through the conviction of its citizens rather than by the enforcement of conflicting theocratic visions."

The issue of Israel's reality is discussed in detail later in this chapter. Here we need to analyze similarity of the approach between the civilian and military "moderates" and their promoters in the US. Haqqani and other secularists' criticism of Musharraf is just for the sake of criticism to curry more favor with Zionists with the use of misleading statements. In his 1200 word essay, Haqqani introduces the idea of anti-Semitism in Pakistan. He wants to score more points than Musharraf by stating: "Violent ideas, including anti-Semitism and sectarianism, should be eliminated to pave the way for a tolerant society" to give the impression that Pakistanis hate Jews.

In promoting such lies, the secularists ignore the basic message of the Qur'an and the fact that Pakistanis have nothing against Jews. The message of the Qur'an is to recognize and defend the rights of Jews and other people of the book whether in Israel or in the diaspora to live in peace, to worship freely, to protect their identity and to express themselves. The people of the book, while they rely basically on God's revelation, have moral precepts and know what is lawful and what is not. For this reason, if one of the people of the book cooks some food, it is lawful for Muslims to eat it. In the same way, permission has been given to a Muslim man to marry a woman from among the people of the book (Qur'an 5:05). Muslims must respect Christian and Jewish places of worship (Qur'an 22:40). In many verses, friendship is recommended even with the idolaters (Qur'an 9:06). Concerning the People of the Book, God gives Muslims a command in the Qur'an to rally to a common formula with Christians and Jews towards peace (Qur'an 3:64).

These commands show that bonds of kinship may be established as a result of the marriage of a Muslim with a woman from the people of the book and that those on each side of the union can accept an invitation to a meal. These are the fundamentals that will ensure the establishment of equitable human relationships and a happy communal life. Since the Qur'an enjoins this equitable and tolerant attitude, it is unthinkable that a Muslim, whether Pakistani or not, could take an opposing view.

When the self-proclaimed "moderates" ignore the core message of the Qur'an and blame Pakistanis as a whole for anti-Semitism, they ignore that every Muslim must oppose anti-Semitism as he would oppose every other racist ideology; he must resist this ideology of hatred and defend the rights of Jews as he would defend the rights of all other people.

Nevertheless, Muslims and all other people of conscience, have the right to justly condemn the cruel and aggressive policies of the State of Israel. But to condemn Israel and criticize its official Zionist ideology has nothing to do with anti-Semitism.[8] The reason Pakistanis object to Zionism is that Zionism is also considered to be a racist ideology. Anti-Semitism is rejected for the same reason.

The crimes committed by Israel in the present day against the Palestinian people are painfully thoroughly documented, but all this must not be taken by Muslims as a cause to feel hostility against the Jewish people. The crimes committed by a group of Jews in allegiance to their Zionist ideology should never be blamed on Judaism or the Jewish people. Muslims who pledge allegiance to the same racist ideology also become Zionists by default and become subject to the same criticism.

The mutual criticism of civilian and military "moderates" and their calling Pakistanis as anti-Semite are all part of the wider "war within Islam" that was so earnestly dreamed up by Thomas Friedman of the *New York Times* and others.[9] It is not only the so-labeled Islamists vs. secularists, but also the self-proclaimed moderates vs. moderates. What else could the Islamophobes desire.

It is a dream of a minority but powerful anti-Muslim lobby to eradicate Islam from the face of the earth. Pakistan was presented as a bastion of Islam and it was quite natural to see all anti-

Islam forces teaming up against this bastion. Their last three centuries of persistent efforts has given rise to pseudo-Islamic cults, new sects, sects redefined, and corrupted orders within Islam. In the last fifteen years, their message has been crystallized. They summed up a new acceptable brand of Islam, called "moderate" Islam as discussed under Musharraf's doctrine in chapter 1, which clearly calls on Muslims to accept part of the Qur'an and stop believing it as the final manifesto of God.

Muslim opportunists are working under the same influence. The political and intellectual moves that we witness are the direct result of this influence of the enemies of Islam. The leading among these forces are pro-Zionist intellectuals. The Pakistani leaders have succumbed to the Zionist influence to different degrees in the past, but Musharraf has surpassed everyone in the degree he has surrendered to the Zionist pressure.

A recent Israeli study, "*Beyond the Veil*," brings to light what Pakistan's own 'pro-Israeli' lobby' has been doing since 1947.[10] "*Beyond the Veil*" is necessarily incomplete, based on only Israeli sources and other published matter. Even so, as they are, parts of the Tel Aviv University study make a disgraceful reading for the Pakistani nation.

According to the Israeli study:

> At one time or another, important Pakistani leaders, such as the articulate Foreign Minister Sir Zafrulla Khan (1947-54), military dictators Ayub Khan (1958-69), Yayha Khan (1969-71) and Zia ul-Haq (1977-88) and Prime Ministers Zulfikar Ali Bhutto (1972-77), Benazir Bhutto (1988-90 and 1994-96) and Nawaz Sharif (1990-93 and 1997-99) were sympathetic toward Israel or facilitated interactions with Israeli leaders, diplomats or officials. They were not alone. A host of Pakistani officials and diplomats have met, discussed and at times dined with their Israeli counterparts. Such contacts were held primarily in Washington, London or at the United Nations headquarters in New York. At the same time, a number of other locations, such as Rangoon, Kathmandu and Tokyo in Asia, Lagos in Africa, Ankara and Tehran in the Middle East, Caracas and Ottawa in the Americas and Brussels and Rome in Europe also functioned

as meeting points for Israeli and Pakistani diplomats.[11]

Quoting the above statement in no way implies that the listed Pakistani leaders were traitors to Islam. They were, in fact, traitors to the cause they publicly stood for. They were traitors to themselves. They could not achieve what they publicly stood for because they were not sincere to the stated cause. They deceived their people and acted against what they stated at public forums, such as their rhetoric at the UN. The details that follow show what has actually made their actions disgraceful. Everyone knows that the American black activists who called for bloody revolution harmed the cause of racial equality. Martin Luther King Jr. with his call for non-violent resistance advanced the cause of civil rights in America. No one says the only solution to the problem in the Middle East lies in killing or exiling all Jews and the above mentioned leaders are wrong because they were exploring other ways of winning justice for Palestinians while accepting the right of Israelis to some living space. The issue is of hypocrisy and deceit. Truth and justice never need concealment or moves under the table. But they were not sincere to their public statements and publicly proposed ways for ensuring justice and equality.

The following facts about the previous Pakistani leadership show that Musharraf stands in stark contrast to them. He seems to be saying: If you could deal privately with anti-Islam forces, I dare to do it publicly. If you could sell Pakistan's interests on the sly, I dare sell it publicly without any fear or hesitation. One can argue that Musharraf's talking to Israelis is not selling anything because the Irish government is not selling the rights of the Irish by talking to the British. Here, one needs to keep the difference in mind. Musharraf is not negotiating any solutions and proposals for peace. He is accepting the unacceptable before reaching any solution, as we will see in detail below.

The reason for this attitude on Musharraf's part is simple. The times have changed. The war on Islam was waged under cover and now it is openly referred to as a crusade without any hesitation.[12]

Muslims are openly told that they have to live by secular laws. Iraqis were clearly told that the Qur'an cannot be the only source of their laws. A reference to the Qur'an in Afghanistan's constitution was a "troubling aspect" for the *New York Times* editors.[13] In such an environment, the modern day fascists do not need covert friends, like the ones listed above. They want overt collaborators. That is the reason Musharraf gets standing ovation as well as Congressional citations, noting him to be a "man of vision," unaware that the *Washington Post* will prove him a liar a week later.[14]

During the days of covert war on Islam, Zafrulla Khan, the first foreign minister of Pakistan, can rightly be described as the ideological father of Pakistan's laid-back and ever-submissive foreign policy. *Beyond the Veil* reveals that the man who was acclaimed all over the Arab world for his eloquent advocacy of the Palestinian and Arab cause at the UN and other international forums was not quite honest to his brief. Zafrulla Khan publicly said in Cairo in February 1952 that Israel must be "regarded as a limb in the body of the Middle East." He further urged Egypt to seek a peaceful solution of the conflict! In other words, to give up any thought of liberating Arab and Palestinian lands and recognize the illegitimate occupation of Palestine.

Israeli occupation of the Arab land is illegitimate because never in history a people has made such claims as the Zionists are making. Look at South Africa. The local population was conquered and enslaved by the Zulus. Some time later, the Dutch arrived and in turn subjugated them. Then the Brits conquered the Dutch. Should everyone be exiled except "the original" inhabitants? Should everyone be making claims on the basis of theological argument dating back to 3000 years? How about the Indians claiming right to the US land and demanding all the aliens to leave because occupation of their land is not even 500 years old? The best way to deal with the inequalities of history is to get over them, analyze the current situation and find the solution that is the most just for everyone. This is typically a compromise, which we don't see on the part of Israel despite the 58 years of occupation, displacement and dispossession of the people it occupied.

Going back in history, there were once Celts, Anglo-Saxons and Normans in Britain. Now, you can be 100% Welsh and live happily with someone who is 50% Norman and 50% Saxon. There are people who cherish their Scottish ancestry, would never marry someone who is not Scottish, and choose to hate the English. As long as they don't impose their views on others, they are free to follow their traditions. Someone must explain how this is not in principle possible in the Holy Land. If, magically, everyone there was given good will and tolerance, we could have a State that cherished the three main religions equally, which is a much vaunted principle of secular state anyway. Instead of rushing into recognizing a racist Zionist regime, which doesn't want anyone other than a single race on its soil, cooler heads ask: Jews could live purely within their religion while their neighbor was a devout Muslims: Is this not better than mutual genocide? Such basic questions don't cross minds of those, who like Musharraf are bent upon seeking legitimacy and recognition for themselves. Musharraf cannot even see what correspondent of the *New York Times* has to tell the world in his famous 1986 book *Arab and Jews: Wounded Spirits in a Promised Land*, David Shipler writes on page 438:

> Non Jews are excluded from sharing authority and participating fully by the basic fact that Israel is a Jewish state, conceived as a sanctuary and vehicle of Jewish life and representing a culmination of Jewish power and self-reliance. Israel has never resolved the contradiction inherent in having an Arab population in a "Jewish state." But two other forces also bolster discrimination against Arabs. One is the obstacle of military preparedness and security, which in a defense-oriented economy closes off important avenues of advancement to Arabs. The other is the culture of poverty, in which a cycle of inferior education, impoverished living conditions, low motivation, and a lack of investment capital renders Arabs economically dependent on Jews.

As a result, the Arabs have become Israel's underclass, a continuation of their inferior position that grew out of the 1948 fighting, when those Arabs who fled were often the wealthiest urban residents who could afford to go and those who stayed were generally the most rural and the least privileged.

The tragedy with Pakistan vis-à-vis Israel that began in 1947 is simply reaching its climax in the 21st century under General Musharraf. Zafrullah Khan was appointed by Jinnah himself. In October 1947, soon after the emergence of Pakistan, Jinnah warned that the partition of Palestine would entail "the gravest danger and unprecedented conflict and that the entire Muslim world will revolt against such a decision which can not be supported historically, politically and morally." Soon afterwards, Pakistan proclaimed at the United Nations that all the Holy Land was being nailed and stretched on the cross. Surprisingly, all these words came from the mouths of those who were being held hostage by the Zionist influence.

Feroz Khan Noon recognized Israel *ex gratia* by declaring "Israel had come to stay" and Zafrullah Khan declared in 1952 that Israel must be regarded as "a limb in the body of the Middle East."[15] Before considering the background of these individuals, let us have a look at the argument that maybe they honestly believed this. Maybe they were right. After all, Jinnah pushed for the partition of India. Why was the same solution not also good in Palestine? The answer is that if these individuals honestly believed so, they were not supposed to say something totally different at the UN in favor of the suffering Palestinians. The world could have reached a solution if they were not saying one thing to the world and another to their Zionist friends. Moreover, in the case of Pakistan, there were no claims laid over the land, nor were any competing claims of different religions over this land. Muslims were in a majority and already living in this part of the South Asia. The situation in Israel is totally different as a result of rejecting all that has been offered to it since its inception, including partition on the basis of equality.

As far their backgrounds, Feroz Khan Noon came from a typically feudal family, the kind of pillars on which the British colonialism had stood. Duly knighted along the way, he had served as high commissioner for (British) India in London (1936-41) and as member of Viceroy's executive council (1941-45).

These serving members of the colonialists dominated affairs of nascent Pakistan and were considered loyal to its objectives. Sir Feroz, an empire loyalist with an Austrian Jewish wife, seemed to have become a Zionist by marriage. We may give Feroz Khan the benefit of the doubt by considering him a tolerant person, accepting of differences. But his committed service to colonialism exposes his real face. He was serving as high commissioner for India in London before the partition in 1936-41, when the colonial secretary, Lord Moyne, asked him to prepare a draft scheme for creating a Jewish state in Arab Palestine, but in a way that British imperialist do not get blamed for being anti-Arab or pro- Zionist. The can-do knight submitted his proposal to the secretary of state for India, Leopold Amery, who too happened to be Jewish. Noon proposed that they first create an Arabian federation, but also slip in an autonomous Jewish state within that federation. This Jewish entity should be a part of the treaty creating the federation.

The full-blown Jewish state would come into existence later, Sir Feroz explained, but the federation would provide the cover that they all needed so that no Muslim ruler could blame England for having created a Jewish state in Palestine or part of Palestine'. According to declassified papers from British Government (file No: F0372-275-E6190/53/65), Noon's proposals were forwarded by Amery to Churchill on 10 September 1945.[16]

Zafrulla Khan also belonged to the heterodox Ahmadi group, created by the colonialists, which made Ahamdis loyal to the British empire by their "faith." Zafrulla also served the colonists and in 1945 represented the British Indian government at a conference on Commonwealth Relations. He met the head of the

Jewish Agency Chaim Weizmann, who organized his six-day visit to Palestine. According to Tel Aviv University's latest study, Weizmann (later president of the Zionist entity) told his men in Jerusalem to "see to it that (Zafrulla's) stay in Palestine, and his contacts with our work, are made as interesting and as agreeable as possible." And so it happened. Having allowed himself to be taken on a conducted tour by the Zionist Agency, it seems Zafrulla did undergo an "agreeable" change of mind. He wrote to Weizmann that he found the problem of Palestine "much more complicated than I had imagined, but let its hope that a just and equitable solution may soon be discovered." Surely any decent person has to agree with such a sentiment. The question, however, is that being in a position to speak truth to power, what did he actually do to help the parties reach a "just and equitable solution." He was just expressing regrets over his public stand on the issue.

Zafrulla did not indicate, though, what complications had since entered his mind, nor, what would make "a just and equitable solution." He was economical with the truth. However, two years later after the UN had adopted the partition resolution (29 November 1947), Israeli orientalist Uriel Heyd, who was also working for the Zionist intelligence in London, reported "noticeable changes in the position of Zafrulla Khan...During his talks in Damascus, Zafrulla Khan indicated that partition, which he [as Pakistan's foreign minister had] vehemently opposed, was the only solution for Palestine. He even counseled the Arabs to allow the establishment of the Jewish state." It was not a volte face, it was a double face.

The sad part of this saga is that Zafrulla Khan and Feroz Khan Noon were not the only individuals who deceived the nation and betrayed the Palestinians. What they were doing then, or Musharraf is doing now, cannot even be justified as using diplomacy in support of Palestinians. There were many others working on their respective projects, who remained unknown. The extent of the Zionist influence can be judged from the fact that in 1950 (May-June) Pakistan's first Prime Minister Liaqat Ali Khan visited the United States and American leaders of trade and industry met him. At the meeting they promised all possible military and economic assistance if Pakistan recognized Israel. The American industrialists also underlined the importance of such a package for the new state of Pakistan. Liaqat Ali Khan in his known gentle tone replied: "Gentlemen! Our soul is not for sale."[17]

Nevertheless, it is extremely surprising to know that Zafrulla had kept telling Israelis that Pakistan was about to recognize Israel. So when Abba Eban saw him in New York on January 14, 1953, as part of their continuing dialogue, Zafrulla "disclosed" to him that while the previous government of Liaqat Ali Khan favored the policy of recognizing Israel, the government now headed by Prime Minister Khawaja Nazimuddin (1894-1964) "'had retreated from the favorable approach adopted by his predecessor." This government "was weaker and more susceptible to public pressure from Muslim extremists." He himself, Zafrulla told Abba Eban, "was attacked for his moderation."[18] It shows Musharraf's moderation is not a new mantra either.

These "founding" figures of Pakistan's foreign services shaped the minds and ideology of a totally raw and unformed diplomatic service. The first batches of the Foreign Service were "trained" in Britain, Canada or the US; when they came back they very well knew how to serve the interests of the new imperial power against the interest of Pakistan. The vision and *raison d'être* of the nation was no more than a joke for them. At best, Islam remained a slogan to make everything acceptable to the masses.

Pakistan's history is replete with hypocrites who provided full support to the views of Feroz Khan Noon and Zafrulla Khan. The prime minister, Husain Shaheed Suhrawardy and the president, Iskandar Mirza, fully agreed with Noon. Mirza, too, had started his career as a British Political Agent in the tribal districts of the North West Frontier. Later on, Ayub Khan, who followed

Noon and Mirza, had to work with the same pro-Zionist and pro-imperialist policy tools.

Musharraf, too, is surrounded by personalities who are either known Ahmadis or have ties with those who are in charge of the modern day crusade. Pakistani hypocrites are not exposed to the nation. But outsiders know them very well. The evidence lies in the world's silence over Pakistan's nuclear weapons and its willingness to even go to war with Iran and North Korea to prevent them from becoming nuclear powers. The outside world knows what Pakistani leaders and representatives tell them in private. Pakistanis can guess it from the incident reported by the Israeli Ambassador to Canada, M.S. Comay. On December 23, 1956, just weeks after the cease-fire between Egypt and Israel, but before Israel withdrew from Sinai, the Indian embassy in Canada hosted a reception in honor of Indian Prime Minister Nehru. Among others, the Israeli and Pakistani ambassadors were invited. Reporting on his conversation with his Pakistani counterpart, Israeli Ambassador M.S. Comay recorded:

> ...the Pakistan High Commissioner Mirza Osman Ali Baig publicly came up to me, shook me by the hand, and warmly congratulated me on the 'wonderful show your splendid little army put up in beating the Egyptians.' His only regret was that the British and the French had intervened, otherwise we might have gone right through to Cairo.[19]

Dr. Shahid Qureshi, London bureau Chief of the *Frontier Post*, argues that it is impossible to assume that Baig was speaking for himself alone: "He certainly represented a certain small but insidious and powerful toady-Zionist-Qadiyani nexus within the country's foreign policy establishment, especially that has continued to blight Pakistan's foreign policy and external relations to this day. Perhaps there is no other country today, which is as friendless and as isolated as Pakistan."[20] Under Musharraf, Pakistan has become totally bereft of its founding vision, which it started losing after the assassination of its first legitimate prime minister, Liaqat Ali Khan. The policy of subservience which passed into the hands of characters like Zafrulla and Noon and their offspring culminated in total surrender at the hands of cronies surrounding Musharraf.

Pakistan and Israel are the only two countries on the globe formed on the basis of religion: Pakistan, on the basis of Islam, and Israel on the basis of Jewish ancestry. Under Musharraf, Pakistan surrendered its *raison d'être* whereas the whole non-Muslim world seems united to defend the Jewish character of the Israeli state. Pakistan, a Muslim country, has gone always with the plea that it will follow the wishes of the Muslim *Ummah*. But Musharraf's doctrine in practice is based on directions and approval from Washington.

Musharraf clearly told the nation on January 12, 2002 that Pakistan is not responsible for the Muslim world. After getting a lesson in Camp David in 2003, he returned home with a message that the heavens won't fall if he recognized Israel and indulged in the rhetoric, "would we be more Catholic than Pope and more Palestinian than the Palestinians themselves"[21] forgetting completely about the Arab League resolution passed in Beirut that Israel should not be recognized unless it completely withdrew from the land it occupied in 1967.

Besides personal motivation, Musharraf has been under a great deal of pressure from his pro-Zionist Western mentors and Pakistani cronies to recognize Israel. The recent Gaza pullout gave them the stick to browbeat the General into taking initiatives that would soon bring about Pakistan's full recognition of Israel. He had also been told that a positive gesture could mean further extension of his absolute hold on power which Washington does not consider an embarrassment to its current campaign for marketing democracy as a global phenomenon. The US has always supported governments that give it financial and political benefits, regardless of ideology or human rights. The talk of Democracy is just that—talk.

The US is now pressing Musharraf due to Israel's obsession

for recognition. As far as Musharraf's dictatorship is concerned, US Secretary of State Condoleezza Rice has defended the use of military force to advance the cause of democracy and liberty as "the only guarantee of true stability and lasting security."[22] Supporting the tyranny of Musharraf is part of this agenda. Hitler made that same claim, and Germany under Hitler was stable and secure for a few months. The US administration hardly realizes that one doesn't make people free by pointing guns at them. The way to set people free is to leave them alone to determine their own destiny and way of life without occupation and dictatorial rulers.

To understand Pakistan and its dictator's position as a pawn in the Zionist game one has to understand the Zionist strategy and its main objectives which are to: 1. Keep the US, UK, India (for neutralizing Pakistan) and Israel under full control; 2. Keep all the countries in the Middle East and South Asia (including Pakistan) unstable by imposing unpopular rulers or discrediting popular rulers, and creating new political parties or infiltrating existing ones with Zionist agents in the name of openness and democracy; 3.Use agents in politics and the press to create or exacerbate civil strife among ethnic groups, regions or sects that seek change in existing political boundaries to create smaller countries that would readily permit control over their resources (oil) and wealth (individual as well as national reserves); and 4. Preclude consolidation of the Greater Middle East (including Pakistan) and its emergence as a strong military power; even resorting to invasion to pre-empt such a possibility.

Pakistan figures prominently in all the Zionist objectives but Saudi Arabia is their most important target. Pakistan is a target because it is the only nuclear-powered nation with armed forces trained to fight a modern war. That is why one finds many schemes to undermine the Pakistani army through moves towards of secularization, internal conflicts and even perpetual dictatorship so as to completely devalue it in the eyes of its nation.

Zionist influence has reached its peak in Pakistan because Bush and Blair won re-elections and the Labour party is still on the sidelines in Israel. Similarly in India, the government is still under the influence of the BJP. Muslims are totally helpless before the traitors and subversives. The press in the Muslim world is subservient to the rulers who, in turn, are serving their Zionists-infected masters. They can hardly expose the Zionist strategy and plans against Islam and Muslims.

It is very unfortunate that under the influence of Zionists, Musharraf and other Muslim dictators and civilian sell-outs— "moderates"[23]—pretend that they do not see or know the realities on the ground. Musharraf and his "moderate" critics and colleagues believe that Israel is a reality that will not go away. To them it is a real estate issue, similar to British history in Ireland, the racial conflict in South Africa, Indians in Fiji, many of the genocidal racial conflicts in black Africa, and so on forever.

Jews somehow reached Palestine, now there are two groups of people with identifiable differences of some kind, sharing the same land and competing for resources. Which is the better way to address the issue: the IRA's, or Nelson Mandela's? The most important point to highlight is that no sane mind advocates genocide in Israel. Nevertheless, Musharraf and his company must be blind not to see the following facts:

- Israel's very foundation is based on racism. It will not exist without racism. It was not anti-Semites, but "most Israelis have argued that Israel cannot remain a Jewish state or a democracy if it incorporates the occupied territories, because Palestinians would alter the nation's demographic balance."[24]

- Not only Israel was founded on racism but through the means of terrorism, brutal murders of men, women and children, exiling 700,000 of them from occupying their lands, homes, gardens and farms. Among those events was the sadistic massacre of 254 Palestinian at Deir Yassin. It was an especially vicious, cold-blooded massacre characterized by

Zionist forces cutting apart the bellies of pregnant women.[25] Former Israel Prime Minister, Menachem Begin, a participant in this horrendous massacre, boasted of the terrorism of Deir Yassin. He wrote that there would not have been a State of Israel without the "victory" of Deir Yassin. "The Haganah carried out victorious attacks on other fronts... In a state of terror, the Arabs fled, crying, 'Deir Yassin.'"[26]

- One of the most important and influential newspapers in the United States, *The Wall Street Journal*, opined that the "right of return" of Palestinian refugees would result in the "demographic destruction of the Jewish state."[27] When the same views of a virtual ban on immigration into his nation were expressed by Austrian political leader, Jorge Haider, he was widely condemned in the mainstream media of the United States and Europe as a racist.

- Not recognizing Israel is not a denial of reality. It is simply a denial to legitimize "an illegitimate child of Western powers."[28]

- Asking to recognize Israel's reality is no less than asking to legitimize Nazism because political Zionism and German Nazism bear some distinct similarities.[29] Joachim Prinz, a former Vice-President of the World Jewish Congress, in 1934 praised the Nazi revolution (1933) in Germany: "Only a state based on the principle of the purity of the nation and the race can possibly endow dignity and honor on...those Jews who themselves subscribe to this principle."[30]

- Zionism remains a political philosophy that is firmly grounded in the anti-integrationist racial thought of the past and present.[31] A former member of Israel's Supreme Court, Haim Cohen, described the system that applies to Jews and Palestinians in Israel as similar to "Nuremberg laws" of Nazi Germany: "...the bitter irony of fate which has led the same biological and racist laws propagated by the Nazis and which inspired the infamous Nuremberg laws, to serve as a basis for the definition of Judaism within the State of Israel."[32]

- Israeli and American scientists are conducting studies to emphasis the biological history of the Jewish people and prove how the latter differ from the non-Jewish world.[33] This information is used to define into existence a "Jewish race" and discriminate against non-Jews. Indeed, Jewish Zionists and their gentile supporters would probably demand immediate annihilation of the countries involved if, for example, it were found that Muslim scientists were attempting to determine how Muslims differ from non-Muslims in genetic-biological sense, and this information would be used to implement racially discriminatory policies.

- These scientific studies have the objective to deny anyone the right to settle in Israel if he does not have "Jewish genes." With this in mind, consider point four of the Nazi Party Program of May 25, 1920. It reads: "None but members of the nationality may be citizens of the state. None but those of German blood, irrespective of religion, may be members of the nationality."[34] In contemporary terms, only those with "German genes" could be citizens of Nazi Germany. Is this reality not enough to show the façade of the Israeli Apartheid state?

- In the words of Uri Davis, who is a Jewish citizen of Israel, but he prefers to describe himself as a Palestinian Jew,[35] to mask Israeli apartheid, it was necessary to present Israel to the world as an advanced form of democracy. Thus, duplicitous legal structures were devised that effectively mask the racial discrimination and apartheid.[36] A study of Israeli and South African apartheid published in the 1980s brought the reality to the forefront that "The parallels between South Africa's system of legalized racism and that of Israel are well-known in academic circles but rarely discussed in the mainstream media, peace community or halls of Congress."[37] Former Congressman George W. Crockett, Jr. noted back in

1985 that "Here in Congress we are fighting against South Africa's repressive measures, and yet closing our eyes to the institutional repression and the brutality that is daily being conducted against the Palestinians in the Israeli-occupied Arab territories."[38]

- Ronnie Kasrils, a Jew, who was active in the fight against apartheid in South Africa from the 60's onwards, told an international conference on Palestine, Israel and International Law at the Institute of Education in London (October 29-30, 2005) that the situation for Arabs in Israel & Palestine is "far worse" than that of the blacks in what was apartheid South Africa. He is currently Minister of Intelligence and Deputy Minister of Defence in South Africa.

- The former editor-in-chief of the *Rand Daily Mail* (the Johannesburg newspaper that fought against South African apartheid), Raymond Louw, further clarifies the reality that the situation in the Israeli occupied territories is worse than the way things were under the South African apartheid regime because under South African apartheid "there was a recognition that the blacks would continue to live in these areas. Here the impression is that the objective is to push the Palestinians out."[39]

It is not that Musharraf does not know the above realities and he is only blinded by self-interest. It is simply that besides opportunism he is under Zionist influence and immense pressure. In short, General Musharraf is as helpless before the Zionist pressure and influence as is his nation before his brute force. He will remain so until he breathes his last or the Zionists achieve their objectives. There is absolutely no hope that he can release himself from Zionist clutches. As long as he remains entangled in the Zionist and the neo-cons web, as long as Pakistan remains under their influence, its sovereignty and independence will remain at stake.

We know that Pakistan is not what it was envisaged by Muslims before 1947. There must not be any doubt that Pakistan will cease to exist if the same timidity, hypocrisy, selfishness and greed remain part of the agenda of its self-appointed leader.

CHAPTER 7

No Will for the Solution

Nations are very much like individuals. More than desire for material gain or fear or love, they are driven by a craving for dignity and respect, by the need to be recognized as valid and just as valuable as the next person or country.[1]

CONTRARY TO the above statement, the unfortunate reality which Pakistan faces today is that Musharraf's "enlightened moderation" is a reflection of the nation's mind-set: focused on material gains and suffering from multiple fears, rather than craving for dignity and pride in self-identity. Except for a tiny fraction of the population worried about the nation's groping in the dark, almost everyone is lost in the struggle for survival or the competition to acquire more material possessions and status.

The nation is at war with its founding ideology. At a time when even non-Muslims agree that it is Islam that has provided political foundation to Pakistan, the secularists in Pakistan argue that the Two Nations Theory is irrelevant and Islam was not the objective or motivating factor behind the struggle for independence. This denial of the reality on the part of some Pakistanis is evident from Hindu analysts' conclusion that:

> The consolidation of a distinct Muslim identity had started even before the idea of Pakistan germinated in the minds of the intellectuals. The quest for such an identity can be identified with the Mujahideen movement which had started under the leadership of Syed Ahmad Brelvi who wanted to purify the Muslims, mostly converts from Hinduism, from the influence of Hindu culture and religion. The madrassas in Deobandh, and the Mohammedan Educational Conference provided awareness to the Muslims as a distinct socio-cultural and religious group and led to the emergence of the pan-Indian Muslim consciousness movement.
>
> Islam, however, became politically useful after the 1857 Sepoy Mutiny. For the first time, the mutiny unified Indians against British imperialism. But the kind of emotional appeal it generated especially among the Muslims (and for that matter, also among non-Muslims) was noticed by intellectuals.[2]

Similarly, B.M. Chengappa points out:

> In the pre-partition phase Islam was used as an effective instrument of political mobilization in order to achieve a Muslim state. However, once the political objective of nationhood was accomplished then there was a marked decline in the leadership's emphasis on the role of religion. As a result, a conflict of ideology arose because the leadership desired a secular state while the people yearned for a Muslim nation… The Muslim elite cherished the concept of a secular state, but could not pursue their ideals since during the pre-partition phase they had sold the line about the formation of a religious state to the masses.[3]

Pakistan didn't exist as a nation until 1947. Until the advent of Pakistan, no one was in fact a Pakistani, for the simple reason that there was no territorial entity bearing that name. Is it just a boundary line that turned Muslims of South Asia into a nation in the first place? Is this nation under the misconception that Pakistan's boundaries are now to stay forever and irrespective of its deeds and divisions, Pakistan will remain forever?

Pakistanis must not forget that the very concept of 'the nation' came to being some 250-odd years ago as a byblow of Europe's industrial revolution. This concept is already dead, except that the world has yet to realize it. In an age of continent-spanning and identity-challenging multinational corporations and globalization, the nation-state is beginning to look more and more like the doddering old family retainer, long past his prime, who continues to hang around largely because no one has got the heart to call an end to this approach of division among people.

In their recent referendums, France and Holland voted against giving up their nationalism—their private limited company, so to speak—to effect a full merger with the Multinational Corporation called the European Union. But the fact that the EU does exist, and that the referendums did take place, suggests that the concept of the nation-state is increasingly coming into question. Curiously enough, even as the idea of the nation-state is being reassessed, nation-states themselves are proliferating like jackrabbits. From 72 in 1900, the number of nation-states in the world has grown to over 190 as of last count. And more are in the making. What constitutes a nation is still a highly debated issue, but a nation most certainly by any definition, transcends geographical boundaries.

Someone might argue that there can be nations, and federations of nations. Countries have split and merged (one way or another) through the ages. That in itself doesn't invalidate the concept of an autonomous country. What would convince the reader is the plentifully available evidence of the way multinational corporations in fact rule governments including the US. Secondly, in the case of Pakistan, one has to go to the roots of what makes it a nation in the first place, and would it remain a nation if that single most factor is taken out of the equation. As discussed in detail earlier, that factor is Islam and all energies are focused on taking it out of the equation.

This seeming paradox—of global agglomeration and mergers on the one hand and national splits and breakaways on the other—can perhaps be better understood if we look at the emerging trend of classifying the world on the basis of civilizations and religion. The approach was instantly adopted after the fall of the Soviet Union. The theory of the clash of civilizations by Samuel Huntington is gradually being translated into a reality. Statements from the US military, political and religious figures in particular and from European figures in general give a good idea as to what they consider as "evil." Individuals adapt to new circumstances by redefining who and what they are in relationship to the rest of the world and themselves.

Likewise nation-states are not immutable monuments like statues. They are changeable narratives and make or break themselves up as they evolve. We—nations and people—are alive as long as we know who we are and what is our objective in life. We live and strive to achieve that overall objective. The day we lose our identity; the day we fail to recognize ourselves and fail to understand the purpose of our existence, our well-wishers take us to a psychiatrist so as to find out further details about our cognitive disorder in which normal connections or associations are no longer present.

Being a collective representation of its individuals, nations ideally reflect the mindset of their people. A people suffering from cognitive disorder make the nation sick. Although symptoms vary, they encompass nearly all domains of function, particularly perception and inferential thinking (delusions). At 58, Pakistan is almost ridiculously young as a nation. In a world where the nation-state may not remain a reality in the near future, losing its identity will cost Pakistan dearly.

There is no other justification for it to declare itself a nation or exist in the first place. According to Ulysses S. Grant, the "greatest general"[4] of American Civil War and 18th president of the US, "nations, like individuals, are punished for their transgressions." Pakistan is destined to pay the price for losing its identity because its cognitive disorder has kept it from understanding the problems it is facing today and the real causes behind these problems. Even if someone tells Pakistanis about the root causes of their ailment, they are not ready to accept the cure.

Pakistanis hardly realize, but the beginning and the end of their ailments lies in taking eyes off the real objective and focusing on personal aggrandizement, material well being and power. Indian analysts are right when they say, "With the emergence of Bangladesh, the frequently tom-tommed two-nation theory, the very *raison d'être* for Pakistan, stood discredited and turned on its head."[5] This was not the defeat of the Two Nations Theory.

It was, in fact, a warning sign for the nation's conduct in the aftermath of the first ever general elections held under direct universal suffrage in 1970. The results were scuttled. Thanks to the same selfishness and the resultant inability of the political establishment, notably Zulfiqar Bhutto, to accept Bengalis into leadership positions. Consequently, the brutal and savage civil war, followed by the Indo-Pak War of 1971, generated two defining events that continue to haunt Pakistan even today: secession of Bangladesh and Pakistan's humiliating military defeat at the hands of India.

Despite that, Pakistanis didn't put our act together to prove that the so-called "objective reality" of Pakistan being a plural, multi-ethnic, multi-lingual society does not close the doors on Muslims living by Islam in an Islamic State. They failed to focus their energies on establishing a model to silence the critics[6] and prove that Islam can definitely find expression in a uniform politico-territorial identity as a single state.

Instead, a majority of disappointed Pakistanis gave up on the hopes that there can ever be an Islamic state and have lost in acquiring more and more material possessions instead. Even members of the religious parties are blindly followers of their respective leaders without any clear objective as to what they want and how their party can help achieve that objective for them in an environment where Musharraf is promoting the idea that Islam is opposed to progress and enlightenment.

The masses have been gradually brainwashed into believing that it was the process of Islamization that has caused severe damage to Pakistan. The self-proclaimed moderates blame the problem of "fundamentalism" on the wrong interpretation of Islam. The first question that comes to a Western mind, which is not aware of the realities on the ground in the Muslim world and receives all information from the so-called mainstream media, is: If Islam is inherently moderate and humane, is an interpretation like that of the Taliban correct?

The simple answer to such confusion is: ask those who have lived under the Taliban, not those who came with pre-conceived ideas and ideological filters. They returned to polish their pre-determined conclusions with select, biased reporting. Or, accept what the media has to say about the Taliban is correct, and then compare those five years with more than the fifty years of Israeli oppression to see whose crimes outweigh the other. Or else, pick up the Qur'an and read it. It doesn't say the Taliban are the role models of Islam, or to follow them. It says follow the Qur'an and *Sunnah* with the best intentions and to the best of your understanding.

Furthermore, in the case of Pakistan, the secularists blame inconsistency and instability in laws on those who called for legislating in accordance with the Qur'an and *Sunnah*. These unsubstantiated allegations and excuses ignore the above mentioned claims from the mouth of non-Muslims who hold the Muslim elite responsible for steering the country away from Islam. Ultimately, today Pakistan finds itself in the middle of nowhere because of the secular zealots. They failed to achieve with their hypocritical approach in the last 58 years what the Turkish Generals could not fully achieve in the last 82 years despite their militant approach.

If the legal system in Pakistan couldn't be transformed, it is simply because the secularists tried to accommodate both godliness and godlessness in one system. The same is true in every aspect of life in Pakistan. The analysts then instantly blame everything on the use of Islam, arguing that Islam, which should have served to unite the people of Pakistan—over 95 percent of them being Muslims—has been, and is being, misused to divide them into mutually hostile sectarian groups and to divert their attention from basic social and economic problems.[7]

These analysts ignore that the root cause is not the use and misuse of Islam and sectarianism. The root cause is the lack of will and misplaced intentions of the leadership at the top. There has never been a sincere, collective effort to gradually evolve Pakistan into an Islamic State. The elite treated Islam like a stigma as if even talking about Islam would somehow devalue their status. Lack of commitment and spirit for establishing an Islamic State has been the root cause for the aimlessness and turmoil in Pakistan today.

Nation-building could not take place in Pakistan because the nation failed miserably at mission-building and providing the masses a direction. A desperate people cannot be made into a solid and cohesive community if successive governments which supposedly establish and consolidate an Islamic Republic of Pakistan are themselves riddled with contradictions and ill intentions. Consequently, in half a century of its existence, Pakistanis could not create a solid nation without a cohesive force that could bind them together.

The rulers are as much responsible for the suppression and distortion of the struggle to establish an Islamic State as for the loss of the sense of belonging that is essential for the survival of a country. They divided the community because there was no central force to keep them on track. Different opportunists appeared to fill the vacuum and exploit public feelings in the name of Islam simply because there was no effort made for this purpose at the central level. Even those who did raise some slogans, like General Zia, simply proved in the final analysis to be insincere. Missing the glue of Islamic brotherhood, people no longer belong to Pakistan but to their ethnic clans or tribes. Their allegiance is to one or another religious sect and they think only in terms of themselves and their families. They see greater benefits by being Pashtun, Sindhi, Balochi, Punjabi and Mohajir, rather than being Pakistanis.

The ultimate result is that the criminalization of Islam is in the offing. We must not be surprised if in the near future, the insatiable greed and unscrupulous ambitions of the military and politicians make them ban every political activity undertaken in the name of Islam in a country established in the name of Islam. The loss of identity is not a trivial matter. It has a clear impact on all state affairs for a long time. Shahid Javed Burki of the World Bank believes that the country is now left with no viable institutions, including that of the judiciary and "we are in danger of losing Jinnah's legacy."[8] This is the direct result of our ideological aimlessness. The government didn't deliberately ruin all institutions. It is due to the lack of a higher objective in a system with no accountability that leaves everyone to pursue their own personal interests. Institutions die and the masses pay the price in the process.

Looking at Pakistan's selfish approach to governance, foreign observers predicted a long time ago that "given the impact of change, Pakistan could cease to exist in its sovereign nation-state form. With the approach of the twenty-first century, Pakistanis may at last find their elusive commonwealth, only it may not be the one envisaged by the nation's creators."[9] The reality, however, remained that no one dared to rise to the occasion to ensure that such forecasts do not come true. Commentators from within have been warning from time to time to no avail.[10] Even Ardeshir Cowasjee, a permanent contributor to *Dawn*, observed that the real fear is that if things slide as they are doing, sometime early in the next century there may not be a State of Pakistan.[11] Above all, the Caretaker Prime Minister, Malik Meraj Khalid, referring to a UN report which stated that Pakistan would break into pieces in two decades, said that Pakistan no longer exists ideologically.[12]

The admitted ideological demise of Pakistan means that successive governments have ignored the reality that Pakistan as a nation-state does not have a political identity outside of Islam, which as a concept is the only tie that seems to bind Pakistan together as a nation and a political concept. It is too late to answer the question whether Pakistan should strive to be an Islamic state as both the masses and the leaders unanimously called for before independence (irrespective of what the elites had in their mind) or a secular state as promised by Musharraf. In the wake of democracies turning to the worst kind of tyrannies human history has ever witnessed, it is a time Pakistanis make a last ditch effort at establishing the best model of human governance. Muslim self-rule is the answer. The most vital question, however, is: Do Pakistanis, or all Muslims for that matter, have the will to do this?

The reality is that even if there is a little will, there seems to be no possibility in the face of the odds in the 21st century. This saps the will and leaves even the willing hopeless. On the other hand, in the absence of self-rule, Pakistan will not survive for long. Musharraf is the critical factor that will remain the major hurdle to working towards the real solution because his mantra of "enlightened moderation" totally negates the right approach. His benighted opportunism further strengthens superficial fears and accusations of Muslims' self rule, and further confuses genuine points of difference with the West. It paves the way for more intrusive interventions in the internal affairs of Pakistan at a time when Pakistan needs a clear and permanent break from Western interference for putting its house in order. Unfortunately, in the near future it seems that if Musharraf disappeared, a copy would replace him that will make a peaceful change impossible and chaos and turmoil inevitable.

Regarding the lack of will for working toward the right solution, Musharraf and his cronies from the secular parties cannot be fully blamed, when leadership of the religious parties is also lost in the petty issues of daily routine. They have no strategy for proceeding toward an Islamic State in the present circumstances at home, let alone helping none-Muslims understand that the objective of a State in Islam is not to annihilate the non-Muslim world or march on country after country to impose the Islamic way of life like the US is doing to the Muslims in the name of democracy.

Presently, most of the Islamic parties and group are unable to offer a consistent and comprehensive plan of action. In fact, many, like the Jamaat-e-Islami, are a spent force. Their *raison d'être* has been thoroughly compromised in every arena—they have failed in their primary mission. Now they are content with mere jockeying for minor positions on the political periphery. The fact of the matter is that even if they win almost every seat in the national and provincial assemblies by working within the current secular system, they will never succeed in establishing an Islamic State because, like anything else, it cannot be imposed from the top. It needs a revolutionary struggle at the grassroots level. In that regard the nation from the top to bottom have wasted 58 years and that's why it has become impossible to find enough people willing to risk working against the mainstream current. A majority finds it convenient to go with the flow of the prevailing trends, because turning back has become almost impossible. Very few feel comfortable living by Islam in all walks of life and no one has the will to do that in an environment where even the Supreme Court has proved itself to stand for the defense of secularism under the present regime. This internally disastrous situation is compounded by external factors, which have made Pakistan the high value target.

CHAPTER 8

Softening the High Value Target

PAKISTAN DID not learn its lesson from the Taliban saga. The demonization of the Taliban started the moment it was evident that they would not serve US strategic interests and would continue to uphold the Qur'an as their constitution.

The problem, in the view of those now targeting Pakistan is not Pakistan. The real source of the problem is Islam, which must be removed from the social and political agenda.

The treatment of the Taliban shows the polarity within American and European society. On the one side are the Islamophobes, who are determined to undermine Islam regardless of the financial, moral and physical costs involved. On the other end of the spectrum are the corporate terrorists, who are willing to co-operate with any kind of regime as long as their financial interests are served.

Sadly, it is the innocent masses pay the price as they are trapped in the middle of these two polarities. When the interests of the war-lords and corporate terrorists are threatened, they can be equally vicious against all types of regimes, and can easily form alliances with the state and other groups. Even when the Taliban received US support with the hope of an oil pipeline and their serving other strategic interests, there was a strong anti-Taliban movement organized by Islamophobes in the name of human rights advocacy.

These very same Islamophobic groups have been totally silent regarding the 58 years of Israeli oppression, occupation and human rights violations against the Palestinian people, and equally silent regarding the well documented US human rights violations and norms of human decency since 9/11. This demonstrates that the real motivation behind these so-called "human rights" movements is hatred towards Islam and Muslims, and now these same groups have turned Pakistan into a problem to be dealt with.

Pakistan's ideological demise is by now a universally accepted reality. But that is not sufficient to pacify the anti-Islam ideologues. Besides its ideological demise, all factors and structures that keep a state intact from within have either given up altogether or are quickly collapsing. Pakistan is presently at the mercy of foreign forces. These factors have made it a high value target. The strategic approach demands that Pakistan should not be treated like Afghanistan.

The forces that keep Pakistan alive are the very forces planning its gradual downfall. They are sustaining it only to achieve specific objectives. The most strategic of these objectives is converting 162 million[1] people to the American version of "moderate Islam." Accordingly, it is better to make most Pakistanis think that the Qur'an is not the final manifesto of God and those believing in its totality are extremists rather than depriving them of a state called "Islamic" and leaving them to "radicalize" and exact their revenge.

Let us have a look at what makes Pakistan a high value target in the first place — a reality which is even recognized by Musharraf himself. Addressing a meeting of businessmen and industrialists in Lahore on January 18, 2003, he said it was being speculated that Pakistan would become the target of "western forces" after Iraq crisis and there were chances of such an eventuality. Musharraf was quoted as saying by *The News* daily (January 19, 2003): "We will have to work on our own to stave off the danger. Nobody will come to our rescue, not even the Islamic world. We will have to depend on our muscle."

Closed to three years later, Richard Norton-Taylor reported in *Guardian* (October 15, 2005) that Mr Bush said he "wanted to go beyond Iraq in dealing with WMD proliferation, mentioning in particular Saudi Arabia, Iran, North Korea, and Pakistan," according to a note of a telephone conversation between the two men on January 30 2003.

The note is quoted in the US edition, released in late October 2005, of *Lawless World, America and the Making and Breaking of Global Rules*, by the British international lawyer Philippe Sands. According to Mr Sands, the memo was drawn up by one of the prime minister's foreign policy advisers in Downing Street and passed to the Foreign Office.

Interestingly, what can save Pakistan is Islam and, at the same time, what has made it the high value target is also Islam. As Musharraf said, "We can talk to the US ... but how can we convince them on our points when the whole country echoes with the slogans of jihad [against the US]" (*Asia Times*, January 23, 2003). To address this "problem," Musharraf's "moderation" is nothing new. Analysts have been pointing out for many years that Pakistan is pretending to be a moderate state. Paula Newberg hinted back in 1994: "No longer a bulwark against falling dominoes in Afghanistan, Pakistan hopes to portray itself as a moderate Islamic state that can buffer extremist Iran, chaotic Afghanistan and an uncertain Central Asia."[2] Indian analysts argued that the face of moderation does not sit well with "Pakistan's decade-long reputation as the epicenter for three major internal security upheavals in India's state of Jammu and Kashmir, Afghanistan and Tajikistan. All these conflicts involve fundamentalist devout who have been clandestinely trained and supported by Pakistan's religious parties or its military."[3] These claims are made to keep fear of Islam and Pakistan alive.

The self-proclaimed moderates are complicating the matters even further, not only for the nation but for the "moderates" in uniform as well. In an attempt to undermine both Pakistan and Musharraf, Hussain Haqqani, for example, told a Zionist gathering on March 02, 2004 that indeed, there exists in Pakistan an underground terror network that Musharraf is not targeting "partially because he doesn't have the capacity to break it down [since] he and many of his military colleagues created this fire. When the ones who lit the fire are asked to put it out they still have some ideas about 'this part of the fire we like.'" Exaggerating the threat of Islam, Haqqani suggested that Pakistan also has, and continues, to serve as the center of an Islamic militant movement.[4]

Pakistan's religious identity has become a liability. Not being able to feel proud of it makes it difficult for Pakistan to get rid of it. The more the elites and military top brass run from this identity, the more the outsiders propagate the idea that an Islamic revolution in Pakistan will have repercussions for the whole region. While making his case against Pakistan, Uma Singh argues: "Besides their obvious repercussions in Central Asia and Afghanistan, these struggles could have potentially spill-over effects on India, with the world's second largest Muslim population and China with its restive Turkik Muslim minorities."[5] Pakistan is presented as a threat, larger than the inflated threat of the Taliban's government at its peak, in the overall geo-economic and strategic configuration, involving West Asia, Central Asia, China and Afghanistan. That's how it turns out to be a high value target.

Similarly, Pakistan's nuclear baggage has become another liability. Serving under the American flag in Afghanistan was supposed to have saved Pakistan from humiliation. Was not the nation told in ringing tones that by joining the Americans the regime had saved Pakistan's nuclear assets and its Kashmir policy? Now it turns out that the most endangered things of all are Pakistan's stand on Kashmir and its nuclear assets. As for those wretched assets, the masses were told that they were meant not for anything as grandiose as national sovereignty but for confronting India. However, when India turned up the heat on Pakistan, the weapons seemed to be of no use in that direction. And when there is a hope of peaceful relations with India, still these weapons are of no use.

On the external front, according to the *Wall Street Journal*, "Pakistan is next on the list, given close historical links between elements in its security services and al Qaeda. Were Al-Qaeda terrorists to acquire a nuclear device, could they successfully seize an opportunity to bring it to Paris, London, Berlin or Rome?... Reviewing this evidence, the world's most successful investor, Warren Buffett, has concluded: 'It will happen. It's inevitable.'"[6]

Writing in *Foreign Policy in Focus*, Michael T. Klare, Professor of Peace & World Security Studies, Hampshire College, made it clear before the Iraqi invasion that a policy "aimed at protecting the United States from WMD attacks would identify Pakistan and North Korea as the leading perils, and put Iraq in a rather distant third place." The reason again is Islam: He argues: "with anti-Americanism intensifying throughout the region, it is not hard to imagine these officers providing the militants with some of Pakistan's WMD weapons and technology. On the other hand, the current leadership in Iraq has no such ties with Islamic extremists; on the contrary, Saddam has been a life-long enemy of the militant Islamists and they view him in an equally hostile manner."[7]

A CATO institute study, released on March 05, 2003 presented Pakistan a greater threat than Iraq. According to the CATO Institute, add Pakistan to the list of "countries who pose a greater threat to American interests than Iraq, yet whom we're happy to cozy up to."[8] Around the same time, former deputy secretary of defense and currently the president of the Centre for Strategic and International Studies (CSIS), John J. Hamre, who is also one of the principal think-tanks, told the New York-based publication *India Abroad* in an interview published the week the US attacked Iraq that in his opinion the situation in Pakistan "poses more threat to the United States than does the situation in Iraq."[9] Mr. Hamre added that General Musharraf is "the best person to work with. We ought to be helping him to have better control over his country...The United States and India would suffer greatly if Pakistan fails."

We must then ask why did the US invade Iraq and not Pakistan? Those who are determined to establish that the invasion of Iraq was motivated by financial interests - not religion, culture or politics - argue in these terms without realizing that Iraq was totally pacified after years of genocidal sanctions and the destruction of all of its weapons which could have hurt the invading armies. Pakistan, on the other hand, is currently too hot for bullies to touch yet. So, before organizing the country's failure, Musharraf has to play a role. The role is pacification of the high value target.

Before going into the role Musharraf has to play, we have to note that for this specific role he is treated totally differently from other dictators and "rouge" states. Dr. Abudul Qadeer Khan's saga has proved this point to a great extent.

Dr. Khan, for his part, confessed that three consecutive chiefs of staff of the Pakistani army were involved in approving the trade in nuclear weapons technology with North Korea. This includes General Musharraf. In a move to silence Khan, Musharraf asked him to sign a confession under duress and then Musharraf pardoned Khan from prosecution. Did George Bush call for the removal of Musharraf from power in Pakistan? Did he call him a grave and impending threat to international security? Of course not! Musharraf is perceived as the only bastion against a growing Islamic fundamentalist movement in Pakistan. As a secular government, albeit one with an atrocious human rights record, Pakistan is deemed a valuable ally in fighting the resurgent Taliban in neighboring Afghanistan. In addition, he has to pacify 162 million Pakistanis.

Pacifying Pakistan is more important than removing it from the world map as a nuclear, Islamic State—no matter how cosmetic the Islamic title may be. Those Muslims who are being promoted as "moderate" and "practicing Muslims"[10] are doing their job to pacify the 162 million under mission "enlightened moderation" and "project Ijthihad." In fact, these highly praised "practicing" Muslims, such as Irshad Manji believe that "an uncritical acceptance of the Koran as the final manifesto of God" is one of the "disturbing cornerstones of Islam."[11]

Since the Qur'an is the threat, working on that project is more important than sweeping Pakistan off its feet. If anyone has reservations that no amount of "moderation," "enlightened moderation," or, in plain words, dilution of Islam will ever please the modern crusaders, then they should read the November 14, 2003 lead editorial of the *New York Times*. It reveals the mentality at work behind the ongoing struggle in the name of democracy and the war on terrorism. The 308 word editorial is sufficient for shattering the philosophy of Musharraf-like neo-mods of Islam who still doubt that terrorism, fundamentalism, Islamism and other such ideas are just ruses with are used to alienate Muslims from the Qur'an.

Commenting on the constitution-formulating efforts in Afghanistan, the *New York Times* writes that the draft includes some "promising aspirations...but there are also troubling aspects of this crucial document." What hurts it the most is:

> it [the constitution] says that no law can be contrary to the sacred religion of Islam. And it says the members of the Supreme Court should be educated in either civil law or Islamic law, a provision that raises the possibility of more judges who base their rulings on the Koran rather than civil law.

So, basing "rulings on the Koran" is a problem because it jeopardizes "the protection of core human rights in this document." The paper asks the United Nations and American officials "to push for language" that does not refer to the Qur'an. The *New York Times* then extends its appeal to the so-called international community: "The time is right for the international community to weigh in. This constitution must provide an enduring promise to all the Afghan people that their most basic freedoms are inalienable, not to be granted or withdrawn easily by a government, its courts or its religious leaders," as if any reference to the Qur'an directly undermines the "most basic freedoms."[12]

The grave concerns shown and the appeals made to the UN, the international community and US authorities in the *New York Times'* editorial are not the result of any direct threat of terrorism against the US. The concern is not because of the "curse" of Wahabi-ism or any other misinterpreted "brand of Islam." It is not because of any calls for *Jihad* against the US, or any other such propaganda themes that have been made the cornerstones of the war on Islam. It directly calls the world to help alienate Afghans from the Qur'an.

This same approach is being followed with the goal of "moderating" 162 million Pakistanis. The grand, multi-pronged, project is underway in which the military, NGOs, media (TV in particular) and politicians are playing a lead role. This grand project, with a slow poisoning effect, is keeping a check on those who want Pakistan quickly eliminated from the world map. Finding a "bold" project manager in the person of Musharraf, the architects of the war on Islam are taking it easy on Pakistan.

In March 2004, Colin Powell unveiled the plan to classify Pakistan as a "major non-NATO ally" and refrained from publicly criticizing Musharraf's handling of the controversy over Abdul Qadeer Khan.

In a reciprocal move, Pakistan's military dictator had to send tens of thousands of troops to occupy South Waziristan, and claim the surrounding of a "high-value target" from Al-Qaeda. Many lives have been lost since then but the "high-value-target" still remains one of the post September 11, 2001 mysteries. Many still do not know that Pakistan, itself a high value target, is implementing the US global designs against Islam at the local level in exactly the same manner. It has long surrendered and is under total control for achieving the higher objectives of the enemies of Islam, and more specifically the neo-cons, in the US.

It is not that Musharraf is in the habit of making claims that later proved to be incorrect. Undoubtedly, he declared the war in Afghanistan over; Osama and Mulla Omar dead; Daniel Pearl alive; 85 per cent Pakistanis his supporters, and the widely criticised referendum as "free, fair and transparent." He has actually made these statements with an intended purpose.

The purpose for lying about a "high value target" in tribal areas was just like the US claims about Weapons of Mass Destruction in Iraq. The objective was to use Pakistani forces for a war on Pakistan—for invasion, occupation, massacres, home demolitions and human right abuses—like any other occupation army. The occupation of South Waziristan was almost like invading another nation. This is the physical aspect of the grand project aimed at promoting the American version of Islam and eliminating all possible sources of future resistance.

Helicopter gunships have been used to fire from safe havens where it is impossible to separate a "terrorist" from accompanying civilians. Heavy artillery—an even more undiscriminating weaponry—are regularly deployed. American U-2 spy planes, flying at 70,000 feet, unmanned Predator drones, equipped with Hellfire missiles, and unattended ground sensors (UGS) dropped from air at passes on the Hindu Kush are examples of the technological weight thrown against a people in the name of getting control of "high value targets."

Well before Musharraf's declaration of a "high value target," the US had forced Pakistan to take all the necessary steps for a successful operation in areas which might produce a future Pakistani Taliban that could potentially launch a resistance against the US occupation of Pakistan. Stephen Cohen, writing in Washington Quarterly, warned that Islam "may now be the vehicle for Pashtun nationalism."[13] He reflected the fear that dwells in the heart of many Islamophobes that Pashtun nationalism might align with "Islamic radicalism." In that eventuality he fears the puppet "regime in Kabul and the integrity of Pakistan could be threatened." [14]

As a result of these fears, we witnessed extraordinary developments in Pakistan. In a sudden move, the Pashtun Corps Commander in Peshawar, Lieutenant-General Ali Jan Orakzai, was retired prematurely. Major General Safdar Hussain, from Punjab, took his place and instantly dispatched troops to South Waziristan.

The outgoing Orakzai was on Washington's black list since 2003, when he openly condemned as "discriminatory" the behavior of US authorities towards Pakistanis. He made these stinging remarks at functions hosted by the Pakistani embassy in the US. Despite being an official guest, Orakzai was forced to go through a plethora of humiliating security screenings and checks at immigration upon his arrival.

There were also some reports about the US authorities' special request of splitting the Pakistani armed forces along ethnic lines. It was proposed that in the next phase of Pakistan's war on Pakistan, all Pashtun officers should be separated from non-Pashtun officers. Pashtun are considered sympathetic to the ethnic Pashtun in the areas chosen for occupation. Being Pashtun, they are viewed as sharing the genes and religious commitment of the Taliban, and thus could pose a threat to the mission of secularizing the rank and file of the armed forces.

Several soldiers and a few officers of Pashtun origin have refused to participate in actions taken against the Pashtun tribes. As an example of who are actually chosen to serve in Wanna, a Major from Punjab, whose appeal for political asylum in Canada was rejected, went back and was instantly sent to Wanna. The decision on the case pertaining to his four-year absence and seeking asylum abroad was kept pending.

Traditionally, a majority of the Pakistani army comes from Punjab, but at the higher ranks the ratio of Punjabi and Pashtun officers was not too different. For the past few years, Pashtun officers have been greatly reduced in number. In recent promotions, 18 Punjabi brigadiers were elevated to the position of major general, while only one Pashtun earned the same title.

A number of colonels were arrested for refusing to fight against their own people in Waziristan. Who are these army officers, what is their background, and what judicial processes have they gone through? This is for journalists and human rights groups in Pakistan to investigate.

Just like all the flimsy and exaggerated reasons and logic for the so-called war on terrorism, justification for the Pakistan army to use force in the tribal areas in order to get rid of "Islamist militants" does not make any sense at all.

Using the US warlords' terminology makes it sound reasonable when Musharraf states he is "clearing Pakistani territory of foreign militants who are pursuing a global *Jihad*." What does not add up, however, is the fact that the same people, if they are there, were fully trained and supported by the US when their *Jihad* was against the Soviet occupation of Afghanistan.

Now the US supported "intellectuals" argue that: "Even those Pakistanis who until recently sympathized with the struggles of fellow Muslims under oppression, for example those of the Kashmiris, Palestinians and Chechens, are beginning to recognize that the methods of the Jihadis are a threat to global order." Do we see any change in the methods from the times of the Afghan *Jihad*? If not, why were they not a threat to global order then?

It is naïve to assume that Pakistanis have changed their minds because they "do not want their country to be subjected to an international military operation, like the ones in Afghanistan and Iraq." Such an argument fails to realize that there is no "global" operation in Iraq. As far Pakistan, it is already subjected to such an operation to the advantage of the US. Actually, it is Pakistan that is trapped as a "high value target," under the occupation of a military kept alive with American financial and logistical support. This military, in turn, is under a commander-in-chief, fully protected and supported by the US like a most valuable target.

Consequently, the desired domestic instability is well before our eyes, thanks to fellow Pakistanis' full participation in the intellectual and physical crusade. Before pulling the plug on Pakistan, its military had to be taken care of. Thus, the military, the only intact institution in Pakistan, is on the way towards gradual and total disintegration. Its public image has already been shattered beyond repair. The family members of Pakistani forces not only have difficulty reconciling to the loss of lives resulting from battles with fellow Muslims, they are also doubtful of their family members' status in the hereafter.

A mere doubt about the objective of killing fellow countrymen is sufficient for sapping the morale of the armed forces and splitting it into different factions. It is even better for the US if it doesn't split over its mission under the grand project because it will confirm effective secularization and ensure success in future adventures. The transition from *Jihad- fi-sabeelillah* (*Jihad* in the cause of Allah) to *Jihad* in the cause of America has put the final nail in the coffin of the army's respect in civilian eyes. Evidence for the rising mistrust of the army is that on June 10, 2004, the Corps Commander's car was attacked in Karachi. Six soldiers and three policemen were killed in the incident along with a civilian bystander.[15]   The chief of the armed forces has never been attacked in Pakistan, whereas Musharraf was attacked twice. Although Al-Qaeda was named instantly, in fact it was a military man, Mohammed Islam Siddiqui, who was charged and hanged.[16]

The negative fallout of Pakistan's military war on Pakistan would have been worth it if it had been an overt part of Musharraf's strategic decision to close the chapter of Pakistan's *raison d'être*, change the motto of the armed forces and openly declare the country a secular state and its armed forces a professional army. It is not that this issue is removed from Musharraf's and his promoters' agenda. It is that the he and his backers think this is the wrong time for such bold declarations. The objective is to keep working toward this eventuality until the nation is soft enough to bear the shock of hearing that they have been perfectly liberated from Islam.

There are always going to be "high-value-targets" before every new operation in the "war on terror" and unbelievable claims, such as "Zawahiri and Uzbek cleric Qari Tahir Yaldash are trapped." These claims are then downplayed at the end of the bloody adventures for pacifying local populations and neutralizing every fear of resistance.

The close to 80,000 Pakistani troops which have been scouring the tribal areas in tandem with the US Task Force 121, CIA cells and British SAS troops will never get the "high value targets," because they are either not there in the first place, or getting them is not a priority at the moment. The real focus is actually on wearing down the "most high value target" of all—Pakistan.

US aggression and occupation, which is a part of the 21st century crusade against Islam and Muslims, will be achieved person by person and tribe by tribe. Like Lieutenant General Safdar Hussain, there would be other commanders, singling out other tribes like Yargul Khel, stating: "I'm determined to punish this tribe and make them an example." More and more innocents will be forced by the thousands to leave their homes and orchards, which are a source of the livelihood and very existence. It is just the beginning of the war on the Pakistani front.

The actual "high value target"—Pakistan—has already been captured. Musharraf, however, believes he will be able to deceive the East and the West simultaneously for a long time without losing the goose that lays the golden eggs for him. Undoubtedly, even the power of America has failed to secure the submission of Iraqis. Earlier, the Afghans brought the Soviet power to its knees. The problem, however, is the cost. In the case of Pakistan, losses would be phenomenal and in the end Pakistan would most probably not remain what it is today. The armed forces ruling and operating without the support of the people will always prove to be powerless in the long run, irrespective of their winning a few battles for the US and irrespective of the US strategic planners' pride over capturing the "high value target."

With so much planning underway to undermine Pakistan externally and so many internal forces working to sell the country out, in the immediate future Pakistan will keep exercising Tony Blair's option of saying yes to every America demand. If, in the words of the *Guardian*'s writer Hugo Young, even Britain is being treated as an American puppet, how much higher can a dictator help Pakistan set its sights? Anti-Pakistani forces will not be needed to bring about the demise of the country, it will be destroyed from within as a result of its acquiescence to American demands and its willingness to sell its soul for a miserable pottage.

Expediting the Demise

PAKISTANIS are still not reading the writing on the wall. They will, however, soon face the music they deserve for losing a golden opportunity of self-rule in an independent, sovereign state. People get the kind of leadership they deserve. At the same time, people with good intentions get equally punished through the effects of unthinking compliance when they refuse to act or fail to make a difference. Iraq and Afghanistan are two clear examples before us.

Iraqis failed to muster enough courage to stand against a weaker Baathist and secularist regime, to establish an exemplary society and a model of governance. They are now paying a far greater price then they would have, had they stood up to Saddam Husain's externally supported tyranny.

Similarly, Afghans lost their opportunity. Instead of collectively working for the common good of their people after having an unprecedented situation of peace, law and order in the country under the Taliban, many Afghans joined campaigns that ended with yet another foreign occupation of their country—this time with the full approval of the United Nations. The result is before our eyes. Afghans, who were delivered from one occupation at a great cost, are now reeling under another indefinite and far worse occupation.

Some analysts have expressed concern that Pakistan is next in line. Others predict Pakistan's failure on the basis of their respective parameters of success and failure of states. From the discussion in the preceding chapters, we can clearly see that Musharraf is the main factor among many others that has made Pakistan's demise inevitable.

The "with us or against us" threat from Bush and subsequent Islamabad policies provide evidence that Musharraf is clearly under pressure. Nevertheless, the list of decisions leading to his willing surrenders is so long that Musharraf can hardly pretend that he is not acting under pressure from within and outside. So far, he is a victim of his delusions, obsession with staying in power and a compulsive attitude of putting everything at stake to achieve his objectives.

This was the case with Mikhail Gorbachev also. Even his adversaries concede that he took the much vaunted initiatives under immense internal and external pressure. However, he had this to say in his famous Nobel Lecture on June 05, 1991:

> Now about my position. As to the fundamental choice, I have long ago made a final and irrevocable decision. Nothing and no one, no pressure, either from the right or from the left, will make me abandon the positions of *perestroika* and new thinking. I do not intend to change my views or convictions. My choice is a final one.

Similarly, advisors to Musharraf ensure that he takes all the blame, thus paving the way for the fall of Pakistan.

In the face of the country's inevitable demise, Pakistanis are still in total denial despite the fact that they cannot provide a single ray of hope that could make them believe that, unlike the great empires of the past, the vulnerable Pakistan is immortal and will survive indefinitely.

The long-term involvement of the military in Pakistani politics and the role it has played for Washington all along is a factor of prime importance in understanding the latest changes as discussed in chapter 5. Musharraf, nevertheless, keeps on gambling on anything he can think of at the moment. His particular theme is "enlightened moderation", which embodies secularism and undermines Pakistan's *raison d'être*.

In *Diplomacy*, Henry Kissinger shrewdly explains the impossible dilemma that Khrushchev eventually perceived, and Gorbachev did not: Gorbachev's gamble on liberalization was bound to fail to the degree that the Communist Party also lost its monolithic character. The same phenomenon applies to Pakistan's losing its monolithic character at the hands of Musharraf. The galvanizing force that brought Pakistan into being was Islam; not culture, nor ethnicity, not even language or geography. Nothing supports its creation and survival.

The loss of faith in Islam has led to the loss one half of Pakistan in 1971, and continues to weaken the rest of the nation with every passing day. There is no other justification at all for separating this piece of land in South Asia, calling it Pakistan, or keeping people of different cultures and ethnic backgrounds together for a long time. If a secular state was the objective, a single independent state of India made more sense than two separate entities, which drained their resources on arms building and bloody wars.

At war with their country's identity, Pakistanis hardly realize it is going through a phase similar to that of the Soviet Union before its demise. After losing its identity and character, the communist party became demoralized. Similarly, masses have become totally demoralized in Pakistan. Just as liberalization proved incompatible with communist rule—the communists could not turn themselves into democrats without ceasing to be communists, an equation Gorbachev never understood—the kind of "moderation" Musharraf proposes is totally incompatible with Islam.

As we discussed previously, Musharaff's "enlightened moderation" has nothing to do with Islam. Musharraf simply wants effective subservience to the continued remote control colonialism of the US. Muslims cannot turn themselves into the kinds of "moderates" demanded by the inventors of these rancid notions without ceasing to be Muslims, an equation Musharraf fails to understand in his pursuit for staying in power at any cost.

The whole idea of the secularization of Pakistan to make it functional is based on the assumption that Pakistan, and other Muslim countries, can survive without being Islamic or democratic in the true sense and that they can endure a compromise on the principles on which Muslims must put the foundation of their collective life. At the same time, a serious attempt to live by Islam could not occur without risking the labels of extremism and terrorism.

Despite Turkey's 80-years experiment with secularization, it has yet to succeed. Countries like Turkey and Egypt, for example, have long histories as nations to survive. Whereas, Pakistan didn't exist as a nation before 1947, nor any other known factor except Islam is there to make it a nation. As such Musharraf's regime took to de-legitimizing Pakistan's entire foundation. He is being rewarded and applauded like a Gorbachev reincarnate for transforming Islam.

Writing about Gorbachev, *Times* magazine noted: "By gently pushing open the gates of reform, he unleashed a democratic flood that deluged the Soviet universe and washed away the cold war." [1] Such inspiring comments are used by the Western media to push their perceived enemies into thinking they would transform their societies into worldly heavens if they toe Washington's line. But that is not what actually happens when push comes to shove. According to Jamie Glazov's analysis: "Within the blink of an eye, the Soviet Union disintegrated. Ten years later, we know that the process of true democratization in post-communist Russia ultimately failed. Boris Yeltsin and now Vladimir Putin, after all, represent a return to the Russian autocratic past. With no tradition of democracy, or even a conception of individuality, Russians, once again, desire order over freedom."[2]

Musharraf attempted simultaneously to contain and transform the country in the image of its enemies, to destroy and reconstruct, right on the spot as per the plans of those for whom existence of Pakistan has been a thorn in the flesh since its inception. Musharraf is doing what Gorbachev did in his six years in power. The changes in what used to be the Soviet Union have been so great that it is easy to forget what the un-reformed Soviet system was like and how modest were the expectations of significant innovation when Gorbachev succeeded Konstantin Chernenko as top Soviet leader in March 1985. Neither Soviet citizens nor foreign observers or advisors to Gorbachev imagined that the USSR was about to be transformed out of existence. So is the case with Musharraf and Pakistan.

While no one predicted the Soviet Union's demise, the greatest skeptics regarding the prospects for change were the first to be overtaken by events. Some, who in more recent years have castigated Gorbachev for his "half-measures," have conveniently forgotten that the actual changes promoted or sanctioned by him exceeded their wildest dreams, making nonsense of predictions that he had neither the will nor the power to alter anything of consequence in the Soviet system. Here, we must keep in mind that the changes under Gorbachev far exceeded their wildest dreams because Gorbachev alone was not responsible. The Soviet Union's demise was also impending, like Pakistan's, for quite some time. The changes and transformation by one man became the last straw on the back of the proverbial camel. In Pakistan's case, as we discussed in previous chapters, the 162 million Pakistanis have already paved the way with their unintentional surrender to the forces that will wash away Pakistan as an entity. Musharraf's gimmicks are going to just hasten its demise.

In his book, *The Gorbachev Factor*, Archie Brown correctly points out:

"When it became fashionable to react against the enthusiastic support for Gorbachev which was widespread in the late 1980s, the same observers who misread Gorbachev's intentions at the outset became the first to scorn an excessive concentration on the part played by Gorbachev while simultaneously, and with scant regard for logic, holding him personally responsible for all the major policy failures. And failures in the Gorbachev era there certainly were—especially of economic policy and in the relationships between the Soviet Union's constituent republics and the centre."[3]

The phenomenon that took place in the USSR well before Gorbachev's taking power perfectly fits the situation in Pakistan before Musharraf's coup. The remarkable thing about change in the Soviet Union during the Gorbachev years was that it occurred peacefully. As we shall see below, unlike the Soviet Union, the transformation in South Asia is more likely to be violent. According to Archie Brown: "Given the failure of all who had openly attacked the system from within the country to make any positive impact on policy outcomes prior to the late 1980s, it is doubtful if change of such magnitude could have taken place with so little violence—especially in Russia—in any way other than through the elevation of a serious reformer to the highest political office within the country."

In the case of Pakistan, the public in general and politicians and military in particular have constantly been either attacking or exploiting Islam, yet no one had the intention to seriously live by Islam and make Pakistan an Islamic State. Musharraf imposed himself on the nation as an intermediary and justified his dictatorship on the basis of being a serious reformer. Yet the political parties and his foreign backers fell into his series of traps. The former acted blindly and the latter just pretending to be blind. Consequently, the Western backers purposely elevated him to the position of a serious reformer. They know that Musharraf has no real vision other than a desire to stay in power. But his promoters, in fact, do have a vision. The public's complacency and helplessness simply exacerbated the situation.

The prospect of a military dictator becoming a "president" acceptable to all is similar to a reformer (Gorbachev) becoming General Secretary of the Communist party—the very idea that such a thing was possible in principle—had been ruled out in advance by many Western observers and by such prominent exiles from the Soviet Union as the writers Alexander Solzhenitsyn and Alexander Zinoviev. Similarly, Bush refused to acknowledge Musharraf by name in his initial interviews after his first inaugurations. When a reporter insisted that the General must have a name, Bush said: "Well, we call him a General."[4]

Yet, just like Gorbachev who had great power concentrated in his hands as part of the Communist Party leaders collectively and as the General Secretary individually, the forces for anti-Islam-transformation in Pakistan realized that a person with many hats, absolute power and opportunist disposition in Pakistan should remain in power to follow their agenda. Without the promotion of a genuine reformer and highly skilled politician to the top Communist Party post in 1985, fundamental changes in the Soviet Union would certainly have been delayed and could well have been bloodier as well as slower than the relatively speedy political evolution that occurred while Gorbachev was at the helm. The same plan is being implemented in Pakistan to make its demise less bloody on the one hand and use the outcome for global struggle against Islam on the other. To the disadvantage of Musharraf's promoters, replication of the same plan is not possible under different situations, particularly when instead of an "ism" a religious faith and a way of life are being targeted: This is the case not only in Pakistan, but on a global level.

Analysts agree that in the case of the Soviet Union, from the moment Gorbachev "was liberated after the August coup, his every political statement, his every initiative, seemed to have preservation of the central structure as its main objective. That freedom from the central bureaucracy was what the republics meant by the independence they were demanding seemed to elude him."[5] In the Muslim world, the US adventures, coupled with relying on "reformation" by a few opportunists is likely to bring about the liberation of Muslim masses—the consequence which the enemies of Islam are actually trying to avoid.

In the past, Western planners wanted to dismantle the Soviet Union and various factors played a role in facilitating this demise. Gorbachev presented the reformation in the name of improving the Soviet economy. The reality, in Archie Brown's words, is:

> No one, though, really needed to be an economist to see that the Soviet economy was going from bad to worse. The man and woman on the street anywhere between Minsk and Khabarovsk could have said the same. And since this was neither Stalin's nor Brezhnev's time but an era of Soviet history of unprecedented freedom, they frequently did.[6]

Western politicians and planners, however, did not base their judgments entirely on the state of the Soviet economy, but accorded a great deal of weight to changes in the language of politics, to new departures in Soviet foreign policy, and to political institutional change, where they did not see any alternative that challenged the supremacy of the West. They mistakenly, and very unfortunately, see this threat now in Islam with Pakistan's nuclear capability at its centre. With their understanding of politics, Western planners were constantly amazed to see Gorbachev pull off what seemed to them virtually impossible feats. Today they see these feats in Musharraf's "chance meetings" with Ariel Sharon and his dining with the American Jewish Congress.

The foreign advisors to Musharraf are more aware than many of the academic observers and the self-proclaimed "moderate" Muslims of the framework of constraints within which Musharraf is operating and of the balancing act which is at times demanded of him prior to his putting sovereignty, independence and the very identity of his nation at stake.

The process of undermining Pakistan is gradual. Many ideas that are openly discussed in the Pakistani mass media under

Musharraf, and in a number of cases translated into public policy, had first been aired in communist and secularist circles in Pakistan before the fall of the Soviet Union. The only difference is that of the use of rancid notions invented in the wake of the end of communism. This terminology now solely focuses on creating divisions among Muslims and demonizing Islam. Moreover, the Soviet Union could not promote its comrades and godless ideology abroad as vigorously as the neo-cons and the millions of Christian Zionists in America are doing in an organized and systematic manner.

That, however, does not mean that this is a simple case of continuity. In fact, the changes of the Musharraf era are more than a continuation of a process the secularists and communists had begun. There was a total lack of positive response to the demands and theories of such elements between 1968 and 1991. A few secularists had dared to speak up. However, many more had decided that discretion was the better part of valour, and stayed quiet until Musharraf had made Pakistan safe for such adventures. Some of them, such as the famous poet, Faiz Ahmad Faiz, didn't even openly challenge the ideology of Pakistan. They were just sending out messages in the name of labor and the working class. Yet they were considered as a threat to national security and were thrown behind bars for years. The measures used against those who made their political dissent unambiguous and public ranged from compulsory exile to incarceration.

Under Musharraf, the world in Pakistan has turned full circle. Former secularists and communists are thriving in the garb of "moderates". Nevertheless, the secular movement retrospectively commands little respect. To see them as the prime agents of pro-US changes in Pakistan is highly misleading and a product largely of wishful thinking. They are playing a role in changing the political consciousness of a part of the intelligentsia after initially donning the garb of liberals and now decorating it with the badges of "moderate Muslims." And that is why the blame for the demise of Pakistan will not go to Musharraf alone. He remains the factor that galvanized the movement that is making the nation's demise inevitable.

On the external front, Musharraf's approach has changed the perceptions and demands of the sustainers-cum-enemies of Pakistan completely. Pakistan has already lost the trust of its neighbors because of the unreliable and unpredictable roles that it plays for the US. Instead of providing them a sense of safety and security, Pakistan became a source of anxiety for its neighbors. It can play a role in attacking Iran for its sustainers in Washington, just as it did in the case of paving the way for the occupation of Afghanistan. Similarly, Musharraf's Pakistan is no longer one of China's staunchest friends as it used to be over the years. Iran would not be too deeply concerned about the fate of Pakistan's large Shi'a minority as the experience in Iraq shows, and India would reap most of the fruits in the absence of a check on expansion of its regional hegemony and without any prospect of violence and disorder on its Western borders.

After bringing Afghanistan to its present state and abandoning even moral support for both Kashmiris and Palestinians, Pakistan is no more needed as a Muslim nuclear power in the region. Totally controlled by Washington, its nuclear program and capability has become completely irrelevant. Instead, it is now the other way round. The rest of the world would not feel concerned about the disposition of a failing Pakistan's nuclear weapons and fissile material, which it already knows is in "safe hands." The US and Europeans' hue and cry about Iran's and North Korea's nuclear programs and a total silence about now occupied Pakistan's nuclear program is a telling sign of the assurance that the weapons are in "safe hands."

In the beginning of the book, we set a simple formula to see if there is any possibility that a positive development can take root in the Musharraf era and lead Pakistan towards safe waters. Our assessment in the subsequent chapters demonstrated that the

Musharraf factor has led to an environment in which any positive development, which can put Pakistan on the right track, has
become totally impossible.

Achieving the objective for which it was created is impossible
(chapter 2). The full restoration of democratic government and
the efficient rebuilding of the Pakistani state in the future is also
clearly impossible (chapter 3). There are no signs of the emergence of a revolutionary or radical political movement. Pakistan
will remain under the occupation of its own military forces: a
kind of sweet occupation. Masses will remain helpless until they
are completely pushed against the wall like the Iraqis and Afghans. Musharraf will continue to dance to the Zionist and neo-
cons' tune until he has absolutely nothing left to gamble with. A
major push will come to turn Pakistan into another Afghanistan
or Iraq when the high value target is completely softened.

Pakistan's disappearance from the world map is actually induced by certain features of the army—its conceptual ability to
plan incremental change. It is mistakenly considered a plus for
reforming the country's ailing institutions. Analysts believed that
Pakistan's army is strong enough to prevent state failure but not
imaginative enough to impose the changes that might transform
Pakistan either in the image for which it was created or the image which the US wants it to adopt. Musharraf calls his mantra
of "enlightened moderation" as a two pronged strategy. Unfortunately, rather than transforming, the strategy and change, which
opportunist civilian and military cronies surrounding general
Musharraf have chosen, will gradually sink Pakistan into oblivion.
This issue was thoroughly covered in Chapter 1.

As for nationhood, despite the dominant position of the armed
forces, including a veto over any attempt to change the consensus view of Pakistan's identity, the army hardly seems willing to
create an identity compatible with the vision of Pakistan, as well
as with the objectives that led to its creation.

Pakistan's most unusual feature is not its potential as a failed state, as we observed from the earlier discussion, but the intricate interaction between the physical/political/legal entity known as the state of Pakistan and the idea behind Pakistan and the Pakistani nation. Few if any other nation states are more complex than Pakistan in this respect, with the Pakistani state often operating at cross-purposes with the original purpose of its creation.

Regardless of all other factors, the US and UK have publicly launched a war on the very basic ideology at the foundation of Pakistan as a nation. It is akin to separating Jewish identity from Israel. Imagine the transformation in the Middle East if Israel were to stop identifying itself as a Jewish State. In that case, would it be able to justify its existence and occupation of the lands, particularly Jerusalem? The problem in the case of any Muslim entity, however, is that it can either be Islamic or non-Islamic (secular). As discussed in the Chapter 2 in detail, it is not possible to have a mix of secularism and Islam and label it as Muslim. Like Israel, the state of Pakistan was thought to be more than a physical/legal entity that provided welfare, order and justice to its citizens. Pakistan was to be an extraordinary state—a homeland for Indian Muslims and an ideological and political leader of the Muslim world. Providing a homeland to protect Muslims from the bigotry and intolerance of India's Hindu population was important, but the real motive behind Pakistan movement was to demonstrate to the world a model of an Islamic State based on the principles of freedom, fraternity and equality of Islam. The Pakistan movement also looked to the wider Muslim world, and its leaders were concerned about the fate of other Muslim communities living under duress, stretching from Palestine to the Philippines.[7]

This is exactly what is now considered as "political Islam" of the "Islamists." This is what the 9/11 Commission has referred to as the "Islamic ideology" and declared a war on it. Accordingly, Pakistan has to be dismantled because its *raison d'être* has no place in the modern world in which a crusade on Islam is now officially and publicly recognized. We observe this from the official report of the 9/11 Commission, statements from Bush, Rumsfeld and British Home Secretary Charles Clark within the span of just one week.[8] Islamic ideology is the threat and a war on it has been declared. In his speech on October 06, 2005, Bush equated all resistance against the US occupation of Iraq, which was made possible through a series of many lies and distortion of facts, to fighting on the part of "terrorists" for the creation of "an Islamic Empire."[9] Now think about the following words and comments by the founding fathers of Pakistan. Imagine any nation under occupation or any Muslim leader now saying the following words. They would perfectly fit the well-defined category on which a war has officially been declared. Also note Pakistan's founder Muhammad Ali Jinnah's reference to the Qur'an, *Mujahids*, Islam and giving protection to neighbors in the following words at a rally on October 30, 1947:

> If we take our inspiration and guidance from the Holy Qur'an, the final victory, I once again say, will be ours... Do not be overwhelmed by the enormity of the task... You only have to develop the spirit of the *Mujahids*. You are a nation whose history is replete with people of wonderful character and heroism. Live up to your traditions and add to another chapter of glory. All I require of you now is that everyone... must vow to himself and be prepared to sacrifice his all... in building up Pakistan as a bulwark of Islam and as one of the greatest nations whose ideal is peace within and peace without... Islam enjoins on every Mussulman to give protection to his neighbors and to minorities regardless of caste and creed.[10]

The same is true today. However, just a vow to make Pakistan, or any country for that matter, into a "bulwark of Islam," taking "inspiration and guidance from the Holy Qur'an," are now sufficient today to instantly declare anyone an "Islamist" preaching "Islamism" at which the US has declared a war. If Jinnah were living today and had uttered these same words he would most certainly have been labeled a terrorist, demonized in the media, hunted down by the US and prosecuted. The US expects from the opportunist dictators and "moderate Muslims" to care about poverty alleviation and forget about their brothers and sisters under foreign occupation. Musharraf has clearly mentioned this in his televised speech on January 12, 2002. Other "moderates" in the pages of *New York Times* tell fellow Muslims: "Muslims must realize that the interests of our sons and daughters, who are American, must come before the interests of our brothers and sisters, whether they are Palestinian, Kashmiri or Iraqi"[11]—an approach which is not only in total contradiction to the message of the Qur'an, but to the basic human values and ethics as well.

At the time of the creation of Pakistan, when the Muslim League adopted the Pakistan resolution on March 23, 1940 calling for the establishment of a sovereign and independent Islamic country, Lord Zetland, Secretary of State for colonial India, wrote of his apprehensions regarding this proposition to Lord Linlithgow, the British viceroy in New Delhi, saying:

> [T]he call of Islam is one which transcends the bounds of country. It may have lost some force as a result of the abolition of Caliphate by Mustafa Kamal Pasha, but it still has a very considerable appeal as witness for example Jinnah's insistence on our giving undertaking that Indian troops should never be employed against any Muslim state, and the solicitude which he has constantly expressed for the Arabs of Palestine.[12]

These apprehensions were ignored for other reasons in 1947. However, the creation of Pakistan on these grounds would have been impossible in the 21st century. So, its survival is at stake today when for the most powerful man in Pakistan, words of its founders and the motive behind the Pakistan movement are no more than a mere joke that can be completely ignored and cast aside.

Both the history and the future of Pakistan are rooted in a complex relationship between Pakistan the "Islamic" state—a physically bounded territory with an Islamic legal and international personality that would be guided by Islamic scriptures and traditions—and Pakistan the nation—mission-bound to serve as a beacon for oppressed or backward communities elsewhere in the world. Pakistan has bitterly failed at both the state and the national level. The rot that started at the top has trickled to the roots and the nation as a whole is as oblivious of its responsibilities as are its leaders.

On the other hand, the forces that undermine Pakistan are nevertheless alive and well focused. Details about how Pakistan has become the high value target were outlined in Chapter 8. Suffice it to present here the following signs that show a large number of forces are bent upon dissolving Pakistan into oblivion.

1. Israelis are topping tourist lists in Kashmir where businesses are changing the language of their outlets' signboards from English to Hebrew.[13] We must note that after Israeli agents' involvement in New Zealand and Canadian passport scams, the visitors in Kashmir could neither be ordinary Israelis nor would they be visiting Kashmir only for vacation purposes.

2. The Pentagon recently stressed that it must recruit and train Pakistani military officers to increase Washington's influence over the country's armed forces. Paul Wolfowitz told the House Armed Services Committee on August 10, 2004 that failure to train Pakistani officers could mean "pushing them into the one alternative, which is the Islamic extremists…It's not as though if we leave them alone, nobody else will go out to recruit them."[14]

3. According to the argument of the US-led "international community": Iran must bring its nuclear program to an end and Pakistan's nuclear arsenal must be in safe hands, but Israel's weapons of mass destruction must remain a "must-have."[15]

4. In total contradiction to the founding vision, the approach of Musharraf's regime is to leave Kashmiris' fate in Indian hands and push Afghan refugees back into occupied Afghanistan. Some 200,000 Afghan refugees have been living in the remote border areas of Pakistan. As the Pakistani operations in the tribal area have risen in strength, countless refugee

homes are destroyed and thousands of Afghans are pushed back into Afghanistan.[16] According to the *New York Times*: "Refugees have been given as little as two hours' notice to leave before their houses were bulldozed, according to officials with the office of the United Nations High Commissioner for Refugees. Some have returned to Afghanistan with no belongings, homeless once again."[17]

5. Almost all Pakistanis in the NGO-sector and many politicians to the level of former Prime Minter Zafrullah Khan Jamali have come to believe that the source of Pakistan's creation, the Two Nations Theory, is no longer valid.[18]

6. After facilitating the occupation of Afghanistan, Musharraf and his inner circle used the SAARC summit as a forum for direct and secret meetings with India's top brass. This was in order to consolidate a US inspired secret agreement to smooth the path for Pakistan in accepting Kashmir as an integral part of India against existing UN resolutions. Musharraf announced the deal after a closed meeting with Vajpayee on January 6, 2003 when he said: "History has been made...The string that was broken at Agra has been repaired in Islamabad". After a phone conversation the next morning with Vajpayee, Musharraf confirmed that: "The deal was sealed". A cautious, secretive and incremental process has been adopted in order for India and Pakistan to work jointly in eliminating the threats to the understanding. Officials from Pakistan and India were very nervous with regards to a leak.

7. Despite Pakistan's surrender on every front, India signed a $1 billion purchase of Phalcon Airborne Early Warning Systems deal with Israel in October 2003. The US, Canada and others have recently extended assistance in nuclear research to India.

8. Despite Musharraf's sacrificing Pakistani soldiers for the US, the US kept on accusing it of a secret nuclear pact with Saudi Arabia, [19] selling nuclear technology and for being insincere

to the US.[20] A CATO study called Pakistan's cooperation "grudging and spotty."[21] These factors amount to keeping options of the US and its allies' open in preparation for the impending U-turn on Pakistan in case there is an attempt to make it an Islamic State according to the mission and vision of the founding masses and the very objective of its creation.

9. As the nation that was supposed to be mission-bound to serve as a beacon for oppressed or backward communities elsewhere in the world is lost in Bollywood or cricket and corruption, the government is devoted to revising the school curriculum for teaching them submissiveness to occupation and aggression.

The above summary may not reflect the extent to which Pakistanis as a whole have undermined Pakistan. What is undeniable and known is that ideologically Pakistan has long been dead. If there are any traces of its still lingering on invisibly, the US war on it will deal with it appropriately. Its leftover physical existence neither makes a difference, nor is likely to survive without its soul for too long.

A combination of factors discussed above will therefore ensure that total pacification and ultimate softening of Pakistan remains a priority while it keeps on acquiring the characteristics of a place in which the ghosts of all legendary dictators would feel at home. That's how the collapse of the present structure and form will take place simultaneously with the emergence of a new order.

The status quo until now has faced no serious challenge in Pakistan, despite the fact that the regime is still fragile, dithering and jittery. The day the simmering rage turns into real resistance in the wake of the masses being pushed against the wall like the case in Iraq or Afghanistan, no one knows if the regime will exercise repression on the scale which we witness by occupation forces in Iraq, Afghanistan and Palestine. The alternative is that the military itself will split into factions. What is known is that the regime is neither sure of itself, nor is the US a credible master to rely on, at least, in terms of its own survival as a super power, as well as in terms of its long record of betraying its "friends." Taiwan is the latest example of the US making a U-turn when there is more money to be made from China. Musharraf and his "moderate" allies are treading a very thorny path by taking themselves out of the fold of Islam when looked in the light of the definitions and requirements put forward by the American promoters of the new version of Islam (refer to chapter 2).

Any major incident or event can explode into a 9/11 in South Asia and become a turning point. More awareness and exposure of the agenda behind Musharaff's "enlightened moderation" increases the possibility of a South Asian 9/11, the day after which life will not be the same. Rather than stability, an increased support for the collaborating "moderates" will bring more turmoil as a result of the increased polarization in the society.

Faced with some unexpected challenges at home and abroad, the regime in Islamabad will initially try to go for the option of repression. With the failure of repressive measures, the regime might then attempt to lurch toward some "democratic" maneuvers. But in the turbulence added from external events and interference, "democratic" antics would not stand much of chance of maintaining the status quo. If Pakistan's Gorbachev is alive, he will be a pathetic figure in this whole saga. He has nothing to offer that would place the Pakistan nation on the right track, except playing the role of a mercenary-in-chief of the final crusade. He will find himself standing as an arrogant disciple of something far worse than secularism at a time when evangelicals and Zionists (including the Bush administration) are busy shaping the world according to their apocalyptic religious perspective. Some analysts still argue that Bush does use religious language sometimes, but that is rhetoric because the same events would be happening if the oil fields were controlled by Christians or Jews or a secular state, who were not interested in selling oil to the USA. In fact, Bush's October 6, 2005 speech proves that the sitting administration wants to destroy Islam and turn it into a Christianity-like religion consisting of a few hallow rituals and strip Muslims of their values concerning morality, economy, social conduct and political ideology. Moreover, we know that Saddam Hussain was a lame duck. He was prepared to surrender anything to come back to the former days of glory. For the US, oil, particularly Iraqi, was not a problem at all.

Anything can spark the South Asian 9/11 and a subsequent movement. It could be a direct foreign intervention after miscalculating the softness of the high value target (chapter 8) or it could be sparked internally on general issues of concern, such as unemployment, poverty, privatization, price hikes and repression of the suffering masses. In the former case, Pakistanis will learn and react the way Iraqis or Afghans are reacting after being pushed against the wall. In the latter case, the demands for addressing general issues will rapidly attain a political and ideological character in view of the greater realization of the objectives behind the "war on terrorism," "enlightened moderation," wars for "liberation" and winning "the heart and minds" of Muslims.

After lying about "Weapons of Mass Destruction" in Iraq in order to justify the country's invasion and occupation, Bush now openly claims that his revised objective is to not let Muslims "establish a radical Islamic empire that spans from Spain to Indonesia."[22] It would enter the political plane and then the whole system that is structured to support the 21st century crusade will become a threat to its own survival. Such an upheaval would actually lead to a real breakup of the elite, military and feudal class lines and the very system they are exploiting to suppress the masses and serve the interests of the imperial-capitalist order.

This whole process will unravel in ebbs and flows, depending on the developments on the external and internal fronts. The masses will learn through the experience and the rapidly changing objective situation on both fronts. The helplessness described in chapter 4 will lead to depression and desperation. As intentions of the totalitarians in Washington and London are exposed, no set of peculiar gadgets, gimmicks and cover ups will help conceal the reality to clutter the political horizon of society with falsehoods. The revolutionary storm of a mass upsurge will wash them away. What we witness at the moment, from liberalism on the left and reformism on the right, from secularism to moderatism, are all different sorts of peculiar smokescreens blown up to cover up despotic dictatorships at home and bloody interventions from outside. The objective of these cover-ups is to hinder and discourage the masses in Muslim countries from establishing an alternative system based on the message of Islam. But this is what will happen as a result of approaches undertaken to sustain the corrupt order.

The oppressed masses of Pakistan have suffered through this ordeal of "democracies" and dictatorships. These are political superstructures of an outdated, exploitative and rapacious socio-economic system of the former colonialists, sustained by the present totalitarians and their global financial institutions. Under the dictatorship, the masses yearned and fought for democracy. The political leadership fooled them into the delusion that democracy would solve all their problems. But it was all loot and plunder. Their miseries intensified. Religious parties also exploited religious sentiments of the masses who cannot tell the differences between them and other exploiters of the godless order imposed on them. With the continued suffering, they have also learnt from the hard school of experience that none of the exploiters in the political parties has a strategy to steer the masses towards establishing a just socio-political and economic order based upon the teachings of Islam.

The helpless masses are quiet but their eyes and ears are open. And they are thinking—developing a new consciousness—a revolutionary one that will inevitably explode unto the scene. Some readers may wonder, from where such a spark would appear to galvanize the masses in such a state of total despair and help-lessness. The answer to this lies in the October 8, 2005 earth-quake in Pakistan, which according to a broad assessment by the World Bank and Asian Development Bank took lives of more than 86,000 people and left 350,000 homeless (Reuters, November 8, 2005). It exposed the worst face of the so-called government and its feet of clay. And the same exposed the potential and the spark in the masses which led to the creation of Pakistan in the first place.

According to the reports thousands of Pakistanis were willing to travel all the way to the far flung areas in the quake hit areas of Balakot or Muzaffarabad to deliver relief goods but they were reluctant to hand over anything to any government agency. So much for the trust in the government and credibility of its institutions! To the contrary, masses were willing to give to such organizations as Jamaat-ut-Dawaah, the Jamaat-i-Islami's Al-Khidmat, Al Badr, Al Rasheed Trust, Al Mustafa Trust, Tanzeem-e-Islami and others which are wrongly labeled as "Islamist" organizations and portrayed as enemies of civilization.

The earthquake also exposed the lack of trust in Pakistan army as a credible institution. Ayaz Amir, writing in *Dawn*, confessed:

> Having been in uniform myself, I say this with a heavy heart. Why have things come to this? In 1971 wherever we went people greeted us, waved at us, gave us food and offered help. Helping the army was considered a privilege and even when Dhaka fell and our eastern command laid down its arms, they didn't blame us soldiers, they said we had been stabbed in the back. People held Yahya Khan and his coterie (and their serious tippling) responsible for the debacle, not the army as a whole. It all seems so long ago.[23]

There is a big difference between criticism of Bush's response to the destruction in New Orleans in the wake of Katrina and criticism of the so-called government of Pakistan's response to the earthquake. That the government was slow to respond immediately after the event is even admitted by General Musharraf. What is "alarming, and quite difficult to understand" for impartial observers "is:

> ...the government's continuing failure to treat this disaster on a war footing. Anything by the name of government is not to be seen in the quake-hit areas. But newspapers are full of the exploits of Shaukat Aziz and his army of cabinet ministers. Seen against the backdrop of what has actually happened, this craze for publicity looks positively obscene.[24]

Musharraf's regime self-praised its work. Around the clock, the state-controlled Pakistan Television (PTV) showed pictures of press briefings, interviews and visits to the disaster zone by government officials, ministers, the prime minister and Musharraf. As usual, PTV acted as a mouthpiece of the regime, with absolutely no criticism of the weaknesses of the relief efforts. Reporters mostly talked with survivors at aid distribution facilities and at hospitals in Islamabad, and only aerial views of the remote villages were screened. Government officials were unhappy with the coverage of private channels, which showed live interviews and the views of survivors. There were reports of the media being denied entry to certain areas.[25]

Ayaz Amir compared the situation to "the Hamas phenomenon happening in Pakistan," where organized authority (in the case of Hamas, the Palestinian Authority, in our case, the organs of government) able to do very little, while the burden of social work (in this case relief work) is taken up by Islamist organizations." What this portends is obvious.

Analysts claim Musharraf's external battle, to be seen to be tackling fundamentalism, will now be overshadowed by his domestic battle, to placate "Muslim hardliners within his own military and government who are angry at his apparent failure to lead his country in its time of need."[26] Others are totally shocked with what the Islamic groups are doing. Writing in Slate Magazine, Mahnaz Ispahani expressed his concerns in these words: "Poised to take advantage of the government's inability to cope with the disaster are the Islamist parties and their extremist cousins."[27]

While expressing fear for the sitting regime, Hassan Rizvi, a political analyst said: "The militants are taking matters into their own hands and winning over members of the public on the ground. Their popularity will soar in these regions as a result and the government will appear directionless. It is a very dangerous situation."[28]

Just two days after the earthquake, when the government's inability to move its resources in the services of its own people was not even known to anyone in advance, Stephen Cohen told his host at the NPR Morning edition on October 10 that Musharraf now faces a deeply uncertain future: "Pakistan is unstable as a government and a society. This is often the case with one-man rule, and especially one-man rule in which serious people - al-Qaeda and its allies inside Pakistan - are trying to kill him. These people are all his enemies and now the public are angry at his response to a major disaster."[29]

This type of propaganda from outside will intensify with the decrease of popularity of stooges working for their imperial masters. Not only the masses will realize the truth but also leaders of the religious political parties will realize the futility of establishing Islam through un-Islamic ways and means. If they don't, under the changed circumstances it would not be difficult for new leadership to emerge. The public response in the wake of earthquake shows the spark among the masses is still alive. They are patiently waiting and observing the state of affairs in which democracy is as impossible as living by Islam; where ending the US interference is as impossible as getting rid of military dictatorship. After 58 years of deception and oppression, it matters little if this explosion is triggered by an Iraqi style invasion from outside or a sparked from within. This is the verdict of history, it is the universal law. Tyranny may be prolonged for some time, but it can not endure forever.

Similarly, Muslims can deviate from the right path and the ultimate Islamic objective, but they cannot be committing *shirk*[30] upon *shirk*; living under a secular system;[31] living by man-made laws;[32] thriving on *Riba*;[33] seeking protection from those who have openly declared a war on living by Islam;[34] supporting the enemies of Islam in butchering fellow Muslims;[35] classifying Muslims into different groups and introducing new forms of Islam that are not based on the sound principles of the Qur'an and *Sunnah*,[36] and still not only deceiving themselves to be living in an *Islamic* republic, but also hoping to see it survive despite undermining it both physically and ideologically.

The Pakistani people can always change their course and hope for the best. But the people's stubbornness to stay the course and all the aforementioned factors, along with the Musharraf factor, does not bode well for the future of Pakistan. Unless Musharraf is stopped in his tracks and both the nation and the political leadership make a 180 degree turn to untangle themselves from the American web and establish a model state according to the vision of the founding masses, the more likely the demise of Pakistan seems.

Notes

Introduction: *The Hard Questions*

[1] BBC Report: Excerpts from General Musharraf's Address," October 17, 1999 Published at 19:36 GMT 20:36 UK . http://icssa.org/landscam.html

[2] Special SAT Report, "The First Hand List of Army Land Grabbers," *South Asia Tribune,* Issue No 5, Aug 19-25, 2002. URL http://icssa.org/landgrab-list.html Accessed October 07, 2005. Also see Annex 1.

[3] Taaffe, Peter. "Musharraf rule shaky as poverty rise," Committee for Worker International, London, March 31, 2005. A total of 48 million people struggle daily on US$2.00 or less.

[4] "Forecasting a 'Yugoslavia-like fate" for Pakistan, the U.S. National Intelligence Council (NIC) and the Central Intelligence Agency (CIA) in a jointly prepared Global Futures Assessment Report have said that 'by year 2015 Pakistan would be a failed state, ripe with civil war, bloodshed, inter-provincial rivalries and a struggle for control of its nuclear weapons and complete Italianization.'" Pakistan will be failed state by 2015: U.S. intelligence, *The Hindu,* Feb 14, 2005. Also published in *Daccan Herald,* February 14, 2005. *Rediff.com* published this report on February 13, 2005. Pakistan snubbed CIA report on February 16, 2005. See: *The Nation*'s report, "Pakistan dismisses CIA report," by Shaiq Hussain.

[5] *New York Times,* September 20, 2004.

[6] "The French president enjoys a much more influential role than the figure-head presidents of many other European countries. This is largely due to General Charles de Gaulle, who beefed up the role to give the president full control in times of national emergency. As in General Musharraf's proposal,

the French president appoints the prime minister who will usually, but not necessarily, be the leader of the largest party after the general election." BBC report: "A different kind of president," Thursday, 27 June, 2002, 17:40 GMT 18:40 UK.

[7] Glazov, Jamie. "Ten Years Since the Collapse of an Evil Empire," *FrontPage Magazine*, August 23, 2001.

Chapter 1: *The Musharraf Doctrine*

[1] Datta, Sunanda. "On the Slow Road to End Kashmir's Trauma," *The Straits Times* (Singapore), February 24, 2004.

[2] BBC Report, "World: South Asia Pakistan's coup: Why the army acted," October 13, 1999 Published at 23:20 GMT 00:20 UK.

[3] BBC Report, "South Asia: Pakistan army pledges interim regime," October 15, 1999 Published at 22:55 GMT 23:55 UK

[4] "The General's Empty Victory," The Economist, May 2, 2002.

[5] Zubrzycki, John. "Musharraf Reshuffles His Trump Cards," *The Australian*, October 10, 2001.

[6] Zubrzycki, John. "Musharraf Reshuffles His Trump Cards," *The Australian*, October 10, 2001.

[7] Cviic, Stephen. "Analysis: Musharraf's gamble," BBC, Saturday, 12 January, 2002, 21:36.

[8] Report by Neturei Karta *International*, June 15, 2003. Presented by Rabbi Yisroel P. Feldman of Neturei Karta Int. at the rally hosted by the New England Committee to Defend Palestine, to protest the "Boston Celebrates Israel Festival" in Boston, Mass. on Sunday, June 15, 2003.

[9] Baker, Mark. "Musharraf's boldest gamble seems to have paid off," *The Age*, May 4 2002.

[10] Abbas, Zaffar. "Games Dictator Play," Herald, April 2002 issue.

[11] "General Musharraf's Lies," Editorial, the *Washington Post*, October 01, 2005. See: http://icssa.org/mushstupid.html

[12] The amendments made to the Constitution by the Legal Framework Order (issued by General Pervez Musharraf on August 21, 2002). URL: http://www.pakistani.org/pakistan/constitution/musharraf_const_revival/ accessed Sept. 24, 2005.

[13] Editorial, the Hindu, July 10, 2002.

[14] Bashir, Sarmad. "Musharraf rejects 'democracy of minority'," *The Nation*, June 28, 2003.

[15] BBC reported on June 28. *The Nation's* Monitoring Desk published its report on June 29, 2003.

[16] Hasan, Khalid. "President won't allow 'vice and virtue' body in NWFP," *Daily Times*, June 27, 2003. See: http://www.dailytimes.com.pk/default.asp?page=story_27-6-2003_pg1_1

[17] *The Nation* reported on June 27, 2003 that President Musharraf told reporters

and editors at a wide-ranging luncheon at the *Washington Times*: "The Islamic world must adopt a strategy of evaluating ourselves, deciding whether we want to follow a militant, confrontationist approach or choose a self-emancipating path away from poverty, away from a lack of production and opportunity." These are two different issues: you fight occupation and oppression on one front and poverty and inequality on another. How could he ask Muslims to allow occupations, be subservient and only worry about poverty? This is not possible without throwing away the yoke of domination and that is not possible with continued submission.

[18] Some Muslims in their zeal to be seen as more moderate than others ultimately cross the limits of and become neo-moderates or neo-mods of Islam.[19] The *New York Times* and its foreign affairs correspondent, Thomas Friedman, are the leading proponents of the "war within Islam."

[20] Musharraf, Pervez. "Islam and West: Time for Enlightened Moderation," *The Khaleej Times*, June 02, 2004. Available at URL: http://yaleglobal.yale.edu/display.article?id=4016

[21] In Afghanistan, a study by New Hampshire professor Marc Herold says 3767 civilians died in the first nine weeks of bombing (Scott MacLeo, "When the body count doesn't count" *Konfrontatie Digital*, Newzeland, 17 January 2002). Estimates also suggested US bombs killed at least 3,767 civilians in the first two months alone. (Seumas Milne, "The innocent dead in a coward's war" the *Guardian*, December 20, 2001). These figures do not include the thousands upon thousands Taliban and Iraqi troops which were targeted with 15,000 daisey cutter bombs and other such arsenal. More than 800 Taliban were systematically killed during a single incident at Qila-e-Jhangi (Associated Press, *Los Angeles Times*, Nov. 28, 2001. http://www.wsws.org/articles/2001/nov2001/mass-n29.shtml). *Newsweek* reported that around 1,000 Taliban prisoners died after they had surrendered to the U.S.-backed Northern Alliance and were in the hands of warlord General Abdul Rashid Dostum (CNN, "U.S. probe mass Taliban 'suffocations'," August 21, 2002).

[22] An Iraqi humanitarian organization reported in July 2005 that 128,000 Iraqis have been killed since the U.S. invasion began in March 2003. Mafkarat al-Islam reported that chairman of the 'Iraqiyun humanitarian organization in Baghdad, Dr. Hatim al-'Alwani, said that the toll includes everyone who has been killed since that time. United Press international. July 07, 2005. URL: http://www.informationclearinghouse.info/article9460.htm In 2004, BBC reported conservative estimates to be more than 100,000 civilian deaths in Iraq> See: "Iraq death toll 'soared post-war': Poor planning, air strikes by coalition forces and a "climate of violence" have led to more than 100,000 extra deaths in Iraq, scientists claim. " BBC News: October 29, 2004. URL: http://news.bbc.co.uk/2/hi/middle_east/3962969.stm

[23] R.J. Rummel, "Death by Government," New Brunswick, N.J.: Transaction Publishers, 1994.

[24] Ibid., R.J. Rummel, *"Death by Government."*[25] See "The Bull Inter Caetera (Al-

exander VI), May 4, 1493 for the background and other details of the Inter Cetra bull: URL http://www.nativeweb.org/pages/legal/indig-inter-caetera. html

[26] See text of the letter: http://ili.nativeweb.org/ricb.html

[27] Cited in Howard Zinn, *A People's History of the United States*, Harper & Row, New York, 1980

[28] Figures cited in Dorris, Michael A., 'Contemporary Native Americans', Daedalus, Spring 1981; also see Zinn, Howard, A People's History of the United States, op. cit., for more on the glorious roots of the United States and the global system largely under its control.

[29] Fallaci, Oriana. "La Forza della Ragione" (The Force of Reason), 2004. Fallaci is an Islam-basher and writes that Muslim terrorists had killed 6,000 people over the past 20 years in the name of the Qur'an and said the Islamic faith "sows hatred in the place of love and slavery in the place of freedom." Reuters report: "Pope met anti-Islam author Fallaci," Tuesday, Aug 30, 2005.

[30] Colonial adventures started with the approval of the Church and continued for 500 years with killing no less than 300 million people which amount to more than 50 holocausts by comparison with what Hitler did to Jews. See: Abid Ullah Jan, "To Hell with Muslim Terrorism," Media Monitors Network, August 24, 2005. http://world.mediamonitors.net/content/view/full/18309, or http://www.amperspective.com/html/to_hell_with.html or http://www.icssa.org/to_hell_with_terrorism.html

[31] The changes which the military made to Pakistan's Constitution.

[32] Walsh, Declan. "Transplant tourists flock to Pakistan, where poverty and lack of regulation fuel trade in human organs," the *Guardian*, February 10, 2005.

[33] Taaffe, Peter. "Musharraf rule shaky as poverty rises," Committee for Workers International, London, March 31, 2005. A total of 48 million people struggle daily on US$2.00 or less.

[34] Musharraf, Pervez. "A Plea for Enlightened Moderation," the *Washington Post*, Tuesday, June 1, 2004; Page A23.

[35] "The suffering of the innocents, particularly my brethren in faith—the Muslims—at the hands of militants, extremists and terrorists has made it all the more urgent to bring order to this troubled scene," writes General Musharraf in the very first paragraph of General Musharraf's speech and widely publicized article. Ibid: Pervez Musharraf, the *Washington Post*.

[36] Benard, Cheryl. "Civil Democratic Islam: Partners, Resources, and Strategies," a Study Supported by the Smith Richardson Foundation, RAND National Security Research Division. 2003.

[37] Ibid., General Musharraf, the *Washington Post*.

[38] M. A. Niazi: "Right Challenge, Wrong Response," *The Nation*, June 04, 2004. http://www.nation.com.pk/daily/june-2004/4/EDITOR/op1.asp

[39] Pipes, Daniel. "The Rock Star and the Mullah, Debate: Democracy and Islam," a PBS debate between Daniel Pipes and Muqtedar Khan. URL: http://www.pbs.org/wnet/wideangle/shows/junoon/debate.html

[40] Irshad Manji, who is promoted as the torch bearer of "moderate" Islam. Daniel Pipes called her a "Practicing Muslim" in his "[Moderate] Voices of Islam," *New York Post*, September 23, 2003.

[41] See, publisher's note on Irshad Manji's book, *The Trouble with Islam.*

[42] Ibid., Publisher note.

[43] Being a Muslim, one has to be moderate. "We made you a nation of moderation and justice"(Qur'an; 2:143) See: *Sahih Bokhari*, Vol 3, Book 40, Hadith # 550; Vol 4, Book 55, Hadith # 629; Vol 7, Book 70, Hadith # 577; Vol 8, Book 76, Hadith # 470, 471 and 474 and *Sahih Muslim*, Book 032, Hadith Number 6243. See http://icssa.org/moderate.html for details.

[44] Qur'an also gives example of those who had accepted the revealed books in parts (5:13-14)

[45] For example, see the preconditions for passing the test of moderation that demand rejection of the Qur'anic view about the court testimony of a man and woman and their share in an inheritance. Another pre-condition for "moderates" is to agree to "scholarly inquiry into the origins of Islam."

[46] Harris, Sam. "Mired in the religious war," the *Washington Times*, December 02, 2004. http://www.washtimes.com/op-ed/20041201-090801-2582r.htm

[47] See Intolerance in the Qur'an: URL: http://www.skepticsannotatedbible.com/quran/int/long.html

[48] Pipes, Daniel. "Identifying Moderate Muslims," *New York Sun*, November 23, 2004 URL: http://www.danielpipes.org/article/2226

[49] Ibid., Pipes, Identifying Moderate Muslims.

[50] Pipes, Daniel. "The Evil Isn't Islam," New York Post, July 30, 2002, http://www.danielpipes.org/article/437

[51] Harris, Sam. "Mired in Religious war," December 02, 2004. URL http://www.washtimes.com/op-ed/20041201-090801-2582r.htm

[52] Cragg, Kenneth. *The Mind of the Qur'an*, George Allah & Unwin: 1973.

[53] Demaria, Andrew. CNN, June 21, 2001.

[54] *The News*, Front-page main headline, July 18, 2002.

[55] Pipes, Daniel. Elections Today, (Spring 2002) [see: http://www.danielpipes.org/article/433, http://www.ifes.org/research_comm/et_spring_02_low.pdf

[56] According to a 2002 study conducted for Unicef Peshawar in Mardan District in connection with establishing Community Information System at local level.

[57] Bystydzienski, Jill M. *Women Transforming Politics*, Indiana University Press, 1992.

[58] Quaid spelled this out to a skeptical young politician, Sardar Shaukat Hayat (d.1998) in April 1943. See: *Early years of Pakistan* by Major General Shahid Hamid Ferozsons, Karachi, 1993 and *Quaid-e-Azam as Seen by his Contemporaries* by Jamiluddin Ahmed.

[59] In his message to other Muslim States, on 27 August 1948, Muhammad Ali Jinnah said: "We are all passing through perilous times. The drama of power

politics that is being staged in Palestine, Indonesia and Kashmir should serve as an eye-opener to us. It is only by putting up a united front that we can make our voice felt in the counsels of the world."

Chapter 2: *The Impossibility of Establishing Islam*

[1] *Deen* is a submission, following and worship by man for the creator, the ruler, the subjugator in a comprehensive system of life with all its belief, intellectual, moral and practical aspects. For details, see: URL http://www.islam1. org/khutub/Defn__of_Deen_&_Islam.htm Accessed October 07, 2005

[2] Haqqani, Husain. *"Pakistan: Between Mosque and Military,"* Washington, DC: Carnegie Endowment for International Peace, 2005.

[3] Ibid., Haqqani, Husain.

[4] Ibid., Haqqani, Husain.

[5] Ibid., Haqqani, Husain.

[6] Editorial, "Questions, Questions, Questions," *Daily Times,* September 24, 2003.

[7] Ibid., Haqqani, Husain.

[8] Ibid., Haqqani, Husain.

[9] "Verily He sent His Messenger with divine guidance and the true Deen in order for it to be dominant over the World" — Al-Qur'an 9:33. Al-Mawardi *The Ordinances of Government (Al-Ahkam al-Sultaniyya)*. Trans. by Dr. W. Wahba. 1996, pp. 3; also see Ibn Khaldun, *"The Muqaddimah: An Introduction to History,"* Princeton University Press, 1967, p. 190,191. Al-Mawardi maintains that the establishment of the *Khilafah* is a religious obligation for the Muslims, because its main object is the defence of the Faith and the preservation of order in the world through the implementation of Revealed Law. In support of his argument he quotes that of the Qur'an in which David was appointed *Khalifah* on Earth by Allah (Al Qur'an 38:27). He is of the view that a secular state is based on the principles derived through human reasoning, and therefore it promotes only the material advancement of its citizens. But since the *Khilafah* is based on Revealed Law, it promotes the material as well as the spiritual advancement of the people. Constitution of Jammat-i-Islami, Pakistan says: "The duty of a Muslim is to strive for establishing the whole of Islam without discretion or division." See: http://www. jamaat.org/Isharat/2000/ish032000.html

[10] *Shirk* is defined as worshipping or submitting to anything (or anyone) else but Allah. To take anything else but God as an object of worship is shirk.

[11] Jafri, Riaz Col. "Islamic Pakistan," *Pak Tribune,* Saturday June 05, 2004.

[12] Ibid., Jafri

[13] Iqbal, Mohammed Allama. "The Wisdom of Moses," from his collection of Persian poems: "What should then be done, o people of the East."

[14] Khatana, Manzoor H. *Iqbal And Foundation of Pakistan Nationalism:* 1992, Lahore, page -110.

[15] Ibid., Khatana, page -119.

[16] " .... Allah has made it Haram for whoever commits *Shirk* to ever enter into heaven. Such (people) will dwell in hell .... " Qur'an, 5:72.

[17] "They took their Priests and Rabbis as Lord-Gods beside Allah; and (they did this in respect of) the Messiah, the son of Mary (as well). But they were not ordered other than to worship and serve one God. Glory is to Him. He is far and above the Shirk which they commit." Qur'an, 9:31.

[18] "The Hypocrites, men and women, (have an understanding) with each other: they enjoin evil, and forbid what is just, and are close with their hands. They have forgotten Allah; so He hath forgotten them. Verily the Hypocrites are rebellious and perverse." Qur'an, 9:67.

[19] "So separate us from this sinful rebellious people!" Qur'an, 5:25.

[20] 'Oh you who believe, obey Allah, and obey the Messenger, and (obey) those from amongst yourselves who are in (positions of) authority...." Qur'an, 4:59.

Chapter 3: *Restoring Democracy Impossible*

[1] Abbas, Zaffar. "Musharraf and the Mullas," BBC report, December 30, 2003. http://news.bbc.co.uk/1/hi/world/south_asia/3357245.stm

[2] Ibid., Abbas, Zaffar. BBC report

[3] BBC Report. "World: South Asia, Clinton urges return to civilian rule," October 14, 1999 Published at 04:02 GMT 05:02 UK. URL: http://news.bbc.co.uk/1/hi/world/south_asia/473507.stm

[4] BBC News: URL: http://news.bbc.co.uk/olmedia/470000/audio/_472803_statedept.ram Web site accessed, October 23, 2005.

[5] Mr Cook said he was "deeply worried" by the situation but added: "The military there must be under no illusion: we will strongly condemn any unconstitutional actions." I call on all parties to respect the constitution, the rule of law and the democratic process." http://news.bbc.co.uk/1/hi/uk/473314.stm

[6] BBC Report. "World: South Asia, Clinton urges return to civilian rule," October 14, 1999 Published at 04:02 GMT 05:02 UK

[7] Norman, Omar. *Pakistan: Political and Economic History Since 1947* (London: Kegan Paul, 1990), p.19

[8] Nadeen Syed, "Punjab PA wants President in uniform," *The Nation*, September 14, 2004.

[9] PCO No 1, 2000, reads "A person holding office immediately before the commencement of this Order as a judge of the superior court shall not continue to hold that office if he is not given, or does not make, oath in the form set out in the schedule, before the expiration of such time from such commencement as the Chief Executive may determine or within such further time as may be allowed by the Chief Executive.". For the text, see *The Herald*, February 2000, p.24.

[10] According to Sharifuddin Pirzada, the main legal advisor to the chief execu-

tive, "The choice was between the imposition of martial law or asking the judges of the superior courts to take oath under the PCO...." See Mubashir Zaidi, "The Case of the Missing Constitution", *The Herald*, February 2000, p.25

11 Nawaz Sharif, during his tenure, had established military courts in Karachi and other parts of Sindh.

12 To have a look at the state of affairs where there is one law for the rulers and the other for the ruled, read the following story as an example: "Rogue Army General Bloodies the Law and Gets Away With it, Publicly," *South Asia Tribune* Report, Issue 63, October 19-25, 2003. http://icssa.org/rougearmy.htm

Chapter 4: *The Height of Collective Helplessness*

1 Mubashir Zaidi, "The Missing Constitution," *Herald* (Karachi), February 2000.

2 "Judges who did not take oath under the military's Provisional Constitutional Order," Pakistan Press International, January 27, 2000.

3 Human Rights Watch meeting with Lt. Gen. (Ret.) Moin-ud-Din Haider, Minister of Interior, Narcotics Control and Capital Administration and Development Division, New York, March 21, 2000.

4 "Government stance on LFO misleading, PPP says" *Dawn* Report, May 12, 2003.

5 Musharraf on "BBC Islam and the West," BBC, Thursday, 11 September, 2003, 13:23 GMT 14:23 UK.

6 Al-Qur'an, Al-Israa: 70.

7 Walter M. Brasch , *"America's Unpatriotic Acts; The Federal Government's Violation of Constitutional and Civil Rights,"* Peter Lang Publishing, 2005.

8 Sam Harris, "Mired in the religious war," *Washington Times*, December 02, 2004.

9 "Islam Sign Outside Latrobe-Area Church Stirs Controversy," *The Pittsburgh Channel,* Posted September 17, 2004. URL: http://www.thepittsburghchannel.com/news/3739274/detail.html Accessed, October 17, 2005.

10 Humphries, Josh. "Church sign sparks debate," *Daily Courier*, May 24, 2005. URL: http://www.thedigitalcourier.com/articles/2005/05/24/news/news01.txt Accessed: October 17, 2005

11 "If any one slew a person - unless it be for murder or for spreading mischief in the land - it would be as if he slew the whole people." Quran 5:32. In a hadith narrated by Abdullah bin Amr bin Al-As, God Told Mohammed (PBUH) You are neither hard-hearted nor of fierce character, nor one who shouts in the markets. You do not return evil for evil, but excuse and forgive. - *Bukhari*, Volume 6, Book 60, Number 362. Fight in the cause of Allah those who fight you, but do not transgress limits; for Allah loveth not transgressors. - Quran 2:190. It has been narrated on the authority of Abu Huraira that the Messenger of Allah said: Do not desire an encounter with

the enemy; but when you encounter them, be firm. - *Muslim* Book 019, Number 4313. Also see: Majid Khadduri, *War and Peace in the Law of Islam*, Baltimore: Johns Hopkins Press, 1955, p. 58.

[12] See the four part detailed report "Serfs on the Plantation," by Jacob G. Hornberger, founder and president of the Future of Freedom Foundation, who proves from various aspects how the US has exactly the same control over its people as the Pharaoh used to have. See: http://www.fff.org/freedom/0693a.asp Similarly, more than fifty years ago in his book *The Road to Serfdom*, Friedrich Hayek argued that Americans were traveling the same road that all others in history, including the communists, fascists, and Nazis, had traveled.

[13] Pitt, William Rivers. "Slaughtergate," *Truthout Perspective*, June 23, 2003. URL: http://www.truthout.org/docs_03/062303A.shtml Accessed: September 29, 2005.

[14] Richard Morin and Claudia Deane, "Poll: Majority Backs Use of Force in Iran," the *Washington Post*, June 24, 2003; Page A16.

[15] Ignatius, David. "Achieving Real Victory Could Take Decades," the *Washington Post*, December 26, 2004, page B01

[16] See "Women's bare-breasted equality," "Canada embraces bare breasts," Global Ideas Bank, *Summarised from a story by Richard Cleroux, entitled 'Judges let topless go over the top', in The Times.* Also see Alexander Chancellor in *The Times (Aug 28th '93)* with additional information from an article by Ben Macintyre, entitled 'Feminists win right to travel topless on New York subway' in *the Times.* http://www.globalideasbank.org/site/bank/idea.php?ideaId=1695. URL Accessed Sept. 29, 2005.

[17] O'Hanlon, Martin. "Bare breasts OK in Saskatchewan, judge rules," *July 22, 1998. See: http://www.geocities.com/CapitolHill/Lobby/6107/Canada/Saskatchewan/Jul2298CFRA.html* Also see, Ritu Bhasin, "Topless ruling allows women to choose." The University of Toronto on Line, Varsity Publications, Inc. URL: http://varsity.utoronto.ca:16080/archives/117/jan16/opinions/topless.html Accessed, September 29, 2005.

[18] BBC report, "French scarf ban comes into force," September 02, 2004.

Chapter 5: *Military Occupation Prevails*

[1] Cohen, Stephen Philip. "The Jihadist Threat to Pakistan," *The Washington Quarterly*, Summer 2003 page 21.

[2] Quoted by Vijay Prashad, "Casual Imperialism," *People's Weekly World*, August 16, 2003. He is professor at Trinity College and author of Keeling Up with the Dow Joneses: Debt, Prison, Welfare.

[3] Sanger, David E. "Bush Sees Transfer as His Fresh Start," the *New York Times*, June 29, 2004. Also see: Paul McGeough, Chief Herald Correspondent in Baghdad, "All eyes on the man who stepped into Iraqi inferno," smh.com, June 30, 2004. http://www.smh.com.au/arti-

cles/2004/06/29/1088487965015.html URL Accessed: October 18, 2005.

[4] Vidkun Abraham Lauritz Jonsson Quisling (1887-1945) was a Norwegian politician and officer. He earned the reputation as one of World War Two's most infamous traitors. He held the office of Minister President of Norway from February 1942 to the end of World War II, while the elected social democratic cabinet of Johan Nygaardsvold was exiled in London. Quisling was tried for high treason and executed by firing squad after the war.

[5] Haqqani, Hussain. "Brainwashing," *The Nation*, June 02, 2004.

[6] See: http://plaza.ufl.edu/nsdighe/Battles_Millenium.html, http://www.prideofindia.net/impbattle.html and http://www.militaryfocus.com/osprey/campaign/35.htm7. "The "battle" lasted no more than a few hours, and indeed the outcome of the battle had been decided long before the soldiers came to the battlefield. The aspirant to the Nawab's throne, Mir Jafar, was induced to throw in his lot with Clive, and by far the greater number of the Nawab's soldiers were bribed to throw away their weapons, surrender prematurely, and even turn their arms against their own army. Jawaharlal Nehru, in *The Discovery of India* (1946), justly describes Clive as having won the battle "by promoting treason and forgery", and pointedly notes that British rule in India had "an unsavoury beginning and something of that bitter taste has clung to it ever since." Battle of Plassey, From a web site created by: Vinay Lal Associate Professor of History, UCLA From: Oliver J. Thatcher, ed., The Library of Original Sources, (Milwaukee: University Research Extension Co., 1907), Vol. VII: *The Age of Revolution*, pp. 59-64. Scanned by: J. S. Arkenberg, Dept. of History, Cal. State Fullerton. Prof. Arkenberg has modernized the text. This text is part of the Internet *Modern History Sourcebook*. The *Sourcebook* is a collection of public domain and copy-permitted texts for introductory level classes in modern European and World history.

[9] In an uprising known as the "Revolt of the Sergeants," Fulgencio Batista took over the Cuban government on September 4, 1933. The coup overthrew the liberal government of Gerardo Machado, and marked the beginning of the army's influence as an organized force in the running of the government. It also signaled Batista's emergence as self-appointed chief of the armed forces, king-maker and favored U.S. strong man.

[10] Mohammad Reza Pahlavi (1919- 1980) was the last Shah of Iran, ruling from 1941 until 1979. At the end of World War II, political unrest dogged Iran and in 1953 the nation's nationalist Prime Minister Mohammed Mossadegh forced the Shah to flee the country. He was quickly escorted back to power and fired Mossadegh through a counter coup, led by General Fazlollah Zahedi, which was supported by the American CIA and Britain's SIS (MI6). On January 16, 1979 he and his family were forced to flee Iran a second time following the Iranian revolution. He was welcomed by President Anwar Sadat of Egypt, and remained there until his death on July 27, 1980.

[11] General Suharto (b. 1921) was an Indonesian dictator and military strongman, who seized power in 1965 through a military coup that had the backing from

the CIA. He was the second President of Indonesia, from 1967 to 1998.

[12] General Manuel Antonio Noriega (b. 1934) was a general and military leader of Panama from 1983 to 1989. He was initially a strong ally of the U.S.A, and was in the pay-roll of the CIA from the late 1950s to 1986. By the late 1980s his actions had become increasingly unacceptable to American law enforcement officials and policymakers, and he was overthrown and captured by a U.S. invading force in 1989. He was taken to the United States, tried for drug trafficking, and imprisoned in 1992. He remains imprisoned in a federal prison in Miami, Florida.

[13] François Duvalier was the notorious ruler of Haiti throughout the 1960s. Duvalier was a physician (the source of his nickname, "Papa Doc") who worked in the Haitian government beginning in the mid-1940s. With the army's support, he was elected to the presidency in 1957. In 1964 he declared himself president for life and indeed, stayed president until his death in 1971, when his son, Jean-Claude "Baby Doc" Duvalier, succeeded him. Papa Doc was an expert in voodoo who ruled Haiti with brute force and terror, with his ruthless security force, the Tontons Macoutes, acting as real-life bogeymen who routinely executed his opponents.

[14] Joseph-Désiré Mobutu (1930-1997) was the President of Zaire (now the Democratic Republic of the Congo) from 1965 to 1997. On September 14, 1960, a coup d'état overthrew Congo's first elected Prime Minister, Patrice Lumumba in support of President Kasavubu. Colonel Mobutu was a key figure in the coup and was rewarded with rapid promotion. It is believed that the CIA had a hand in this coup.

[15] For a historical analysis of Horthy's strategy, see Ian Kershaw, Hitler (1936–45): Nemesis (New York: W. W. Norton, 2000), pp. 734–35.

[16] Quoted in Kux, p. 268. The quotes are taken from a State Department memorandum and talking points for Secretary Shultz's meeting with Zia that Kux obtained through the Freedom of Information Act.

[17] Mahir Ali in *Dawn* (11 December 2002 writes, "[Kissinger] threatened Z.A. Bhutto with dire consequences for pursuing a nuclear program." In his book, "*If I am Assassinated*" that he wrote in his death cell, Zulfiqar Ali Bhutto gives the following account of his encounter with Kissinger, "He [i.e., Kissinger] told me that I should not insult the intelligence of the United States by saying that Pakistan needed the reprocessing plant for her energy needs. In reply, I told him that I will [sic] not insult the intelligence of the United States by discussing the energy needs of Pakistan, but [by] the same token, he should not discuss the plant at all" (Page 138).

[18] "Lydia finds herself in a place of deep internal conflict about her children's military service. One son is permanently disabled because of military service. Another is in Gaza at this time. She hopes that the values that they learned at home will help them treat Palestinians with respect and to moderate others in the military who believe that Palestinians are subhuman." These are the observations of Dr. Rucharma Marton, President and Founder of

Physicians for Human Rights, Israel in an article entitled "The Psychological Effect of the Second Intifada on Israelis." *The Palestine-Israel Journal of Politics*, Economics and Culture, March 2004.

[19] *The Statesman* report, May 17, 2001.

[20] *Dawn*, Sept. 26, 1999.

[21] Djerejian, Edward P. "The US Policy towards Islam and the Arc of Crisis," James A. Baker III Institute at Rice University, No 1, 1995.

[22] Mahmood-ul-Hasan Khan, "Defence Expenditure and Macroeconomic Stabilization: Causality Evidence from Pakistan," State Bank of Pakistan Working Papers No 6, December 2004. Page 7.

[23] Policy Analysis, No 436, May 8, 2002.

[24] See "CIA and FBI operating freely in Pakistan," *Daily Times*, August 04, 2004 http://www.dailytimes.com.pk/default.asp?page=story_4-8-2004_pg7_2; Pakistan: FBI rules the roost," *Asia Times*, October 04, 2003; and "Over 300 netted in post-7/7 hunt," *The Nation*, July 21, 2005.

[25] Frida Berrigan and William D. Hartung, with Leslie Heffel, "U.S. Weapons at War 2005: Promoting Freedom or Feuling Conflict? U.S. Military Aid and Arms Transfers Since September 11," A World Policy Institute Special Report, June 2005

[26] Congressional Budget Justification for FY06 Foreign Operations, Request by Region: South Asia, State Department, Bureau of Resource Management, February 2005.

[27] "The U.S. Designates Pakistan a Major Non-NATO Ally," Reuters, June18, 2004.

[28] Bake, Peter. "Bush: U.S. to Sell F-16s to Pakistan," the *Washington Post*, March 26, 2005.

[29] Wayne, Leslie. "Connecting to India Through Pakistan,"the *New York Times*, April 16, 2005.

[30] Sengupta, Kim. "Afghanistan: Unraveling of a Nation Liberated by the West," *Independent* (UK), June 30, 2004.

[31] Congressional Budget Justification for FY05 Foreign Operations, Request by Region: South Asia, State Department, Bureau of Resource anagement, February 2004.

[32] Cooper, Robert. "The new liberal imperialism," in the *Observer* on April 07, 2002. URL http://observer.guardian.co.uk/worldview/story/0,11581,680095,00.html

[33] Ibid., Cooper.

[34] "Since September 11, the United States has set up military bases housing sixty thousand troops in Afghanistan, Pakistan, Kyrgyzstan, Uzbekistan, and Tajikistan, along with Kuwait, Qatar, Turkey, and Bulgaria." U.S. Military Bases and Empire, *Monthly Review*, Volume 53, Number 10. URL: http://www.monthlyreview.org/0302editr.htm. Also See: Patrick Martin, "US bases pave the way for long-term intervention in Central Asia, WSWS, January 11, 2002. http://www.wsws.org/articles/2002/jan2002/base-j11.shtml URL

Accessed September 30, 2005.

[35] Associated Press Report, "Pakistan Denies CIA Has Bases in Tribal Areas," Monday, December 13, 2004. URL: http://www.foxnews.com/story/0,2933,141328,00.html

[36] Loeb, Vernon. "Footprints In Steppes Of Central Asia: New Bases Indicate U.S. Presence Will Be Felt After Afghan War," The *Washington Post*, February 09, 2002.

[37] Visit this web site to read US Central Commands' acknowledgement of Musharraf's surrendering Pakistan to make occupation of Afghanistan possible: http://www.informationclearinghouse.info/pakistan-uscentcom.htm

[38] Dina Nath Mishra, the Pioneer, May 22, 2002.

[39] See, for example, Douglas Frantz, "The Rogue to Fear Most Is the One Following Orders," New York Times, January 13, 2002, p. WK1

[40] "Now for an Equally Hard Part," The Economist, November 17, 2001, p. 15

[41] "F-16s in Exchange for US Intelligence Bases Against Iran," DEBKA-Net-Weekly, April 01, 2005. http://www.debka-net-weekly.com/

[42] Ramtanu Maitra, "US-Pakistan: An elaborate pas de deux," *Asia Times*, September 21, 2005.

[43] Fear expressed by many, such as Christopher Hitchens, "On the Frontier of Apocalypse," *Vanity Fair*, January 2002, p. 153

[44] Hoagland, Jim. "Nuclear Enabler, Pakistan today is the most dangerous place on Earth," the *Washington Post*, Thursday, October 24, 2002; Page A35

[45] As analyst Victor M. Gorbarev argued in a policy paper, "India could become a strategic counterweight to China and a crucial part of a stable balance of power in both East Asia and South Asia." Victor M. Gobarev, "India as a World Power: Changing Washington's Myopic Policy," Cato Institute Policy Analysis no. 381, September 11, 2000, p. 2.

[46] Leon T. Hadar, Pakistan: Strategic Ally or Unreliable Client? Policy Analysis, No 436, May 08, 2002.

[47] Kamran Khan and Thomas E. Ricks, "U.S. Military Begins Shift from Bases in Pakistan," the *Washington Post*, January 11, 2002.

[48] *Baluchistan Post*, June 29, 2002.49 The *Statesman*, June 30,2002, Front-page story.

[50] Berenbaum, Michael. editor. *Witness to the Holocaust*. New York: HarperCollins. 1997. pp. 112 – 113.

[51] Zaidi, Abbas. "Is Pakistan on America's hit list," Letter from Pakistan, *GOWANUS*, Simmer 2003 issue.

[52] See www.punjabilok.com/pak_newsletters/pak_generals.htm. Also see "Granting Lands to Pakistan Army Generals Continues Unabated" in *South Asia Tribune*; the article refers to Pakistan's defense budget and the Army's wealth: URL: http://icssa.org/grantingland.html

[53] Ismi, Asad. "A U.S.-Financed Military Dictatorship: Pakistan has Long, Bloody History as Terrorist Arm of U.S.," Canadian Centre for Policy Alternatives published a report in June 2002

Chapter 6: *Zionist Influence Intensifies*

[1] Iqbal Hussain Khan Yousafzai, "US Congress eulogizes Musharraf," *Asian Tribune,* September 19, 2005.

[2] "Musharraf breaks new ground, meets Jewish leaders in NY," Agency France Presse, September 18, 2005.

[3] Ibid., Agency France Presse: comments of Jack Rohen, the chairman of the American Jewish Congress, who is also chairman of the Council for World Jewry.

[4] See Hurley, Andrew. *One Nation Under Israel,* Truth Press, 1999. Husain Haqqani at Spring 2003 Board Meeting (07-09-2003) http://www.jinsa.org/articles/articles.html/function/view/categoryid/2102/documentid/2109/history/3,2359,2166,1306,2074,2102,2109 and see the real face on JINSA at http://www.rense.com/general18/JINSA.htm and at http://www.rense.com/general37/behind.htm

[5] See Haqqani at JINSA Forum talking on "Islamic militancy" on March 02, 2004. URL: http://www.jinsa.org/articles/articles.html/function/view/categoryid/1930/documentid/2478/history/3,2359,2166,1930,2478. Husain Haqqani at Spring 2003 Board Meeting (07-09-2003) http://www.jinsa.org/articles/articles.html/function/view/categoryid/2102/documentid/2109/history/3,2359,2166,1306,2074,2102,2109 and see the real face on JINSA at http://www.rense.com/general18/JINSA.htm and at http://www.rense.com/general37/behind.htm

[6] Aamer Ahmed Khan, "Pakistan and Israel—new friends?" BBC News, Karachi. http://news.bbc.co.uk/2/hi/south_asia/4205750.stm

[7] Complete article of Hussain Haqqani is still available at the Indian Express Web site under the title "General's Global Obsession," published July 25, 2003. http://www.indianexpress.com/full_story.php?content_id=28258 URL accessed October 01, 2005

[8] See *The politics of Anti-Semitism* by Alexander Cockburn and Jeffrey St. Clair, AK Press, October 15, 2003.

[9] After the *Washington Post's* editorial "The war of ideas' (December 29, 2001) and after his first appeal for a war within Islam in the *New York Times* (December 12, 2001), Thomas L. Friedman came out with another column "war of ideas" (the *New York Times* June 02, 2003) demanding that the US must "take on" the Muslim world's "ideas in public." The targeted "idea people" are "religious leaders, pseudo-intellectuals and educators." Jed Babbin, writing in the *Washington Times* (January. 17, 2002), was quick to appreciate Musharraf after his January 12, 2002 speech and tell the world: "Italian President Silvio Berlusconi's remarks, while undiplomatic, got so much attention because they were true. What is most shocking about Mr. Musharraf's speech is that some of the things he said sound like Mr. Berlusconi wrote them." On January 21, 2002, Mr. Friedman wrote that the world "needs a

war within Islam, not with Islam." The reason for his jubilation was: "At least one leader has finally declared it. It would be nice if some Arab Muslim leaders now did the same."

[10] Kumaraswamy, P. R. "Beyond the Veil: Israel- Pakistan relation," Jaffe Centre for Strategic Studies, Tel Aviv University, Tel Aviv, March 2000)

[11] Ibid., P R Kumaraswamy

[12] Two-and-a- half years after assuaging Muslim anger over US President George Bush's use of the word "crusade" to describe anti-terror efforts, Secretary of State Colin Powell used the term in March 2004. Specifically mentioning Musharraf he said: "We gave them 24, 48 hours to consider it and then I called President Musharraf and said: 'We need your answer now. We need you as part of this campaign, this crusade'." He said these words in testimony before a commission investigating 9/11 on Capitol Hill, March 23, 2004. Published on Tuesday, March 23, 2004 by Agence France Presse. Similarly, General Boykin has become infamous for making public appearances, in full military uniform, during which he declares that America's wars in Iraq and Afghanistan are part of a Christian Holy Crusade against Islam, a religion that Boykin suggests is aligned with Satan. The March 3, 2004 letter, which Bush-Cheney Campaign Chairman Marc Racicot sent to new campaign charter members in Florida, lauded the Republican president for "leading a global crusade against terrorism" while citing evidence of Bush's "strong, steady leadership during difficult times." Also see Jim Lobe, "Anti-Islamic Crusade Gets Organized," March 2, 2005 URL: http://right-web.irc-online.org/analysis/2005/0503pipes.php and The Coming War Between Catholicism and Islam: URL: http://www.thetrumpet.com/index.php?page=magazine&id=68

[13] Editorial, the New York Times, November 14, 2003.

[14] "When Gen. Musharraf's statement provoked an uproar, he responded with another lie: He claimed that he had never made it. In fact, a recording of him speaking is available on The Post's Web site, washingtonpost.com. His words are quite clear. 'These are not my words, and I would go to the extent of saying I am not so silly and stupid to make comments of this sort,' the general said. Well, yes, he is." Editorial, the Washington Post, October 01, 2005

[15] Ibid., P R Kumaraswamy

[16] Quoted by Dr. Shahid Qureshi, "Pakistan & Musharraf Under Siege Of Qadyanis And Zionists," Daily News Monitoring Service, Bangladesh. September 07, 2005.

[17] "When the question of recognition was broached along with an offer of aid in 1949, Quaid-i-Millat Liaquat Ali Khan's response to the US officials was: 'Gentlemen, our souls are not for sale'. One may ask the present military-dominated regime whether three billion dollars plus fringe benefits is now an acceptable price for the soul of the nation." Mahjabeen Islam & Saif Hussain, "Debate on Recognizing Israel," Dawn, September 04, 2003.

[18] Ibid., Kumaraswamy P R

[19] Ibid., Kumaraswamy P R

[20] Ibid., Dr. Shahid Qureshi

[21] Musharraf first broached this idea with Ted Koppel of ABC in his June 24, 2004 interview: "We should not be more Catholic than the Pope" by holding out on diplomatic recognition of Israel.

[22] "Rice: Force necessary for democracy," Aljazeera Net, Saturday 01 October 2005, 15:24 Makka Time, 12:24 GMT

[23] The best example of their escapade is Husain Haqqani's article in the *Nation*, July 23, 2003, which is representative of the research papers being produced from American think tanks, the State Department and even the White House these days. Haqqani, Hussain. *"Israel on the home front," The Nation*, July 23, 2003. Even the most naïve readers can understand the real objectives behind this kind of write-up. Wrapped in nicely worded prescriptions for the well-being of Pakistan, there are well-studded gems for pleasing the masters of our destiny, the Zionists in the U.S.

[24] Jewish Middle East analyst, Mitchell Bard, says in Ohio's most important newspaper *The Plain Dealer*, January 19, 1989, p.3-E.

[25] De Reynier, J. (1950). Chief Representative of the International Committee of the Red Cross in Jerusalem. (A Jerusalem Un Drapeau Flottait Sur La Ligne De Feu', Geneva.

[26] Begin, M. (1964). *The Revolt: The Story Of The Irgun*. Tel-Aviv: Hadar Pub. p.162.

[27] *The Wall Street Journal*, February 7, 2001, p.A26.

[28] In the words of Founder of Pakistan, Israel is an illegitimate child of the Western powers. (25th October 1947).

[29] Nicosia, Francis R. *The Third Reich and the Palestine Question*, pp.16-21.

[30] Quoted in Uri Davis, *Israel: An Apartheid State*, pp.1-2.

[31] Roselle Tekiner, Samir Abed-Rabbo, Norton Mezvinsky, eds., *Anti-Zionism: Analytic Reflections* (Amana Books, 1988); Uri Davis, *Israel: An Apartheid State (Zed Books, Ltd, 1987); The International Organization For The Elimination Of All Forms Of Racial Discrimination, Zionism And Racism* (North American, 1979); Francis R. Nicosia, *The Third Reich And The Palestine Question* (University of Texas Press, 1985); Lenni Brenner, *Zionism In The Age Of The Dictators* (Lawrence Hill, 1983); Regina Sharif, *Non-Jewish Zionism: Its Roots In Western History* (Zed Press, 1983).

[32] Badi, J. (1960). *Fundamental Laws Of The State Of Israel*. New York. p.156.

[33] See *Nature*, 21 March 1985, p.208; See Pro*ceedings' Of The National Academy Of Sciences*, 9 May 2000, as reported on in Nicholas Wade, *"Y Chromosome Bears Witness to Story of the Jewish Diaspora," New York Times*, 9 May 2000.

[34] See Robert Vexler's *Germany: A Chronology And Fact Book*: 1415-1972, p.129.

[35] See Uri Davis biography at Palestine: Information with Provenance which gives background information on every author, speaker, journal or broadcaster whose opinions they publish. URL http://student.cs.ucc.ie/cs1064/ jabowen/IPSC/php/authors.php?auid=1 Accessed November 3, 2005.

[36] Davis, Uri. *Israel: An Apartheid State*, pp.4, 25, 44, 49, 53, 55, 58, 60.

[37] Cainkar, Louise. ed., *Separate And Unequal: The Dynamics Of South African And Israeli Rule* (Chicago: Palestine Human Rights Campaign, 1985), see Preface.

[38] Ibid., Louise Cainkar, page 49

[39] Quoted in *Ha'aretz* (Israel), 24 May 2001.

Chapter 7: *No Will for the Solution*

[1] Prestowitz, Clyde. *"Rogue Nation: American Unilateralism and the Failure of Good Intentions,"* Basic Books, 2003.

[2] Pattanaik, Smruti S. *"Islam and the Ideology of Pakistan,"* Strategic Analysis: A Monthly Journal of the IDSA December 1998 (Vol. XXII No. 9).

[3] Chengappa, B.M. *"Pakistan: The Role of Religion in Political Evolution,'* Strategic Analysis: A Monthly Journal of the IDSA March 2001 (Vol. XXIV No. 12).

[4] Hiram Ulysses Grant, more commonly called Ulysses Simpson Grant (April 27, 1822– July 23, 1885) has been described by military historian J. F. C. Fuller as "the greatest general of his age and one of the greatest strategists of any age." He won many important battles, rose to become general-in-chief of all Union armies, and is credited with winning the war.

[5] Kak, Kapil. "Pakistan: A Geo-Political Appraisal," Strategic Analysis: A monthly Journal of the IDSA, November 1988, (Vol. XXII No. 8).

[6] Critics such as J.N. Dixit were of the opinion that Islam is not monolithic and cannot become a basis for organization for Muslims. See, J. N. Dixit, "Pakistan's India Policies: Role of Domestic Political Factors", *International Studies,* July-September 1995, p. 236.

[7] Karam Ali and B.M. Kutty, "In the lap of bureaucracy," *Dawn,* February 14,1992.

[8] *Dawn*, December 06, 1995.

[9] Ziring, Lawrence. 1980. Pakistan: The Enigma of Political Development. Boulder, Colorado: Folkestone. Pp 257.

[10] Akhtar, Humayun. "Politicians beware! Lest Prof. Ziring's predictions come true," *Dawn,* March 18, 1994.

[11] Cowasjee, Adreshir. "The bare bones," *Dawn,* September 01, 1995.

[12] *Dawn*, January 05, 1997.

Chapter 8: *Softening the High Value Target*

[1] According to July 2005 estimates, Pakistan's population is 162,419,946 See: http://www.cia.gov/cia/publications/factbook/geos/pk.html

[2] Newberg, Paula. "Date line Pakistan: Bhutto's Back", *Foreign Policy Summer* 1994, p.161.

[3] Kak, Kapil. "Pakistan: A Geo-Political Appraisal," Strategic Analysis: A Monthly Journal of the IDSA, November 1998 (Vol. XXII No. 8.

[4] Dardashti, Shai. "Dealing with a Difficult Ally; Pakistan's Tenuous Role

in American Foreign Policy," Jewish Institute for National Security Affairs (JINSA), April 27, 2004. URL: http://www.jinsa.org/articles/articles.html/function/view/categoryid/1930/documentid/2478/history/3,2359,2166,1930,2478 Accessed October 03, 2005

[5] Singh, Uma. "Pakistan's Foreign Policy", *World Focus,* February 1997, p.12.

[6] Allison, Graham. "Nuclear Terrorism Poses the Gravest Threat Today," *The Wall Street Journal Europe* (14 July 2003): A10.

[7] Klare, Michael T. "The Coming War with Iraq: Deciphering the Bush Administration's Motives," *Foreign Policy in Focus*, January 16, 2003.

[8] Subodh Atal, "Extremist, Nuclear Pakistan: An emerging Threat," Cato Policy Analysis No. 472, March 05, 2003.

[9] Reported by Khalid Hasan, *Daily Times*, April 23, 2003.

[10] Pipes, Daniel. "[Moderate] Voices of Islam," *New York Post*, September 23, 2003.

[11] See, publisher's note on Irshad Manji's latest book, *"The Trouble with Islam."*

[12] Editorial, the *New York Times*, November 14, 2003.

[13] Cohen, Stephen Philip. "The Jihadist Threat to Pakistan," *The Washington Quarterly*, Summer 2003 page 14.

[14] Ibid., Stephen Cohen. Page: 22.

[15] Masood, Salman. "Pakistani General survives attack that killed 10," the *New York Times*, June 10, 2004.

[16] "Man hanged, who plotted suicide-attacks on Musharraf," *Pakistan Times Monitoring Desk, August 21, 2005.*

Conclusion: *Expediting the Demise*

[1] Tolstaya, Tatyana. "Mikhail Gorbachev," *Times*, April 13, 1998.

[2] Ibid., Jamie Glazov

[3] Brown, Archie. *"The Gorbachev Factor,"* Oxford University Press, 1996.

[4] Quoted by British MP, George Galloway in his speech in Boston on September 17, 2005.

[5] Calabresi, Massimo. "Mikhail Gorbachev's unintended consequences—demise of the Soviet Union," *National Review*, Jan 20, 1992

[6] Ibid., Archie Brown

[7] In October 1947, its founder Mohammed Ali Jinnah warned that the partition of Palestine would entail "the gravest danger and unprecedented conflict and that the entire Muslim world will revolt against such a decision which can not be supported historically, politically and morally." Once Pakistan was created, Jinnah stressed the need for cohesion among Muslims all over the world and a broad-based policy of cooperation inspired by Islamic identity. In his last *Eid-ul-Fitr* message, he warned the Muslim world: "We are all passing through perilous times. The drama of power-politics that is being waged in Palestine, Indonesia and Kashmir should serve as an eye-opener to us. It is only by putting up a united front that we can make our voice felt in the

counsels of the world."

[8] One: "Those voters are demonstrating again today that there exists no conflict between Western values and Muslim values. What exists is a conflict within the Muslim faith—between majorities in every country who desire freedom, and a lethal minority intent on denying freedom to others and re-establishing a caliphate." Rumsfeld September 30, 2005.

Two: "Some call this evil Islamic radicalism; others, militant Jihadism; still others, Islamo-fascism. Whatever it's called, this ideology is very different from the religion of Islam. This form of radicalism exploits Islam to serve a violent, political vision: the establishment, by terrorism and subversion and insurgency, of a totalitarian empire that denies all political and religious freedom. These extremists distort the idea of jihad into a call for terrorist murder against Christians and Jews and Hindus—and also against Muslims from other traditions, who they regard as heretics." George Bush October 06, 2005.

Three: "What drives these people on is ideas. And unlike the liberation movements of the post World War II era in many parts of the world, these are not in pursuit of political ideas like national independence from colonial rule, or equality for all citizens without regard for race or creed, or freedom of expression without totalitarian repression. Such ambitions are, at least in principle, negotiable and in many cases have actually been negotiated. However there can be no negotiation about the re-creation of the Caliphate; there can be no negotiation about the imposition of *Shari'ah* law; there can be no negotiation about the suppression of equality between the sexes; there can be no negotiation about the ending of free speech. These values are fundamental to our civilization and are simply not up for negotiation." The British Home Secretary, Charles Clarke on the 5th October 2005.

[9] "President Discusses War on Terror at National Endowment for Democracy" Ronald Reagan Building and International Trade Center, Washington, D.C.White House, October 06, 2005. http://www.whitehouse.gov/news/releases/2005/10/print/20051006-3.html

[10] Speech by Jinnah [I assume]at a rally at the University Stadium, Lahore, October 30, 1947.

[11] Khan, Muqtedar. "Putting the American in American Muslims," *the New York Times*, September 07, 2003.

[12] India Office Library, Document No. 609, and others, cited in *Speeches and statements of His Excellency Syed Sharifuddin Pirzada*, Organization of the Islamic Conference, 1988.[13] "For 2nd year, Israelis top tourist list in Kashmir," *Haaretz*, 19 August 2004. http://www.haaretzdaily.com/hasen/spages/466713.html

[14] "Pentagon: US must train Pakistan officers," *Aljazeera*, Wednesday 11 August 2004.

[15] "Israel's must-have," editorial, *Washington Times*, July 22, 2004.[16] Carlotta Gall, "Pakistan Army Ousts Afghan refugees in Militants' areas," *New York Times*,

July 21, 2004.

[17] Ibid., Carlotta Gall

[18] Haq, Faizul, "Two-nation theory not valid today," *The Nation*, March 01, 2003.

[19] Arnaud de Borchgrave, "Pakistan, Saudi Arabia in secret nuke pact," *Washington Times*, October 22, 2003.

[20] "Pakistan without illusions," editorial, *New York Times*, July 09, 2004.

[21] Atal, Subodh. "Extremist, nuclear Pakistan; an emerging threat," Policy Analysis No. 472, March 5, 2003

[22] "President Discusses War on Terror at National Endowment for Democracy" Ronald Reagan Building and International Trade Center, Washington, D.C.White House, October 06, 2005. http://www.whitehouse.gov/news/releases/2005/10/print/20051006-3.html

[23] Amir, Ayaz. "The best and the worst," *Dawn*, October 28, 2005.

[24] Ibid., Amir, Ayaz.

[25] Rizwan Atta, "Pakistan: Government fails in earthquake response," *Green Left Weekly*, October 26, 2005.

[26] Dan McDougall, "Government's earthquake aid failure fuels calls for holy war," *Scotsman*, October 16, 2005.

[27] Ispahani, Mahnaz. "Getting Things Done: Pakistan's self-help society mobilizes; President Musharraf faces his own crisis," Slate, posted Friday, Oct. 14, 2005, at 1:33 PM ET

[28] Dr Shabir Choudhry, "New role for quake victims," *Asia News International*, October 21, 2005.

[29] NPR Morning Edition, October 10, 2005, Steve Inskeep interview with Stephen Cohen, senior fellow of foreign policy studies at the Brookings Institution, about the political impact of the massive earthquake that shook Pakistan over the weekend: "South Asia Earthquake's Political Ramifications."

[30] *Shirk:* Many Islamic scholars have clearly declared embracing secularism as political *Shirk*. See Chapter, "Islam Impossible," for details.

[31] Ibid: *Shirk*.

[32] Allah emphasized His ability and states that whoever reverts from supporting His religion and establishing His Law, then Allah will replace them with whomever is better, mightier and more righteous in Allah's religion and Law (Al-Qur'an 47:38. Explanation of the verse—"If ye turn back (from the Path), He will substitute in your stead another people; then they would not be like you! (Al-Qur'an 47:38)—given in Tafsir Ibn Kathir, Vol 3, page 207.

[33] Like the Jews before them (Qur'an , 4:160-1) Muslims are clearly forbidden in the Qur'an from engaging in interest based transactions. Al-Qur'an 2:278, 79: "O ye who believe! Fear Allah, and give up what remains of your demand for usury, if ye are indeed believers. If ye do it not, Take notice of war from Allah and His Messenger: But if ye turn back, ye shall have your capital sums: Deal not unjustly, and ye shall not be dealt with unjustly." Yet, the

Supreme Court in a State established in the name of Islam approves *Riba*.

[34] Allah prohibits Muslims from supporting or taking disbelievers as protectors. Allah warned against such behavior when He said: "and whosoever does that, will never be helped by Allah in any way" (03:28). At another occasion, the Qur'an says: "O ye who believe! Take not my enemies and yours as friends (or protectors),... And any of you that does this has strayed from the Straight Path." (60:01).

[35] Muslims today are providing full assistance to those who are engaged in exterminating their fellow Muslims in Afghanistan, Iraq, Israel and elsewhere. The Qur'an clearly says: "lend not thou support in any way to those who reject (Allah's Message)" (28:85).

[36] And finally because Allah says you are Muslims—one could be a Momin if he strives—but nothing more or less (See Al-Quran 22-78, 41:33, and 2:128). Yet Muslims refuse to get out of their stubbornness of classifying themselves as "moderate," "liberal," "enlightened moderate," etc only to please their worldly gods. About them Allah says: "The parable of those who seek protectors from other than Allah is that of a spider..." (29-41).

Index

Annex

This list shows some of the military men in civilian positions until Nov 2002 under Musharraf regime. A complete analysis would show far worse face of the military domination than what we can imagine from the following incomplete list.

1. General Musharraf (Chief executive, president and army chief),
2. Major General (Retd) Muhammad Anwar (President of Azad Kashmir),
3. Lt Gen (Retd) Khalid Maqbool (Governor Punjab),
4. Lt General (Retd) Syed Iftikhar Hussain Shah (Governor NWFP),
5. Lt General (Retd) Moinuddin Haider (Federal interior minister),
6. Lt General (Retd) Javed Ashraf Qazi (Federal communications minister),
7. Col (Retd) S.K. Tressler (Federal minorities & culture minister),
8. Lt Hamid Javed (Chief executive's chief of staff),
9. Major General Muhammad Yusuf (Chief executive's deputy chief of staff),
10. Major General Rashid Qureshi (President's information adviser),
11. Lt General Muneer Hafeez (Chief of NAB),
12. Major General Usman Shah & Major General Shujaat Zameer (Deputy chiefs of NAB),
13. Major General Abdul Jabbar Bhatti (Chief of regional RAB Punjab), Air Vice Marshal Zakaullah (Chief of regional RAB NWFP),
14. Major General Tariq Bashir (Chief of regional RAB Sindh),
15. Major General Owais Mushtaq (Chief of regional RAB Balochistan),

16. Lt General (Retd) Syed Tanvir Hussain Naqvi (Chief of national reconstruction bureau),
17. Lt General (Retd) Hamid Nawaz (Secretary defence), Air Marshal (Retd) Zahid Anees (Secretary defence production),
18. Lt General (Retd) Saeedul Zafar (Secretary railways),
19. Major General (Retd) Fazal Ghafoor (Ambassador to North Korea),
20. Brigadier (Retd) Abdul Majeed Khan (Ambassador to Tajikistan),
21. Major General (Retd) Salimullah (Ambassador to UAE),
22. Major General (Retd) Muhammad Hassan Aqeel (Ambassador to Thailand),
23. Lt General (Retd) Asad Durrani (Ambassador to Saudi Arabia),
24. Vice Admiral (Retd) Shamoon Aslam Khan (Ambassador to Ukraine),
25. Air Marshal (Retd) Najeeb Akhtar (Ambassador to Brazil),
26. Major General Syed Mustafa Anwar Hussain (Ambassador to Indonesia),
27. Lt General (Retd) Muhammad Shafeeq (Ambassador to Bahrain),
28. Lt General (Retd) Zulfiqar Ali Khan (Chairman WAPDA),
29. Major General (Retd) Agha Masood Hassan (DG of Postal Services),
30. Major General Farrukh Javed (Chairman National Highway Authority),
31. Rear Admiral K.B. Rind (DG Ports & Shipping),
32. Rear Admiral Ahmad Hayat (Chairman Karachi Port Trust),
33. Rear Admiral Sikandar Viqar Naqvi (Chairman Port Qasim Authority),
34. Vice Admiral Tauqir Hussain Naqvi (Chairman National Shipping Corporation),
35. Major General (Retd) Muhammad Hassan (Chief of National Fertilizer Corporation),
36. Lt Colonel (Retd) Afzal Khan (Chairman Pakistan Steel Mills),
37. Lt Colonel (Retd) Akbar Hussain (Export Processing Zone Authority),
38. Major General Shehzad Alam Malik (Chairman Pakistan Telecommunications Authority),
39. Air Vice Marshal Azhar Masood (Chairman National Telecommunications Authority),
40. Brigadier (Retd) Muhammad Saleem (Chairman NADRA),
41. Brigadier Mirza Babar Aziz (DG NADRA),
42. Brigadier (Retd) Muhammad Anwar Khan (DG NADRA NWFP),
43. Major General Raza Hussain (Chairman SUPARCO),
44. Major General Sabihuddin Bokhari (Surveyor General of Pakistan),
45. Brigadier Javed Iqbal Cheema (DG National Crisis Management Cell),
46. Air Marshal (Retd) Shafeeq Haider (Chairman Federal Public Service Commission),
47. Lt General Arshad Hussain (Member Federal Public Service Commission),
48. Lt General (Retd) Jehangir Nasrullah (Chairman Punjab Public Service Commission),
49. Major General (Retd) Arshad Chaudhry (Member Punjab Public Service

Commission),
50. Major General (Retd) Arshadullah Tarar (Member Punjab Public Service Commission),
51. Air Vice Marshal (Retd) Aliuddin (DG Civil Aviation Authority),
52. Air Vice Marshal (Retd) Arshad Saleem (Deputy DG Civil Aviation Authority),
53. Major General Zafar Abbas (DG Anti-Narcotics Force),
54. Major General Syed Haider Javed (DG National Logistics Cell),
55. Major General (Retd) Inayatullah Khan Niazi (DG Auqaf),
56. Major General Pervez Akmal (MD OGDC),
57. Brigadier (Retd) Rizvan Ashraf (General Manager OGDC),
58. Brigadier (Retd) Ishtiaq Ali Khan (MD Pakistan Mineral Development Authority),
59. Major General (Retd) Hamid Hassan Butt (Chairman Pakistan Railways),
60. Lt General (Retd) Syed Shujaat Ali Khan (Rector Engineering University Lahore),
61. Lt General (Retd) Arshad Mehmood (Vice chancellor Punjab University),
62. Air Vice Marshal (Retd) Sardar Khan (Vice Chancellor Engineering University Peshawar),
63. Captain (Retd) U.A.G. Isani (Vice chancellor Islamabad University),
64. Lt General (Retd) Sardar Ali (DG National Institute of Public Administration),
65. Brigadier (Retd) Maqsoodul Hassan (DG Directorate of Education),
66. Brigadier Muhammad Ejaz (Home secretary Punjab),
67. Brigadier Abdur Rehman (Director health NWFP),
68. Brigadier Shadab (Secretary C&W Punjab)
69. Brigadier Anees (chairman Punjab Privatisation Commission),
70. Colonel (Retd) Shahid Qureshi (DIG Sindh Telecommunications),
71. Colonel (Retd) Ghulam Hussain (Secretary S&GAD NWFP),
72. Brigadier Mukhtar (Home Secretary NWFP),
73. Brigadier Zaheer Qadiri (Secretary C&W NWFP),
74. Brigadier (Retd) Akhtar (Secretary to Governor Sindh),
75. General Muhammad Aziz Khan (Chairman Pakistan Hockey Federation),
76. Lt General Tauqir Zia (Chairman Pakistan Cricket Board),
77. Air Marshal Mushaf Ali (Chairman Pakistan Squash Federation),
78. Major General (Retd) Imtiaz (Chairman Pakistan Athletics Federation),
79. Brigadier Saulat Abbas (DG Pakistan Sports Board).